EXPEDITIONS
to
THE HEBRIDES

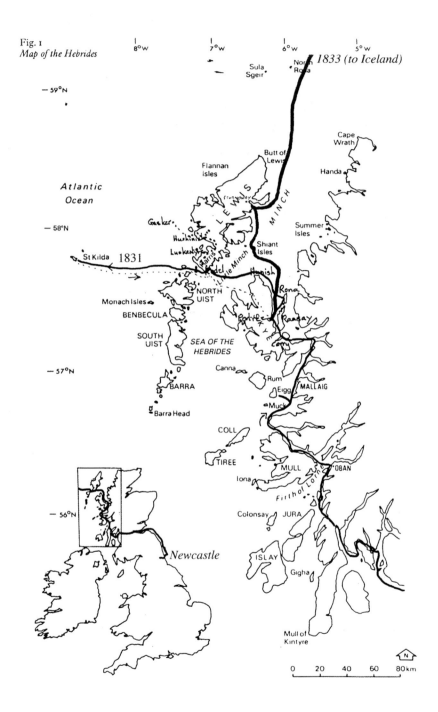

Fig. 1
Map of the Hebrides

8°W	7°W	6°W	5°W

Sula Sgeir

North Rona

1833 (to Iceland)

— 59°N

Cape Wrath

Butt of Lewis

Flannan Isles

Handa

Atlantic Ocean

LEWIS

MINCH

— 58°N

Gasker

Summer Isles

Hushinish

Shiant Isles

Luskentyre

Harris

St Kilda *1831*

Little Minch

Harris

Rona

NORTH UIST

Raasay

Monach Isles

BENBECULA

SKYE

SOUTH UIST

SEA OF THE HEBRIDES

Corry

— 57°N

Canna

BARRA

Rum

MALLAIG

Eigg

Barra Head

Muck

COLL

TIREE

MULL

OBAN

Iona

Firth of Lorn

Colonsay JURA

— 56°N

ISLAY

Gigha

Newcastle

Mull of Kintyre

N

0	20	40	60	80km

map

EXPEDITIONS

to

THE HEBRIDES

by

GEORGE CLAYTON ATKINSON

in

1831 and 1833

Edited by

David A. Quine

MACLEAN PRESS

First Published 2001
by Maclean Press
10 Lusta, Waternish,
Isle of Skye. IV55 8GD.
Tel 01470 592322
E-mail macleanpress@btinternet.com

ISBN 1 899272 06 2

British Library Cataloguing-in-Publication Data
A Catalogue record of this book is available
from the British Library

Designed and typeset in Caslon 10.5 on 13 by
Eric Mitchell, Glasgow

Published with the generous support of
The National Trust for Scotland

❀ ❀ ❀

Printed and Bound by Oriental Press, U.A.E.

❀ ❀ ❀

CONTENTS

CONTENTS

ACKNOWLEDGEMENTS

I OWE a tremendous debt of gratitude to Dennis Atkinson and Bridget Scott, the great-grandchildren of George Clayton Atkinson, first for allowing me to see the original Journals, which I found so exciting, and then for the privilege of working on them with a view to having them published, enabling a larger body of those interested in Islands and in Natural History to enjoy them too.

The chapter headings and daily titles are mine with a view to helping the reader into the parties location and activity. GCA had some titles at the tops of his pages. The individual sketches of the people have been moved to be linked to their reference within the text.

I would also like to express my thanks to Dr Richard Fawcett, Principal Inspector of Ancient Monuments for Scotland for information relating to the 'French King', and to F. MacLeod, R. A. MacLeod and Dr. A. Maclean who have kindly gone out of their way to comment on the text and individuals mentioned there, sharing their knowledge relating to their own particular fields on Skye and the Outer Hebrides; also for assistance received from Alastair Garvie, Honorary Curator at the Tobermory Museum and Professor W.M.(Bill)Lawson of Northton, Harris, specialist in Highland genealogies.

I greatly appreciated the opportunity to be permitted into the store rooms of the Laing Art Gallery, Newcastle upon Tyne and the Shipley Art Gallery in Gateshead to see the original paintings by Edward Train. My thanks to the Natural History Society of Northumbria for kindly supplying me with the Accession Numbers for Atkinson's donations to the Hancock Museum and for giving me permission to photograph the engraving of Thomas Bewick by Edward Train. I have received a tremendous amount of help from David Gardner-Medwin, Chairman of the Council of the Hancock Museum, in pursuing the Brunnich's Guillemot skins and other matters and from David Noble-Rollin, the Secretary of the Natural History Society of Northumbria, for making much information available. The staff of the Mitchell Library in Glasgow were also extremely co-operative.

The bibliography gives some idea of those who have stimulated my interest in preparing the background notes for these Journals and have fascinated me by their knowledge and research.

Robin Turner of the National Trust for Scotland was kind enough to recommend a local publishing house, and Roger Miket, for Maclean Press, has been most helpful in every way, and encouraged me to explore the historical figures mentioned in the text. Last but by no means least, my wife, who has supported me in this fascinating project; she has become a meticulous proof reader and has shown incredible patience and stickability!

DAVID A. QUINE

Newcastle in 1830

❖ ❖ ❖

INTRODUCTION

Access to the 1831 Journal

MANY of the old documents about St Kilda are deposited at the head-quarters of the National Trust for Scotland in Edinburgh and kept in the Bute Box, so called since the islands were bequeathed to the Trust by the Vth Marquis of Bute in 1956. The Box contains old editions of books by Martin Martin, Buchan, Macaulay, Connell and others, the school logs, newspaper accounts of visitors, lists of boats and their skippers as well as memoirs of some who emigrated to Australia in 1852. There are lists of plants and copies of research carried out on St Kilda covering archaeology, geology and botany.

While I was delving in the box in 1980 I came across a thick wadge of paper stapled together, a very faint carbon copy, which was almost impossible to read in places. It was part of an account of George Clayton Atkinson's (GCA) exploration of the Western Isles of Scotland and a voyage to St Kilda in 1831, which he entitled, *A Few Weeks Ramble among the Hebrides in the Summer of 1831*.

I obtained a photocopy and at home tried to decipher some of the words which were practically illegible. The typescript had been made by James Fisher and a hand-written note on the cover explained that he had given a copy to the Marquis of Bute. James Fisher, reputed to have started bird watching on his father's knee at the age of two, became the leading ornithologist in the UK in the post war years and the author of several books, including one of the first bird monographs in the Collins *New Naturalist Series*. It was on the Fulmar and contained 496 pages with 28 about St Kilda. He was a lecturer at King's College in Newcastle upon Tyne and went out to St Kilda to gather information for a book. At the same time he was researching for a book on the Gannet. I had spent several days camping on the Bass Rock, (home to 8,000 pairs of Gannets then, 30,000 pairs now), taking a number of unusual photographs of Gannets landing, taking off, performing their mutual greeting ceremonies and feeding their young in the most precarious nest sites. I sent him some enlargements in case they could be useful. Sadly, he was killed at a young age in a car accident before these two projects could reach fruition.

James Fisher was a friend of the Atkinson Family and, as he lived just round the corner from them in Newcastle, he was lent the original Journal. The typescript he made covered only the St Kilda section of the expedition and made no mention of the outward journey or eventful return. Interspersed in the text were tantalising references to sketches in the original *A View of St Kilda from the East, Fowling for Guillemottes, Village of St Kilda, Stack Biorach, Stackanarmin and Soa Stack* but there were no sketches attached to the copy and no indication of their quality. I longed to get a glimpse of some of the earliest known sketches of the St Kilda archipelago. The only sketches of that period I had seen were the twelve by Sir Thomas Dyke Acland painted in 1812 which I was able to reproduce in colour in *St Kilda Portraits* (Quine D.A. 1988). I would have liked to have included a chapter on Atkinson's expedition with some of the sketches if the quality were reasonable. After a long series of enquiries over several months I eventually made contact with GCA's great grandson, Dennis, only to discover that the document was not in his possession nor available at that time. As my book *St Kilda Portraits* was nearing completion I reluctantly decided that the Atkinson expedition and sketches would have to be omitted.

Sixteen years elapsed before I made another effort to see the original document. This time Dennis Atkinson had it in his possession and offered to bring it over to the Lake District when he came on holiday. The great day arrived and from a plastic carrier bag he brought out a large, thick, black, hard-backed book. The spine had disintegrated, otherwise it was in extremely good condition. It was much larger than I had imagined, 321 pages, gold edged, of splendid copper-plate writing, in the form of a diary – 90 pages were on St Kilda although GCA was there for only three days out of his five and a half weeks' expedition. If that was not enough even more exciting were the sketches, many in colour, no fewer than 47 pages. Sketches of mountain and island scenes, tiny cottages and mansions, people they met on their travels – shepherds, guides, whisky smugglers, helmsman, seasick passengers and Sir John Macrae. His sketches of St Kilda are of particular interest showing the natives' method of Bird Fowling, the impressive sea-stacks and one of the Village before its re-planning, but after the recently built Kirk and Manse. It contains a compendium of the scenery and of contemporary dress and architecture. I did not know that GCA had taken with him a promising young, professional artist, Edward Train, to illustrate and capture all aspects of the expedition. I was absolutely thrilled by the quality and attractiveness of the illustrations. GCA was also a painter, more of an amateur, but of considerable recognition. He came into his own on several occasions, but particularly on St Kilda as Edward Train had been so seasick crossing the Minch that nothing would induce him to face a further 50 miles in an open boat in order to reach their destination.

The text is no less fascinating, GCA describes the problems and frustrations of travel in those days, the limited accommodation away from the cities, the attempt by some lads in Glasgow to snatch their baggage as it was unloaded from the coach. He writes about the early smoky steamships and the people on board, and their attempts to identify the different fellow passengers. Due to three leaks in the newly repaired Crinan Canal their boat, the *Highlander*, was wedged in the lock for two hours; passengers and luggage had to be unloaded and they lost one of their dogs as they whiled away the time hunting rabbits. They explored the islands and caves near Portree and were excited by the impressive mountain scenery of the Storr. They were forced to land on the islands of Rona and Raasay and they enjoyed exploring Harris, observing the varied fauna.

Then they hired a boat to take them out to St Kilda, met the people there and admired their cliff-climbing skills. GCA was one of the few to witness and describe the scaling of Stack Biorach, the Pointed Stack, a steeple-like rock 240ft high, the most difficult of all the St Kilda climbs. It has only been climbed by one non-St Kildan, R.M. Barrington in 1883; it was rarely climbed by the St Kildans. GCA watched two lads make the treacherous ascent to the summit to catch Guillemots and he recorded his eye-witness account. The party also landed on Boreray and Soay and with the help of the Rev Neil MacKenzie recorded the status of the breeding birds as well as the customs of the people. They left St Kilda after only three days.

The party had an uncomfortable voyage back from St Kilda and a rough first night on Harris. They then had to track down Edward Train. Having met up again, they crossed the Minch by a shorter route and returned to

Portree, explored the Storr once more and wished they had more time to climb around Loch Coruisk and the Cuillins. In a gale they were forced to land on the island of Raasay where they renewed their acquaintance with Sir John Macrae. Later they had a fascinating evening at the MacKinnons of Corry and on their voyage back to Glasgow were pleased to meet McLean of Coll and McNeil of Canna. From Edinburgh they returned by coach to Newcastle upon Tyne after five and a half eventful and fruitful weeks.

Access to the 1833 Journal

In the summer of 1832 GCA explored the Shetland Islands aboard a top-sail schooner, *Magnus Troil*. For a number of years his sights had been set even further afield and in 1833 the opportunity came for him to mount a major expedition to Iceland. The route as far as Portree was the same as in 1831 and they had the added bonus of meeting Dr. William Hooker, the Professor of Botany in Glasgow. From Portree they took the steamboat to Stornoway on the Island of Lewis, calling at the Shiant Islands on their way. At Stornoway they were delayed for a whole week as their chartered sloop, the *Peggy*, was not ready for the sea. GCA was not one for wasting an opportunity and in his Journal he gives us a fascinating account of his peregrinations and observations in Lewis – the agricultural methods, the archaeological sites of Clach an Truiseil, Dun Carloway and the Stones at Callernish, meeting up with some illegal whisky distillers.

Eventually his boat was ready for sailing and they left Stornoway heading for Torshavn in the Faeroe Islands. He visited many of the islands before going to the Westmann Islands and then spent several weeks in Iceland. He did not take an artist with him this time. He made many sketches and on his return employed three of the top professional artists in Newcastle to turn his sketches into finished watercolours for his Journal. They were T.M.Richardson and his son, George, and Henry Perlee Parker. T.M.R. and H.P.P were *the two most famous artists in the North East. Their names had been made not only through their work, which was much in demand among the local gentry, but also by their attempt to establish a Northern Academy of Arts in Newcastle, on the model of the Royal Academy in London* (Seaton, 1989).

It wasn't until January 1998 that I had the opportunity of seeing the original MSS of this 1833 Expedition. Once again I was most impressed by GCA's output, his care and accuracy in recording his observations in a rough note book before writing it up fully at home, and the paintings, developed from his sketch book, are superb. Mrs. Bridget Scott, GCA's great grand-daughter kindly gave me the opportunity to see the document and allowed me to take it home. Volume 1 included the early part of the expedition with the exploration of Lewis. I was delighted when she kindly gave me permission to include extracts from this period, together with the beautiful illustrations. Having explored parts of Skye and Harris in 1831, as it were with him, the addition of the Island of Lewis and the Shiants has been a great bonus. I have spent many happy hours transcribing GCA's copper-plate handwriting, which has caused a few textual problems, but I have been delighted to work from the original and have been quickly transported to many of my favourite haunts.

George Clayton Atkinson (1808–1877)

'GCA', as he was affectionately known, comes over as a very fit young man, aged 23, confident, adventurous, from the upper class of Newcastle society, a knowledgeable ornithologist, an accurate observer and a copious note-taker.

He had a great sense of humour and a lively and, to us, a quaint turn of phrase using some intriguing words which have fallen out of modern use – *clept, anent, philippic, eleemosynary*, etc. His spelling and punctuation are rather irregular. I have kept both on the whole apart from a few minor adjustments to improve the clarity of the sentence. In 1831 he follows Dr. McCulloch's island spellings – *Egg* and *Sky* (now *Eigg, Skye*) but by 1833 he is using *Skye. McLoud*, he occasionally uses for *MacLeod*; *McCray* and *McCrae* should be *Macrae*. With few relevant maps available of the areas visited, distances, and the heights of the mountains, proved difficult to estimate but his own compass bearings were put to very good practical use in rescuing his party from a tricky situation.

The original objective in writing the journal was to aid his memory, but he later realised its possible benefit for other travellers. He could share his experiences, giving advice and information, including compass bearings, with other travellers in the Western Isles of Scotland. He also gave lectures to local learned societies on St Kilda and other topics of natural history.

Links with Thomas Bewick and the Natural History Society.

GCA was encouraged in his study of natural history by a neighbour, Thomas Bewick (1753–1828) the wood engraver, an elderly man in his seventies when GCA was in his early teens. Bewick had a lifelong love of nature and birds in particular. His first book, published in 1790, the *General History of Quadrupeds* was very well received. This was soon followed by his *History of British Birds* in two volumes (1797–1804), illustrated by his meticulous engravings, and combined his love of nature with his great attention to detail. The result was far superior to anything seen before and became the model for all successive authors during the 19th century. He was a genius as a wood-engraver, but few people realise that behind these were the most exquisite little water colour paintings. He worked from life where possible, failing that from stuffed specimens in museums. Bewick Swans were named in his honour. He commented, 'My own efforts were directed to the rising generation and my object was to enveigle youth onwards by the vignettes to the study of natural history.' (Allen, 1976) In GCA he had a captivated pupil, visiting him two or three times a week. Bewick's care in observation and his desire to depict what he saw, together with his urge to collect specimens, was to have a lasting influence on the young Atkinson. GCA writing after his death commented, 'I look back now with feelings of the greatest satisfaction to the pleasant and instructive hours I spent with him'. Bewick often expressed a great sense of wonder, investigation and reflection in the presence of the marvels of the natural world; he also showed a lively sense of humour. On one of GCA's visits he was offered a small packet of paper which, on being unfolded, displayed – a tooth, the paper contained the following inscription *I departed from the Place – from the place I held in the Service of Thomas Bewick, after being there upwards of 74 Years on the 20th November,* 1827. On the back was written 'Bewick's Tooth, 1827'. On the death of Bewick GCA wrote his biography from which these quotations are made.

GCA became an avid collector of specimens for the museum of the newly formed Natural History Society of Northumberland, Durham and Newcastle upon Tyne of which he was a founder member. In 1829 he was appointed the curator of the ornithological section at the museum. The *Transactions of the Society* frequently refer to specimens he had donated from the Highlands and Islands of Scotland, including St Kilda and the Shetland Islands, New South Wales, the Faeroes and Iceland.

These specimens are now housed in the Hancock Museum in Newcastle, which possess one of the largest assortment of stuffed mammals, reptiles and birds outside London. The Founders of the Natural History Society, now based at the Museum, boasted many of the leading Natural Scientists of the Day – Sir Walter C. Trevelyan, Botanist, Geologist with an interest in Fine Arts, William C. Hewitson, Curator of the Insect Collection and Author of *British Oology*, Albion Hancock, who, with Joshua Alder, produced the monumental work on *British Nudibranchiate Mollusca* and later one on Brachiopods, and published papers on fossil fishes, reptiles and amphibians, – 74 papers in all. John Hancock played a prominent part in the planning and construction of the Museum, and was a writer, taxidermist and Vice President. GCA profited from the company of these leading natural scientists.

Life during Newcastle's City Development

This was a time of great importance and excitement in the history of Newcastle. Great industries were beginning to flourish – the Lemington Iron Works, the Northumberland Glass Works, second only to Coal and Ship Building – Newcastle was becoming the key city of the North East. The whole city was in the process of transformation from an old medieval market centre with timber framed buildings, old garrets, dirty narrow streets and slum cottages to an urban based society. 'In 1800 there were no towns outside London with a population of over 100,000, by 1837 when Queen Victoria came to the throne there were already five.' (Ayris, 1997). The change in Newcastle was brought about under the inspiration and direction of Richard Grainger, the son of a *porter pokeman gannin' on the quay*. Richard was apprenticed to a master carpenter and developed into an extremely successful builder. He was aided by a brilliant architect and surveyor, John Dobson, and had the backing of John Clayton, the Town Clerk, who was not only a leading solicitor, able to attract wealthy business men, but was also alert to the needs of the Town. GCA's sister, Mary Ann, married John Dobson and John Clayton was his cousin. Grainger, Dobson and Clayton all have streets named after them in the centre of the city. The end of the Napoleonic Wars had brought a time of peace and stability from 1815 onwards with a period of prosperity and build-

John Dobson's plan of the Central Station, Newcastle

ing programmes to an unprecedented degree. The whole centre of the town was undergoing a new birth in the Classical style – *Under the magic hand of Grainger a city of palaces had suddenly sprung up.* – words from a speech at the opening of the Grainger Market on October 22nd 1835. The dinner at this amazing event is depicted in a large oil painting in the Laing Art Gallery by Henry Perlee Parker with the Mayor, Richard Grainger and 2,000 men seated, and 300 admiring women watching the banquet from a balcony. Where was GCA, surely he must be there somewhere, he was the Sheriff only two years before?

Early Travellers to the Hebrides

In 1831, when GCA was visiting the Hebrides and St Kilda, tourism in Scotland was in its infancy. Very few people had the inclination to venture far afield or had the money to carry out their pipe dreams. During the previous 150 years there had been a few who had braved the elements but in each case they had a specific object in view.

Martin Martin, a native of the Hebrides (Skye) and tutor to the MacLeod's of Dunvegan on Skye, travelled widely around the Western Isles. He saw a need for a native Scot to visit and describe the islands since most of the previous writers had reported on hearsay alone. *The Isles I describe are but little known and considered,* he commented, and bemoaned the fact that *the young travel to foreign Countries whilst they are absolute strangers at home.* His masterpiece, published in 1703, *A Description of the Western Islands of Scotland* is a classic, covering in detail the natural history as well as describing the natives and their customs. In 1697 he had visited St Kilda with the tacksman who was collecting the rent paid in birds' feathers, dried fish, tweed and fulmar oil and in the following year published his first splendid book, *A Late Voyage to St Kilda – The Remotest of all the Hebrides.* After his visit he sent a package to Sir Hans Sloane, the British physician and naturalist (whose amazing collection formed the basis of the British Museum which opened in 1753), containing an egg of a Solan Goose (Gannet) and one of the Gairfowl (Great Auk), these were deposited in the British Museum, and remain there to this day.

In 1758 the Rev Kenneth MacAulay, minister of Ardnamurchan, was sent out by the Society for the Promotion of Christian Knowledge to *catechize the natives, preach among them and to see into the state of the Charity School and to collect all the observations which*

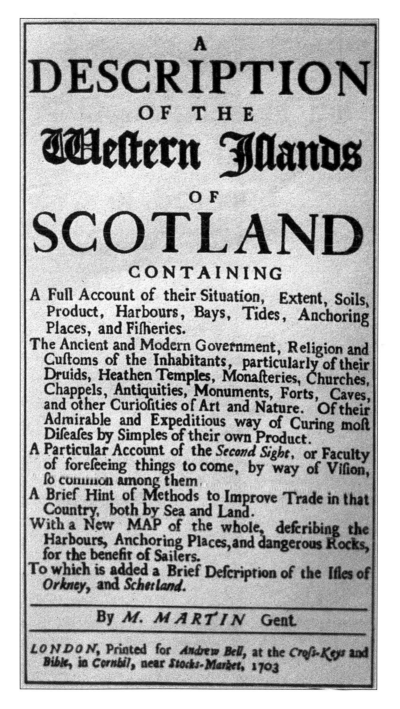

Martin Martin's title page 1703

might interest the public. His book, *The History of St Kilda* is fascinating.

Sir Joseph Banks had accompanied Captain James Cook in 1768 in circumnavigating the whole world, but four years later on his way to Iceland he 'discovered' Staffa. He was awe-struck by the sheer magnificence of the spectacle of the columnar basalt rock formations and caves. He was the first to describe them and his account was included in the Rev Thomas Pennant's second Book, *A Tour in Scotland and Voyage to the Hebrides in 1772*. This and his first book, *A Tour in Scotland in 1769*, became the standard travel guides of the times.

Perhaps the first 'Tourist Party' was that of Johnson (1709–1784) and Boswell (1740–1795). Johnson had the desire to visit the Hebrides for so long that he could not remember 'how the wish was originally excited'. The two adventurers spent August to November 1773 exploring. They spent one night in Raasay House, and also stayed at the Inn at Portree and with the McKinnons at Corry. GCA also stayed at these places. Johnson published his *Journey to the Western Isles of Scotland* in 1775 but Boswell, who had assiduously written his daily journal on the spot, refrained from producing his volume, *The Journal of a Tour to the Hebrides* until 1785. Henry Brougham and his party from Edinburgh were heading for Iceland in 1779 but the stormy weather forced them to land on Islay. They had to abandon their primary objective, but managed to reach far off St Kilda. That evening they visited Boreray and returned to Hirta at 1am to be refreshed in the priest's house, *A more wretched hovel never sheltered beast from the storm than this,* was his observation. The party returned *via* Stornoway, Denmark and Scandinavia.

Sir Thomas Dyke Acland, escaping from the pressures and cares of his estates in Devon, was touring central Scotland in 1812 when the urge took hold of him and he, his wife and son aged three decided to extend their tour to St Kilda. Travel and painting were his ways of relaxing and on this visit he produced the first known watercolour paintings of the archipelago, twelve in all. He was shocked by the islanders' poverty in their wretched huddle of thatched huts and, as he reached the boat, he promised to return again. He returned in 1834, on his own boat, *The Lady of St Kilda*, in which he circumnavigated the whole of England, Wales and Scotland on a six weeks' tour. He left £20 with the Minister, the Rev Neil MacKenzie, a gift which set in motion the planning of a new village.

Dr. John MacCulloch's purpose for visiting many of the Western Isles including Rum and the remote islands of North Rona and St Kilda (1815) was a careful study of the geology. To make his account, which covers three volumes with illustrations, more readable he included matters of more general interest. The poet John Keats visited Mull and Iona in 1818 and the Rev. Dr. John MacDonald, the Apostle of the North, made several pastoral visits to St Kilda between 1822–30. He was greatly appreciated and raised £600 for the building of a Kirk and Manse on St Kilda which were completed in 1830, ready for the arrival of the Rev. Neil MacKenzie, with whom GCA stayed.

With the development of the steam packet vessels in the 1820s, the Western Isles, particularly the Inner Hebrides, were now on the Tourist's route. Felix Mendelssohn was 21 in 1829 when he visited Mull and went out to Staffa where he was so moved by the majestic sights and sounds of the breaking and booming waves and sea birds that he immediately began the score of his Hebridean Overture. Two years later, in the summer of 1831, other distinguished artists arrived, one painting in oil the other with words. J.M.W. Turner was invited up to Scotland by Sir Walter Scott as the publishers of Scott's new book of poems thought that his sketches would considerably increase the sales. He completed his task, went to Glasgow and then on the steamer to Kyleakin and painted Loch Coruisk, then to Tobermoray and out to Staffa. William Wordsworth also visited Scott and went on Mull commenting, *I never saw Scotland under a more poetic aspect.*

Keats, Mendelssohn, Turner and Wordsworth did not venture further west than Mull, Staffa, Iona and Skye; very few others reached the Outer Hebrides and it required a special breed and motivation to go the further 50 miles west out into the Atlantic. GCA was one of these. Great determination was required to overcome the problems and frustrations to be faced – large distances on foot, bone-shaking journeys in the stage coaches, smoky paddle steamers, soaking trips crossing the Minch on board sloops with no protection, often with very primitive accommodation, many inns noted for their bed-bugs, fleas and indifferent meals. Only two of GCA's party of four who left Newcastle reached their destination. The voyages on the *Highlander* and the *Maid of Isla* were more than enough for brother

Paddle Steamer Inverary Castle *built 1830 and similar to the* Highlander

Isaac – he parted company on the way out at Portree and returned home. Crossing the Minch proved such an awful experience for Edward Train, as for many others, that nothing would induce him to face a further ten to fifteen hours bobbing about in a tiny boat in the Atlantic heading for St Kilda. On their return it took GCA and his brother Richard about 48 hours to get back to the safety of the Sound of Harris.

It was another seven years before the first steamer from Glasgow reached St Kilda. The *Vulcan* arrived on 25 July 1838 from Glasgow carrying the first party of genuine tourists – thirty four passengers in all, making a one-off trip. More importantly for St Kilda, the Rev Neil Mackenzie was on board together with his purchases using Acland's initial gift of £20 for the newly built houses – 47 bedsteads, 24 chairs, 21 stools, 21 tables, 21 dressers, 21 glass windows, pieces of Delftware. A new era was emerging for St Kilda – with mixed blessings.

Important Historical Document

People: GCA relied a great deal on letters of introduction to influential people when exploring a new area. One of the most interesting people he visited in Edinburgh was William MacGillivray (1796–1852) the artist and ornithologist. William was brought up on his uncle's farm at Northton, Harris overlooking the Luskintyre sands. Aged 11 he went to school in Aberdeen, his birthplace, and in his early 'teens' he entered the University, in due course obtaining his MA. Then for several years he studied medicine before giving that up to devote his energies to natural history. In 1819, 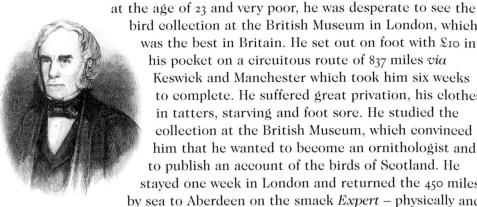 at the age of 23 and very poor, he was desperate to see the bird collection at the British Museum in London, which was the best in Britain. He set out on foot with £10 in his pocket on a circuitous route of 837 miles *via* Keswick and Manchester which took him six weeks to complete. He suffered great privation, his clothes in tatters, starving and foot sore. He studied the collection at the British Museum, which convinced him that he wanted to become an ornithologist and to publish an account of the birds of Scotland. He stayed one week in London and returned the 450 miles by sea to Aberdeen on the smack *Expert* – physically and mentally exhausted.

In the spring of 1830 John James Audubon, the famous American bird painter, unable to get his book published at home, came to Edinburgh searching for help with the text of his *magnum opus, Birds of America*. He was introduced to William who agreed to assist him. In the next nine years five volumes of Ornithological Biography were published with more than 3,000 pages of text and detailed descriptions of almost 500 species. There were 98 anatomical drawings by William. The first volume appeared in April 1831, one month before GCA visited MacGillivray, leading to the discussion reported in the Journal for May 17th. MacGillivray was working on his own first book, *Description of the Rapacious Birds of Britain* which he published in 1837. In 1841 he was appointed Regius Professor of Natural History at Marischal College, Aberdeen, lecturing in zoology and geology during the winter and botany in the summer, as well as leading exhausting field trips! He also published books on Molluscs and his five volume *History of British Birds (1837–52)* established his reputation as the 'father of British Ornithology' – a title well earned.

GCA met Sir John Macrae on the *Maid of Isla* during their outward journey to Portree in 1831, and again on the island of Raasay when they stayed with him for a few days having been storm-bound on their return journey. Sir John was a Colonel in the Cameron Highlanders, who spent part of his retirement on Raasay, deeply interested in the Gaelic oral tradition. He was an accomplished player on the bagpipes and is said to have played before Queen Victoria.

In 1833 in Glasgow GCA called on Dr. William Hooker, then Professor of Botany, who became the first Director of Kew Gardens in London, and obtained from him considerable valuable information. Dr. Hooker introduced him to Dr. John Scouler, Professor of Natural History at the Andersonian Institute in Glasgow, who gave GCA a skin of a Brunnich's Guillemot, one used to establish this as a different species from our Common Guillemot. This skin was collected and labelled by Captain Sabine, later Sir Edward Sabine, President of the Royal Society from 1861–71. Most of GCA's collection made its way to the Hancock Museum in Newcastle. There is a possibility that this skin may have perished during their lengthy expedition in Iceland. The Staff of the Museum have hunted high and low but can find no details of one donated by GCA. Of the thirty-three Guillemot skins in their possession, three were Brunnich's, two had no place of origin noted, but the third was in winter plumage and came from one of Sabine's old haunts – the Davis Straights in the Arctic between Baffin Island and the West coast of Greenland. The date of entry was not specific but would have been contemporary with GCA as it was in the handwriting of Albion Hancock himself, one of the founders of the Museum.

GCA's background and his contacts with Bewick and other leading scientists of the day enabled him to make accurate, well based observations and records of the natural history. Eagle Clarke who was the Keeper of the Natural History Department of the Royal Scottish Museum, having spent years in isolated outposts of Scotland, produced a two volume work *Studies in Bird Migration* in 1912. Summarizing the contribution of past writers he had this tribute for GCA, *Of the older writers, Martin (1697) and Macaulay (1758) stand pre-eminent, and their information afforded the basis of all that followed until the year 1831, when Atkinson ushered in the modern era in St Kildan ornithology.*

Sketches: The sketches are a wonderful record of the scenery and the places visited as well as being a valuable resource of information about contemporary dress and architecture. Apart from William Daniell's two views of Portree (1819), the sketches of Portree are the earliest known of the expanding township. Train's three illustrations of the Storr offer a far more realistic representation than other contemporary views, such as that made by MacCulloch during his visits between 1811–18. Some of the earliest known sketches of St Kilda are to be found in the 1831 Journal. The originals of these must have been drawn by GCA but it is possible that they may have been redrawn by Train on their return to Newcastle. The scenes of the Stacks and the Bird Fowlers are brilliant and the view of the Village is particularly interesting. It shows the Village as a small huddle of old houses in the foreground at the foot of Oiseval and in the distance on the right the new Kirk and Manse. Both these had been built during the last 18 months prior to GCA's arrival. He stayed in the manse with the Rev Neil MacKenzie (who had just been in residence for one year) and his wife, a non-Gaelic speaking Glaswegian. Neil became the driving force behind the newly planned village although the original stimulus came from a gift of £20 from Sir Thomas Dyke Acland. On his second visit in 1834 he saw the impressive new Kirk and Manse and was concerned for the ordinary inhabitants who were still living in their primitive and filthy hovels. His gift was for the first person to pull down his old house and build a new one. This gradually resulted in the careful planning of the new settlement with the houses in an arc round the bay in the middle of field strips stretching from the Head Dyke down to the sea wall.

Songs: GCA records two songs which he heard on his voyage. One, the *Vari Dheum*, or in standard Gaelic, *A Mhairi Dhonn*, a Love Song which was sung at a musical evening in the McKinnon's house at Corry on Skye. The other, the *St Kilda Wedding*, was sung enthusiastically by Ian McLeod on the way out to St Kilda. The words are incomprehensible and were intended to be to make them easier to learn and to sing. The tune of the *St Kilda Wedding* must be one of the earliest St Kildan songs to be noted. There is a lovely arrangement of the melody which has been played on Radio Scotland by the group called *Ossian*. The tune is quite beautiful and in recent years has been recorded several times by groups in Scotland and Canada. It is the tune being danced to at the very beginning of the BBC film, *Am Posadh Hiortach* – St Kilda Wedding screened in 1996.

Shanties: GCA must have had a very good ear. On May 31st he described landing on St Kilda and how everyone joined in hauling the boat up the beach to the *heaving chorus* of the leader which he recorded as *Hoy sho wallosho, wallosho* meaning 'here with her altogether'. I asked a Gaelic specialist, Calum Ferguson, to comment on this. He replied, *The leader's exhortation, as recorded by Atkinson, is very interesting indeed. 'Hoy sho, etc' is exactly what the St Kildans would have shouted, markedly different in pronunciation from what Atkinson might have heard in similar circumstances elsewhere in the Western Isles. The difference I suppose is attributable to the St Kildans' famous lisp.*

Standard Gaelic would be: *Shin sibh a bhalachu, bhalachu!*
Phonetic. *Hin-shoov a vallocho, vallocho!*
Meaning *There you go lads, lads*

Notice that the St Kildans did not pronounce *bh* of *bhalachu*, as a *v* but as *w*. They also dropped the *n* sound from *Shin*.

Pertinent Observer: Of exceptional interest is the way in which Hebrideans, known to us historically for other reasons, are depicted through the eyes of a traveller, who then illuminates aspects which have eluded or been ignored in the historical record.

Conservationist: In his early years GCA was an ardent collector of specimens for the Hancock Museum but his interests changed. In 1846 he became a founder member of the Tyneside Naturalists' Field Club which was concerned with the observation and recording of natural history data rather than the collecting of specimens of flora and fauna. In the 1860s he was in the forefront of the atmospheric pollution debate which was at crisis point.

As President of the Field Club, at the end of their Annual Meeting in April 1872, he delivered a blistering attack on the state of atmospheric pollution caused by the thirty factories along the Tyne, *'There is a lamentable amount of destruction going on wholesale, incessantly, and increasingly by our manufacturers – I speak not at this time of the fish in our rivers – but much that is beautiful of the vegetable creation; a destruction that can never be repaired. We can only lament and remember the beautiful denes and hanging woods, or the handsome single trees that were but are not . . . many are gone, many are going; poisoned gradually by the smoke or more suddenly by the chemical fumes from our manufacturers.'*

'Atkinson made an outstanding contribution to pollution control at his

Lemington factory by pioneering a method of processing smoke produced in the iron manufacturing process. This successfully eliminated the worst atmospheric effects of iron production and made Lemington a model factory at the time when all other iron works were still producing uncontrolled emissions of acid smoke.' Seaton, 1989.

At the 1872 meeting GCA proposed that the Club should carry out a Tree Survey to monitor the damage being caused by pollution. This would involve describing and photographing individual trees in the county. The Survey took 5 years, most of the photographs were by GCA but he died in the year the survey was completed and did not witness its effect on industry and the community.

In the Journal of his Icelandic Expedition in 1833 GCA was delighted by the pleasure expressed by those who had read his earlier Journals. He commented, *it is particularly gratifying to me to consider that my former ones have in some measure answered my intentions in writing them; I mean in inducing others to visit the remote and neglected scenery which appeared to me so well worthy of observation. Several parties of my friends, during the last summer have visited the fine scenes of the Hebrides, and returned well pleased with their expedition.*

ST KILDA

St Kilda enthusiasts will be surprised by his comments, *St Kilda, except to the ornithologist, is not worthy of a journey, for though even sublimer and more uncommon than any of the scenes in Skye, the difficulty in attaining to it – though generally much exaggerated – renders a special visit scarcely worth while.* No doubt his impressions were tainted by the fact that they nearly came to grief in thick mist just off the rocks of Hashkir. They also spent two gruelling days rowing practically the whole way back – 50 miles – from St Kilda to the Sound of Harris.

I have thoroughly enjoyed studying the journal, accompanying the three explorers and getting to know the individuals mentioned with the help of the wonderful sketches. I do hope many others will also derive tremendous pleasure in entering into the same experience.

DAVID A. QUINE
Ambleside, 1999

GCA, SHORT BIOGRAPHY

MY GREAT-GRANDFATHER, George Clayton Atkinson, was born in 1808 in Newcastle upon Tyne, the eldest son of Matthew Atkinson of Temple Sowerby, Westmoreland and Anne Littledale of Whitehaven, then in Cumberland, now Cumbria. The Atkinson family lived in Temple Sowerby since at least the 16th century and had risen from Statesmen (yeomen farmers) to leather merchants and bankers with a business in Penrith. A branch of the family operated a sugar estate in Jamaica until the begining of the 19th century and it is interesting to speculate whether this activity subsequently promoted my great-grandfather's urge for island travel! In 1727 Matthew's father, George, built Temple Sowerby House which was the family home until 1980 (when it was occupied by my cousin). Over that period members of the family were some-time Sheriffs of Westmoreland and Receivers General of Revenue and *de facto* Lords of the Manor.

Matthew, being a younger son, moved to Tyneside around 1790 and lived at Carr's Hill, Gateshead and later Ovingham Vicarage where Thomas Bewick, the famous naturalist and engraver, had been educated fifty years before. G.C.A. was educated at St Bees School followed by Charterhouse. At about the age of sixteen, to prepare and qualify for the more intense business of adult life, he joined the Tyne Iron Company at Lemington, one of the largest industries in the area. His father anxious to get him in set-tled work purchased a share in the great firm. It provided him with a steady income but with a reasonably flexible use of his time which did not divert his interest from natural history. He later became a director of the company.

From a child, great-grandfather had been a student of nature and spent his boyhood exploring the Tyne valley and adjacent countryside with his brother, sketching and collecting the flora and fauna of the area. These included *collections of birds' eggs, insects, and whatsoever was new, curious, or interesting to an inquiring mind.* (Welford, 1893).These activities caught the attention of Bewick who befriended and encouraged him. He used to visit Bewick *two or three times in the week and always met with the same cordial welcome or kind reproval for not coming more frequently.* From those days I inherited one of the first four prints of the Chillingham white bull which were produced before the engraving block cracked, signed by Bewick to *my young friend G.C.Atkinson.* On the death of Bewick Atkinson read a paper to the Natural History Society on the *Life and Work of the late Thomas Bewick.* He was only twenty one at the time but he completed a thorough work which included a brief history of engraving, a summary of Bewick's prolific output and closed with some interesting personal reminiscences.

Circumstances stimulated scientific nature studies on Tyneside at that

time. For thirty years from 1803 the Rev William Turner had lectured on science and philosophy, and others had done similar work. Lectures both informed G.C.A. and provided a platform and he soon became known. He made donations of specimens to the museum from 1825 onwards, the catalogue recorded a note of his donations of a tippit, or great crested grebe, caught on the Tyne, and a piece of ironstone with plant impressions, found locally. In 1829 the Natural History Society of Newcastle upon Tyne was formed with his name as a member together with many prominent and older scientists and authors.

In 1831 he went on the first adventurous journey with his brothers Richard and Isaac to the Hebrides and St Kilda taking the local artist Edward Train with them, collecting specimens and making sketches of both the wildlife and the inhabitants, to be worked up into paintings upon their return home. They were one of the earliest parties of visitors on record to visit these remote parts. The following year with two friends, William Hewitson and Edward James, he visited the Shetland Isles in a topsail schooner, the *Magnus Troil*; and in 1833 with William Cookson, son of the founder of the Cookson's Lead Works (now Associated Lead), and Mr Proctor explored Lewis in the Outer Hebrides, the Faeroes, Iceland and the Westmann Isles in the sloop, *Peggy*.

Of these expeditions he wrote copious Journals, initially for the entertainment of his sisters and personal friends but, with their encouragement, he submitted them to the Natural History Society and the Hancock Museum (opened shortly before) in the form of Transactions and accompanied by gifts of specimens brought back from the tours, birds' eggs from St Kilda: insects, minerals and curios from the Faeroes and Iceland, shells from Van Dieman's Land and other islands. On his return from Iceland he was persuaded to enter local political life and was elected Sheriff of Newcastle in 1833. He soon found that his scholarly tastes were not compatible with council room debate and retired in 1835.

In 1840 he married Sophie Hutton of Gate Burton, Lincolnshire and, after her death, Elizabeth Carr of Whickham, living first at West Denton and, from 1854, thereafter at Wylam Hall. Whilst there for 35 years he carried out a series of weather observations on rainfall, snowfall and temperature which are recorded in the Transactions of the Tyneside Naturalist's Field Club of which he was a founder member. He remained an active member and in due course became President. During this period he became increasingly interested in arboriculture and got to know the trees in the four northern counties very well. These he photographed, having taught himself, and he invented an instrument, small enough to be carried in the pocket, to measure their height. He also made a careful study of trees to explore the potential of their qualities and uses. With increasing industrial pollution he became much concerned about the effect on the trees and as an ardent conservationist carried out research on this

Wylam Hall

xxvii

subject. As a hobby he took up, and became very skilful in, decorative wood turning and invented numerous improvements to his lathe, which for a time I inherited and used, and in his industrial life he became an important iron-master and inventor of such things as a ball and socket joint for the tuyeres, (the nozzles through which the blast is forced) of the blast furnaces to replace the old leather hoses.

In 1874 he moved to 12 Windsor Terrace, Newcastle, since demolished, became a JP for Northumberland, a director of the Newcastle and Carlisle Railway and a member of the Society of Antiquaries and of the Merchant Adventurers Company. He died in 1877 and is buried in Jesmond Cemetery leaving an only child, Matthew Hutton Atkinson, my grandfather.

His talents and interests are carried through to this day. Matthew was sent in 1874 by Lord Armstrong to Egypt for several years to advise on electric torpedoes for which he held patents. He filled several sketch books in his free time. His grandson, George, was sent to Japan before World War 1 to show how to make large calibre naval guns (they were our allies at the time!). He came back with a large collection of artefacts. His grand-daughter, Sophie Mildred Atkinson, became a well-known water colourist in Canada where she lived for many years and had pictures in the Canadian archives including a commissioned one of the Prince of Wales' (later Edward V111) Cattle Ranch. She also broadcast on art over the Canadian radio and published *An Artist in Corfu* after a visit there. My sister, Mrs B.J.Scott, has inherited the talent and has made a small collection of our aunt's pictures.

Sadly, the talents have by-passed myself! I cling with my finger-tips to membership of the County Wildlife Trust and the Merchant Adventurers Company as shades from the past and live in hope of my children and grandchildren.

GEORGE DENNIS ATKINSON B.Sc.
Ponteland, 1998

❖ ❖ ❖

THE ARTISTS

1831 Expedition

Edward Train (1801–1866)

Edward Train, the artist who went in GCA's party to the Hebrides, was a whimsical character reciting poems and singing songs particularly when he was in a threatening situation – a delightful person to have in one's company. He was aged 30 at this time and not nearly as fit as GCA, who was frequently frustrated by his slow progress on the hills. Seasickness was another vexation and limitation as it came upon him only too quickly in any appreciable swell in a small boat.

He was born in Gateshead but lived most of his life in Newcastle upon Tyne. He served his apprenticeship as an engraver under Edward Scriven in London, a specialist in the stipple technique. He was soon to return to Newcastle and here developed into a well known land-scape, portrait and figure painter. He exhibited mainly in Newcastle and Edinburgh where his Highland scenes, which formed a large percentage of his work, had a ready market. His Hebridean expedition with Atkinson in 1831 was the inspiration and the stimulus for much of his work in the future. *A Northern Stream, Isle of Harris* was exhibited in the Carlise Atheneum in 1850. One of his paintings *A View in the Isle of Skye* was hung in the Royal Scottish Academy Exhibition in 1837.

He is represented in the Darlington Art Gallery by an oil painting, 43 x 56 cm of a fishermen in action, titled, *On the Esk*. The Shipley Art Gallery, Gateshead contains four oil paintings (*Mountain Torrent*, 1849. Accn. SH 79; *Scottish Lake Scene*, 1851. Accn. SH 214; *Waterfall*, 1854. Accn. SH 216; *Mountain Scene*, 1857. Accn. SH 192). The Laing Art Gallery in Newcastle also holds four oil paintings by him (*Landscape with Waterfall*. Accn. L05-130(A); *Landscape with Lake*. Accn. L05-130(B); *Landscape with Gypsy Encampment*. Accn. L05-142; *Mountainous Landscape*. Accn. L13-9) He occasionally combined his Scottish Landscapes with theatrical and historical matters, as in his *Macbeath and the three Weird Sisters*.

He grew up at a time when Newcastle could boast a large group of artists, Thomas Miles Richardson (Senr) being the finest, but with others close on his heels, Henry Perlee Parker, John Dobson and John Wilson Carmichael. Edward Train does not feature among the names in such high company, but he was very well gifted and greatly appreciated by many of his contemporaries

He also became an able portrait painter, and some excellent examples of his early work adorn this journal. Later he painted many well known Northumbrians, including Robert Roxby the Northumbrian poet. One of Thomas Bewick, from a bust by Bailey, was included as an engraving in the *Sketch of the Life and Work of the late Thomas Bewick* written and published by his erstwhile travelling companion G.C. Atkinson.

1833 Expedition

An artist did not accompany GCA on this expedition, but he drew copious sketches himself and then, to turn them into finished paintings for his Journal, he employed three of the top professional artists in Newcastle.

Thomas Miles Richardson, Senior. (1784-1848)

T.M.Richardson Senior is considered, *One of the most highly regarded painters in watercolours produced by the North of England.* (Hall M.1973). He painted landscapes, marine subjects, figures in oil and watercolour, he was an illustrator, engraver, lithographer and etcher.

He was born in Newcastle, the son of a schoolmaster, and spent seven unhappy years apprenticed to a firm of cabinet makers in Newcastle pursuing art in his free time. When his father died in 1806 he followed him as drawing master at St Andrew's Charity School. Visiting London he was inspired by Turner and other great painters. From 1813 he devoted himself to his art work and in 1814 exhibited *A View of the Old Fish Market, Newcastle* at the Royal Academy in London. He struggled on, success came slowly. In 1822 with Thomas Bewick, Henry Perlee Parker, John Dobson and others he founded the Northern Institution for the Promotion of Fine Arts. In 1827, he established the first purpose built Gallery and also the Northern Academy of Arts which held its first exhibition in 1828. He also founded other bodies for the Promotion of Fine Arts. Later he painted many large oil paintings, the one 2.5m x 1.25m of *Newcastle from Gateshead Fell* was bought by the Corporation for 50 guineas and now hangs in the

Laing Art Gallery. He is best known for his superb paintings in oil and watercolour of Northumbria, Scotland and the Lake District. In 1845 he last exhibited at the Royal Academy, but his work can now be found in the British Museum, the Victoria and Albert and all over the country, particularly in the Laing in Newcastle and the Shipley in Gateshead. He became known as the *Turner of Newcastle* .

George Richardson (1808–1840)

The eldest son of T.M.R. above, showed very early prowess and by the age of 18 was an established drawing master in Newcastle opening an academy with his brother T.M.R. Junior. He gave private lessons and evening tutorials and continued to paint landscapes. He exhibited at the British Institution between 1828-33. He was only 32 when he died.

Henry Perlee Parker (1795-1873)

Portrait, figure, landscape and marine painter in oil and watercolour, a drawing master. He was born in Devonport, Devon, the son of a wood engraver and guilder who became a professional artist and teacher. Henry began work as a tailor and coachmaker, and also painted portraits and made drawings for his father's pupils to copy. He illustrated C. T. Gilbert's *Historical Survey of the County of Cornwall* published in 1815. In 1814 he moved to Plymouth as a professional portrait painter, staying there a year before going to relatives in Sunderland and on to Newcastle. Here he was very successful and became one of Northumbria's best known artists. He was a founder member of the Institution for the Promotion of Fine Arts in Newcastle, exhibiting at the Royal Academy between 1817-59, with 23 works in all. He was patronised by many of the most important men on Tyneside. He also painted smuggling subjects, animals, landscapes and special events. The Laing Art Gallery has some magnificent examples of his work, *Pitmen playing Quoits*, 1840, showing men with their black faces, lit by a brazier hanging above their heads, and the *Opening of the Grainger Market* which is at least 1.25m x 0.73m. In 1838 he painted Grace Darling in the attempted rescue of the *Forfarshire* off the Farne Islands. He moved to Sheffield in 1841 and to London in 1845 where he died penniless in 1873. His work is represented in the Victoria and Albert Museum and in Galleries, mainly in the North East.

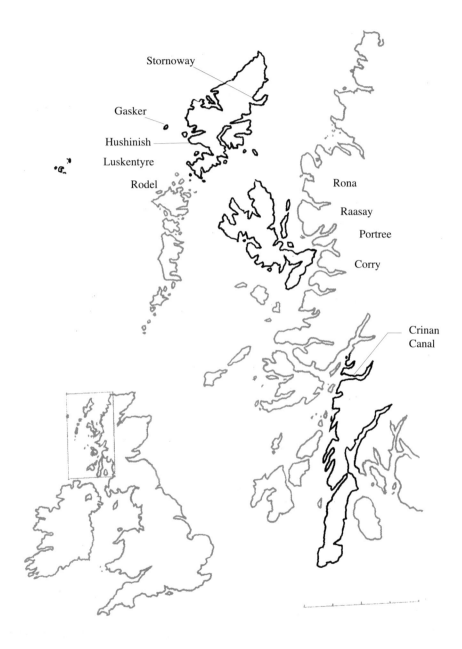

Stornoway

Gasker

Hushinish

Luskentyre

Rodel

Rona

Raasay

Portree

Corry

Crinan
Canal

FEW WEEKS RAMBLE

among

THE HEBRIDES

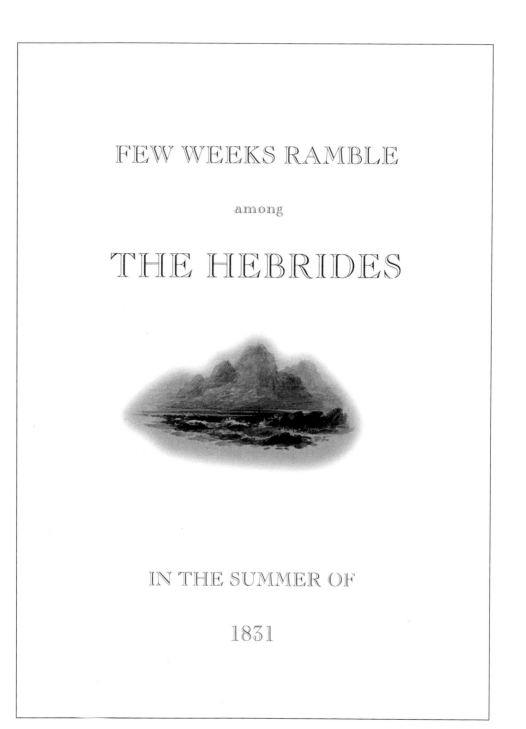

IN THE SUMMER OF

1831

Original Title page

ATKINSON'S PREFACE

A WEEK'S RAMBLE on the isle of Arran, in the summer of 1829, left so
forcible an impression on my mind of the beauties and grandeur of
the Scottish island scenery, that I determined to devote a longer period, at
some future time, to a tour among the more northern and remote ones.

In this expedition my brother Isaac was my companion, and as his
enjoyment of it was little inferior to mine, we anticipated much satisfaction in the execution of our scheme. The spring of 1831 presented us an
opportunity as there was a prospect of his almost immediate departure for
Jamaica, where his stay might interpose many years before we should see
each other again, and as the intercourse afforded by a residence in the
same city is small, and decimated by diversity of occupation or amuse-
ments, we arranged for an excursion together, and reverted to our long-
talked of intention of visiting Skye and Harris.

My remaining brother Richard got leave of absence for 6 weeks to
accompany us, and a young artist of much promise, Mr. Edward Train
completed the party, except, 'Jack' and 'Crab' two pet Terriers belonging
to the 'boys'.

This excursion, we commenced from Newcastle in May partly that we
might visit some of the great breeding places of the sea fowl, at the time
of nidification, and partly because this was Dick's most leisure time in the
course of the year: it occupied between 5 and 6 weeks, I was replete with
pleasure and gratification.

In former rambles, I had always kept memoranda of each day's proceedings, as the means of more firmly fixing the recollection of them on my
memory: this plan I pursued on the present occasion; but the places we
saw, are so little known and the information contained covering them and
matters relating to them, of so much greater comparative interest, than
what it has hitherto occurred to me to see on record, that I have been
induced to copy out in a legible hand – at least as clearly as I could make
it – the journal I kept while away. Since our return, Mr. Train has most
kindly taken the trouble of drawing for its illustration nearly all the
sketches we made, and if any interest presents itself to the general
peruser, I may without any false modesty, attribute it to their presence.

As St Kilda is certainly the most interesting point, herein made mention of, it naturally occupies a comparatively large portion of the Journal though much of the matter relating to it, will be uninteresting except to the ornithologist, and therefore I recommend the reader to skip it.

Some apology should also be made for the egotistical character which I find, despite my endeavour to the contrary, to pervade what novel writers call *my pages*: I can only explain it as arising from being the work of an individual unaccustomed to writing, and a detail of events which though occurring to the whole party it devolved entirely on him to relate, without any comparison of feeling on the subject of what was seen, with his fellow travellers.

He therefore presents it to his friends, in the certainty that indulgence will be extended to it, as he hopes that it is destitute of pretension – the only naturally ridiculous and contemptible quality; which is equally so under all circumstances, – bookmaking, as well as the more every day actions of life – and which may be presumed to be the natural food of the critic.

If this volume has the effect of interesting any of his friends or inducing them to visit the scenes depicted or described, it will be cause of satisfaction to him, as it may tend to a more general acquaintance with scenery, to which he knows nothing at all equal, and which has been hitherto neglected from not being known.

The sketches occur throughout this volume, in a very unconnected and promiscuous way; this however may be fully as amusing as a more systematic arrangement to the *reader* who does not *read* but only skims over the pictorial part as one does over the contents of an album.

Such as it is I confide it to the good nature and indulgence of those who read it, and need say no more on the subject of so little consequence.

1. Newcastle upon Tyne to Rowdill, Harris

May 16th – 30th

Newcastle to Edinburgh on the Ardincaple, *Coach to Glasgow,*
Highlander *to Oban, Jammed in the Crinan Canal,*
Maid of Isla *to Portree (Skye), Explore Storr, Sea Caves and Islands,*
Sloop to Rona and on to Rowdill (Harris).

☞ **Monday, 16th May** ⚜ ⚜ ⚜

    Newcastle to Edinburgh on the steam ship
    Ardincaple.

EMBARKED on board the
Ardincaple[1] at 6.30 am
in the morning in high
spirits at the prospect of the
pleasure we anticipated in our
excursion.

In lack of other occupation we
amused ourselves with speculations
on our fellow passengers, who were
uninteresting enough, and had not
the advantage of seasickness to eluci-
date the sharp and more striking points of character,
more commonly developed by wine, or some other
agent overcoming the natural artificiality of human
nature.

5

There was a very beautiful child of whom Mr. Train made a sketch, and its papa who exceedingly discomposed my admiration of a favourite song , *'They say my love is dead'*, by declaring the air to be one and the same with a vile local Newcastle song *'Mr Mayor'*.

The Captain was a nice obliging fellow and indulged a propensity we displayed, by taking us near any flocks we saw on the water – Isaac's weapon was a double barrel gun and mine a rifle, we did no execution, which I was glad of, as there was nothing rare enough to be desirable.[2]

We had a delightful sail, the weather being as fine as possible and enjoyed the fine scenery of St Abb's Head[3] and the Bass,[4] Wolf's Craig[5] to the north of the former, Dunstanborough[6] etc. very much.

Dunstanborough Castle

From Ewbank's[7] frequent representations of the Bass, I had formed a pretty correct opinion of it: it is one of the only breeding places of the

Wolf's Craig

Gannet, which are carefully protected by the person who rents it. They, the Razor Bill and Kittiwake, are most numerous though the Guillemotte is in great numbers, and on some of the small rocks higher up the firth the Puffin, Cormorant and other common sea fowl are constantly to be met with. Jackdaws inhabit the Bass and on one or two of the rocks, the Black Guillemotte is found. The Bass forms a striking object from whatever point it is seen and the historical associations created by it, tend considerably to increase its interest. After passing it, the hill called North Berwick Law presented itself on the left: it is of considerable elevation and rises alone from a comparatively level country.

They gave us an excellent dinner on board, and all went well with us. We landed in Newhaven[8] at 10.30, squabbled with every porter, boatman, and coachman we had anything to do with, got some porter at a public house, and walked up to Edinburgh at 11 with our captain, where we settled ourselves comfortably at Ambrose's,[9] had supper and went to bed.

☞ **Tuesday, 17th May** ✿ ✿ ✿

Stay at Ambrose's Hotel, Edinburgh, coach to Glasgow

DICK and I rose at 7. I rambled forth to enquire about conveyance to Glasgow. The number of coaches seemed few, though from all places in the early coaches being taken, there would seem to be work for more of

7

them. We were obliged to take 4 places in an afternoon coach at 4 o'clock, which vexed us a little at the time, though the delay was eventually fortunate and gave me an opportunity of calling on McGillivray[10] and getting an introduction from him to his brother, a young surgeon, gone for the vacation to his home in the Island of Pabbay. This of course procured much as an introduction to a young man in the very place where in order to get to St Kilda our own exertions and the acquaintance of friends would be most required was more than we had ventured to hope for. Breakfast at 8.30 am and at 10 called on Mr Allan the Banker with an introduction from Mr Hutton:[11] he had been at St Kilda and is the only man I ever met with who had been there. He regretted that he knew no one among the islands, but at length recollected Col. McQuarry of Glenforsa,[12] Mull, to whom he gave us a note. Mr. Train and Isaac went to see Holyrood and the French King[13] or anything else worthy of observation. In our return from Mr. Allan's, bought a small portable fishing rod off an old fellow called Mr. McKenzie, evidently a character, and a sort of person who would be apt to talk of older times and address his junior customers as *'you young men'*. Thence to call on Mr. McGillivray who is engaged in a work on British birds on the scale of Audubon's American Ornithology: in fact Audubon and he are jointly concerned in it: it is to commence in about two years, and if they keep clear of that straining after effect, which has induced Audubon to represent his birds in attitudes which they could scarcely ever assume, it will be a splendid undertaking. When we called he had on his table a drawing for this work which was superior to almost any of Audubon's: it was Razor Bills and Guillemottes on a mass of rock where they breed, and their eggs are nicely represented beside them. He showed us some more of the drawings, but none so good. Some young blackbirds were ruined by unnatural attitudes, so were some blue-tit-mice and others I don't remember. One of Audubon's great faults, which McGillivray has fallen into, is representing his birds stepping and stretching with one foot extended: this though natural in man, whose heavy limbs serve to balance the extended upper part of the body, is peculiarly ill-conceived in represen-tations of birds, whose light limbs could avail nothing for this purpose, even though they be birds which do step, and nine out of ten I think hop and do not proceed by alternately moving the legs: in addition to this it is representing them in an attitude which is so rapidly changed, when they do assume it, as to elude very close observation, and is one so uncommon, as to be entirely unknown to general observers.

Dined at 2.30 and having enjoyed Ambrose's nice accommodation and civility left him at 4 by a heavy Glasgow coach: one young lady, Isaac, a raw-boned vulgar Scotsman and myself occupied the latter part of this

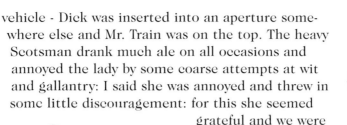

vehicle - Dick was inserted into an aperture somewhere else and Mr. Train was on the top. The heavy
Scotsman drank much ale on all occasions and
annoyed the lady by some coarse attempts at wit
and gallantry: I said she was annoyed and threw in
some little discouragement: for this she seemed
grateful and we were
soon excellent friends:
like many of her
country, though
in a middle
station in life
she proved
herself well
informed and
intelligent, and
amused me by
repeating snatches of poetry in the
Scotch dialect: one little thing in praise of *'our ain fire side'*, was
peculiarly pretty, and was repeated in excellent taste.

Got to Glasgow at 9 and stopped in the coach at the
Bucks Head in Argyle Street:[14] our luggage was no
sooner taken from its place of storage and
placed in the street, than it was seized on by 4
or 5 fellows who under pretence or carrying it
for us would in all probability have stolen one
half of it, as it seemed matter of small import
to them to ascertain where we wanted to go to;
however in the midst of our perplexi-
ty a policeman came forward and
ordered them to put everything down
and stand back, and then turned and
asked where we wanted it taken: this
was all done without any noise or fuss
and saved us I dare say some inconvenience: we determined our next move
would be an aquatic one to station ourselves near the Broomie Law from whence

the steam boats go: so we put up very comfortably at McLean's
Hotel,[15] the low end of Broomie Law, had some supper and then sent for
the Captain of the steamer which goes to Oban tomorrow to enquire

9

about the time etc., he was an unprepossessing priggish fellow and departed without giving us much information. To bed at 11.

☞ Wednesday, 18th May 🌺 🌺 🌺

Glasgow, down the Clyde on the steam ship Highlander.

AFTER breakfast Isaac and I called on Mr McKinnon, the Columbian consul,[16] with an introduction from Mr. Gilfillan, Isaac's master in Liverpool. He received us very kindly, gave us a further one to his mother at Corry on Skye and expressed a wish to see us on our return. Called on Tidy (a son of the East Indian Col. Tidy) whom I had known in Newcastle: found him away from home. Went to Museum but found we were too soon for admittance, the hour for which is 12 o'clock till 3. Met at 1.30 dinner. I went on board *Highlander*[17] steam boat at 2.30; it was however an hour before we had got a hundred yards from the quay, and all seemed so uncomfortable and ill managed that we nearly determined to leave her and go the next day in the *Maid of Isla* direct to Skye. However we remained and I had a most uncomfortable passage to the east end of the Crinan Canal[18] which we reached about 2 in the morning, experiencing by the way every possible misery and discomfort incidental to small dirty steam boats.

Few characters worth memorializing occurred: perhaps the only one was a fine wild looking girl, 14 or 15, who came on board enveloped in her plaid at Glasgow; from the practical expression of her features and costume, and not appearing to bestow one thought on anything that was passing, we had made up our minds she must be bound for some lonely glen, or distant island; all this interesting fancy work, she soon put an end to, by landing at Greenock: not however before Mr Train, struck by her romantic appearance had got an excellent likeness of her.

In descending the Clyde, groups of washer women and lounging men afforded him likewise little odd fanciful subjects for his sketch book, which with some common street characters he got in Glasgow from the window are all we got today and are faithfully represented herewith.

☞ **Thursday, 19th May** ✿ ✿ ✿

Jammed in the Crinan Canal on the way to Oban

AFTER tossing about in the hot frowsty cabin of the *Highlander* for an hour got out on the canal side, close to which we were lying and walked on to while away the time and see the country until we should be over-taken by the boat. This was a distance of 4 miles in which we caught beetles for William Hewitson,[19] and sketched and hunted ducks for ourselves: there is a gentleman's house about two miles from the east end of the Crinan, to the south of it, a very nice situation, and further on, the view to the North lighted by the rising sun, formed a fine view; after this the canal takes its course along the south side of a very extensive morass, which I should imagine a great resort of wild fowl in winter. The west end of the Canal is much finer and with the Loch of Crinan and the hills, and castle on the north side is well worth seeing if you are passing, and it is only the trouble of coming on deck for that purpose.

Mr Train

In coming along Dick and I ran the dogs after a Rabbit, and in spite of all our endeav-ours we could never find Jack again: he is rather a sulky dog and as Isaac had been jaw-ing him in the morning while we were hunting young wild Ducks, Dick thought he had pre-tended not to hear our calls for him and had just sauntered in the wood. As it was we were a good deal vexed as Jack was a fine Dog, a great favourite of Isaac's, and this was our first misfor-tune. The steam boat stuck in a lock for two hours, and this we devoted to seeking him, but unsuccessfully. I never saw such a hopeless stick as that our boat made, for it absolutely jammed against the walls of the lock on each side, and not until the lug-gage and passengers had been landed could they get her out of this awkward situation: nothing could exceed the cool-ness and apathy of the captain all this time: he never made a suggestion for her extrication, but idled about the deck in the most unconcerned way, and then sauntered lazily down below where he remained till she got loose. The reason of the mischance was the extreme lowness of the canal, which has three leaks and has not been so low for many years – I cannot imagine anything much worse than sticking there for a day of two, and our prospect of such an event was decidedly brilliant at one time. In general it takes about 3 hours to come through it, but in our case from 3 till 9 in the morning.

The remaining part of our day's journey compensated for all our canal miseries, as from hence to Oban is an excellent specimen of the best style of Hebridal navigation; you have got to the mouth of L. Crinan when Jura and Scarba open up on the left: Jura is a long mountainous island remarkable for its conical hills called the Paps, and rich in Geological curiosities, Grouse and Red Deer. Scarba presents little that is envious to the eye of the passer-by, but between these islands, the whirlpool of Corryvrechan, or rather its situation is easily seen from the steam boat: the danger in sailing over it only exists at certain times of the tide, and most of those with whom we talked about it, had passed at one period or another. The mountains in the southern extremity of Mull now appear, of which Benmore is the highest; they are a striking group, but our boat did not go very near them, leaving them on the left for Oban; in our way we sailed within the island of Kerrera, a long, low uninteresting piece of land once favoured for smuggling, which as in almost every other district has now given way to the vigilance of the excise: this is the finest thing we have yet seen: the latter part of it particularly, from the slate quarries to Oban.[20] On entering the bay on which this pretty little town stands, there is something in the arrangement of the hills which reminded me a good deal of the Trossachs on Loch Caterain (Katrine), and the castle of Dunally[21] to the north tends to make a beautiful piece of island scenery of its kind, as can be seen anywhere. The houses of the town are low, and generally white resembling in situation and general effect, those of Rothsay, Tobermoray, and Portree in Skye, though the two latter stand higher and have the advantage of a little wood near the town.

One sad bore in these steam boats is their frequent deviation to land passengers: thus one may fairly calculate on occupying an hour or more in each day's journey with them, and except that it now and then present opportunities of seeing what would otherwise be passed at a distance, is

rather irksome to those who are considerably possessed by the true
English feeling of getting on.

During the day we had a strong easterly wind, which though divested
here of its chilling Northumberland character is cold and unsatisfactory
enough, and came with tremendous violence from the hills on our right:
this with the state of discomfort in which everything was, on
board the *'Highlander'* since we left Glasgow, induced us at
1.30pm when we got to Oban to land and put up at an inn
there, and take the chance of catching the *'Maid of Isla'*
in the morning direct for Skye. Dined, and after dinner
walked 3 miles to the north east to Dunstaffnage[22] –
sketched, caught beetles, returned, tea'd
and went to bed.

Only one worthy fell beneath Mr.
Train's pencil today: he was a rough
looking man in a very rough looking dress and asked Mr. Train if he
was in the cattle line.

Nothing more this day of much
importance, except that I had
toothache pretty bad, and looked so dowdy with a
Welsh Wig on and my cap tied over it, that when
Mr. Train found his repeated attempts at conversation with me fruitless, he took his pencil and put me
down among his characters. Mem: pay him off for it
when he is in trouble.

☞ **Friday, 20th May** 🌼 🌼 🌼

From Oban to Portree, Skye on the steam ship Maid of Isla

UP and aboard the *Maid of Isla* Steamer[23] for Skye at 4.30 am – happy to
find her a great improvement on our vile conveyance of yesterday, in
point of size, cleanliness, accommodation, and attention of officers. She
only travels between Tarbert (a *'boat-carrying'* or narrow isthmus) in the
Mull of Kintyre and Portree in Skye, but she meets the Glasgow boat at
Tarbert and receives their passengers, who walk, or are conveyed over the
neck of land, not a mile in width to the West Loch Tarbert. She comes
through without stopping as she has excellent beds and does it if there is

13

not much digression in 27 or 30 hours; the sail to East Loch Tarbert in a goodish boat will occupy 6 or 7 more, so if the passenger be not long detained at Tarbert, Portree may be attained in 37 or 38 hours from the time of leaving Glasgow.

The Captain appeared a very civil fellow and boasted much of the superiority of his boat to the *Highlander*: he more than insinuated that all the respectable people came with her in preference, and instanced his now having Sir John McCray[24] on board: as 5 o'clock in the morning is an uninteresting time in a steam boat, we found no better amusement than in speculating on our fellow passengers as they made their appearance. We could not form any satisfactory preconception of the dignitary mentioned by the Captain and after a good deal of amusing disquisition on the subject made up our minds that he would be a very grand and supercilious personage, rather little in person, but very trim and neat, with two servants and a very perfect travelling equipage. Ridiculous as it may seem, we felt fully persuaded at 9 when we went down to breakfast that he was not among those who had come on deck, and in fact felt it would be quite consistent with the opinion we had formed, that he would remain below till that time, probably in a private cabin if there was such a thing. When we got beside the cups and saucers, a single glance convinced us that this must be still the case, so we formed silent notions of his great consequence, and devoted ourselves to the more real and substantial occupation of breakfast: scarcely was the anxiety we felt on the important subject beginning to slumber, when all our doubts and speculations and anticipations were concluded by a pretty looking lady on my right *'troubling Sir John for a mutton chop'* – now I had so fully settled that the gentleman who responded, was not Sir John, that in my anxiety to catch a first glance of that illustrious man, I had been aware of an inclination not to be bothered by the remarks which a gentleman with a shabby hat, had been making on my rifle before we came down: however I had been civil, and promised him a shot with it, if any sea fowl should occur, and after breakfast we became capital friends. He knew Mrs McKinnon of Corry, to whom we had an introduction. They were a nice family etc, and the ladies whom I had seen at

breakfast were going there. He was plainly dressed even to shabbiness, smoked cigars, had been much in India, and was Sir John McCray.

He lives at Rasay House, the proprietor of which McLeod is a young man in the army and lets it to his friend Sir John who amuses himself with farming and yachting, for which latter pursuit no spot seems to be so well adapted as these islands; few of them not affording the most excellent harbour in the numerous lochs with which they and the coast of Inverness-shire abound.

Reached Tobermorey[25] in 4 hours and staying a few minutes for passengers, had an opportunity of admiring the pretty clean looking town, and the excellent house of McLean of Coll to whom we have an introduction from Mr.Gilfillan: he is a man of considerable property; Coll, of course belonging to him, as well as Rum and nearly a third of Mull: his house and pleasure ground are situated half a mile from Tobermorey to the south of the bay – we hope to see more of them in the sequel. I cannot imagine a finer natural harbour than this bay; it is completely landlocked and would hold many a navy or two with ease.

After leaving the Sound of Mull there is more open sea, till the narrow straight between Skye and Inverness is attained; this takes about 6 or 7 hours and about 4 o'clock we found ourselves within it; at particular periods of tide, the current in these narrows is exceedingly strong; I believe as much as 7 or 8 knots, and steam boats have been compelled to lay to till the turn of the tide after unsuccessful attempts to steam it. The peculiarity of the scenery however compensates for any length of time in passing it – the mountains are fine and at one or two points, the boat appears com-

Scuir of Egg

pletely locked among them, not an appearance of egress presenting itself to the eye of a stranger.

As we had a passenger to land at Egg, an island to the south of Skye, we had an opportunity of remarking and sketching the rock called the Scuir of Egg, [26] and certainly a striking object, though not so wonderful as one who had formed his sole opinion on Mr. McCulloch, and would be inclined to imagine. In one part of this island there is a cave, narrow at the entrance, but widening internally till it is large enough to shelter some hundred men. A few centuries ago the men of Skye and Egg being at feud, the former landed on Egg and having at length discovered that their enemies had taken refuge in the cave, they collected straw and other combustible matter, and piling it on the beach at the mouth of the cave, set fire to it and smoked every soul within it to death: their bones remain within it to this day and it is a fashionable excursion just now to see them!

Rum, Egg, and Muck constitute this group of islands. The former is 4 or 5 miles in diameter, mountainous, and like the isle of Arran in its style of outline: Eagles, Ptarmigan and Loon game abound upon it and it belongs as I before observed to McLean of Coll. Egg is remarkable only for the Scuir and cave mountain mentioned before; and Muck or Monk (a whale, or saw according to association – in this case the former) is a low island affording good pasturage, and to its proprietor a good rent. In consequence of considerable care having been bestowed in Rum, upon the breed of ponies, [28] which have been crossed with Arabian horses, that island now affords by far the finest ponies in the Hebrides.

Got to Portree [29] at 10 o'clock, and hearing that in consequence of a fair in the village, it would be difficult to procure beds and accommodation ashore, we ordered supper and went to bed on board; for the latter the steward charged us 2d a piece, for which and sundry other little exorbitances, I jawed him somewhat mercilessly.

In coming along today, an old fellow called Martin who has the Salmon fisheries in Skye and some other islands, overheard some conversation of mine on the merits of my rifle, and joining in showed so much wonder and incredulity that I told him I was sorry no chance of convincing opportunity was likely to occur, and it was then almost dusk, and we had seen few sea birds that day, upon this hint he insisted on my firing at a bottle slung at the head of the foremast; I objected partly because if I missed it, I was pretty sure to cut some of the tackle of the ship and loose my own credit. However, this was all over argued and a ginger bottle sent up, hitched on the signal haulyards. I made a good shot, but as I feared, though I broke the bottle, the signal haulyards, to which it was attached were cut, and the head of a respectable old Nanny Goat sentimentalising below, considerably maltreated by the fragments of the bottle.

There was a gentleman on board who proved eventually to be Mr. Reeves[30] inspector of Post offices in the islands, and of whom Mr. Train obtained a most ridiculous likeness: if these likenesses which we occasionally took, had been caricatured, or had been induced from any motive of ridicule or ill nature, this and most of the others would have been omitted, as nothing could exceed the wish to inform and oblige displayed by Mr. Reeves, where local knowledge, from constantly having to visit the islands, was most valuable and interesting to us. He was a good deal addicted to humming scraps of songs and bravura pieces of his own, and knew the name of every loch, hill and island we passed.

Portree: Isle of Skye

☞ **Saturday, 21st May** 🌸 🌸 🌸

Exploring the rocks and caves around Portree.

ALTHOUGH we had ordered breakfast at 7.30am we did not get till two hours later and then went on shore - our next step was to get a boat to take us somewhere, and on making inquiry for one, a fellow with a face full of roguery came and offered as we were gentlemen to give us a sail for

£2.2-! We declined, even when he reduced his demand to fifteen shillings; we thought there was too much London in his appearance to encourage any doings with him, and set off to walk round the shallow south part of the bay, in order to attain some caves among the cliffs, where abundance of Cormorants and pigeons breed; in coming upon an unexpected group of cottages on the shore we found that the caves were inaccessible without a boat and we then hired two lads to take us for 5/-.

For some time before we set off from Carr Hill, Isaac had evinced a carelessness about the excursion, which if it did not promise ill for its execution, threatened very much to interfere with the activity requisite to attain the more important object we had in view. Today he fancied too much fatigue likely to be incurred, and declared his resolution to return home by the *Maid of Isla* on Monday morning: it is perhaps better for us that he should go, as being obliged to devote alternate days to resting ourselves would curtail our time too much.

I was wrong in saying the Cormorant inhabited these caves to the south of Portree Bay for we did not see more than two nests today. The Rock Pigeon and Black Guillemotte seem to be the only fowl which breed there, and both in places difficult of access: the former on the earth among the mass of rock, deposits its two white eggs and rears its young. The latter builds its nest in the most difficult chinks and holes of the rock it can meet with, often within the caves, but almost as frequently on stacks (rocky pinnacles) or inaccessible gullies among the cliffs; unlike the others of this genus which have only a single egg, it lays three of the size of a Guinea fowl's, though of a more tapering and elegant form, the ground colour, a greenish white and spotted and blotched with sepia and rust coloured marks. We shot a couple of Rock Pigeons and procured two eggs.

After leaving the caves, round a little further to the south, to a cliff where a pair of Eagles have their eyrie: situation of it seemed so easy of access that I wanted very much to send the boys home for a rope, and a man or two to hold it, and descend the cliff for the Eaglets which must now be in it, but the youngsters very coolly laughed at me and said if the men came they would

Peat Carrier in Skye hold me to prevent me from risking my life in such an attempt – so we came away and landed to dinner at 4.30.

Rambled afterwards up a little burn to the north east of the bay, where Dick and Isaac groped for trouts and Mr. Train sketched a little.

☞ **Sunday, 22nd May** ❀ ❀ ❀

Went to the Gaelic Service in Portree, Isaac leaves for home.

I ATTENDED Gaelic service this morning with a young scotch gentleman
of the name of Forbes who was staying at the Inn, I was much pleased
with the attention displayed in the congregation. The poor box is fixed
near the door, and few of them passed without dropping in a trifle: their
psalms are pleasing and nicely sung, in fact in one of them I recognised
one of our own church tunes. The Minister's family occupied a pew near
the pulpit and the old lady seemed devoted to her snuff box, as she made
frequent applications to it. I was amused by an old woman who occupied
the pulpit steps, and patiently waited till her superior had taken a pinch,
to thrust a long bony hand and arm through the rails for the purpose of
participating in it. This was not at all resented, but the box extended to
her in the most friendly way.

Mr McLachlan's House in Portree

After the Gaelic service, some psalms and a sermon in English were
performed, which with the other detained us from 11 till 3, had a walk
afterwards, dinner, and at 10 tea; after which Isaac left us and went on
board the '*Maid of Isla*' again, which sails at 4 every Monday morning from
Portree Bay. Sent home two 'Rock Pigeons'[31] for the Museum and a letter
for Mary Ann.[32]

☞ Monday, 23rd May ✿ ✿ ✿

Exploring Prince Charles' Cave and Holm Island, north of Portree.

ACCORDING to an agreement we made on Saturday, our two young boatmen waited on us this morning at 8, and persuading Mr Forbes to accompany us, we set off to the north to see Prince Charles'[33] cave and the Storr

The cave is between 3 or 4 miles from Portree by sea, but not so much I should think by land, and is well worth seeing. It is scarcely perceptible from the sea as the entrance is closed almost entirely by a huge mass of Stalactite covered with ivy and no symptom of the cave is visible, but two or three apparently trifling crevices in a rugged front of rock: one of these however is sufficiently large to admit a person to the interior which in a sunny day is fine from the effects of light through the irregular apertures at the entrance and extreme brilliancy of the Ferns and wild flowers which grow within it. The green I have even observed assuming its gayest tints where the sun does not shine.

Prince Charles' cave interior

The cliffs about here rise from a steep grassy slope at some distance from the sea and are in many places grand. They are Basaltic and have somewhat the character of a mighty wall. We saw eagles soaring among them in two or three places, but they seemed so wary that even my rifle did not promise to avail much against them.

We landed on a small island called Holm island, about 6 miles from Portree and nearly opposite the Fox-hunter's Cottage at the foot of the Storr, but though we sought diligently upon it for the eggs of seafowl which evidently abounded on it, we didn't succeed in obtaining any; I had some shots at the Black Guillemotte in the water from the island but with equally bad success, for though very abundant my single ball did not procure one.

From Holm island we rowed to the Fox-hunter's Cottage and through the interpretation of our boatmen procured some milk, a most acceptable thing always, but where you get it in such excellence and abundance, as in the highlands

Prince Charles' cave exterior

and islands of Scotland, where nothing but water and whiskey divide its sway, it is unquestionably the most satisfactory thing a traveller often has to depend on.

Angus the Fox-hunter had 10 or 12 of the Skye Terriers[35] running about him; they are long in the back and short-legged, strongly made and would average from 14 to 16 pounds in weight. They have almost dew claws and do not seem finely bred; in fact we afterwards learnt that the gentlemen who are considered to have the best breeds are so negligent in keeping the breed uncontaminated that the father of a litter of pups is never known. Colour seemed of no consequence, as among Angus' pack there were black, brown, liver and grey dogs, differing considerably in appearance, and all good dogs. Some gentlemen on this island and Rum have a variety of the Skye Terrier nearly white; but it is exceedingly scarce, and valued accordingly. They must be very courageous as one or two of them were cruelly tattooed. Angus had just shot an otter in the sea opposite his cottage and was skinning it when we visited him. They were going that night to watch a fox earth for the old dog fox, whose family they had dispatched a few days before.

Rowed about 3 miles further to some caves where Scarfs and Cormorants abound, taking with us a visitor and fellow croftsman of the Fox-hunter, who had come to see him from Loch Torridon, and who tells a correct tale, shot the otter this morning. This man with two of his dogs and his terrible looking gun, we took in the boat with us. When we came to the part of the shore where there were fowl, nothing could equal the interest and excitement displayed by our young boatmen in their pursuit; no exertions seemed to be too great for them, and without seeming for one moment to consider themselves, they urged and entreated us to go on to new places, and evinced such delight in our success, that I think we stayed longer than we should have done, for their amusement and edification. In consequence of one or two fairish shots I made with the rifle, I was in particular esteem, and it was somewhat increased by the zeal and activity I displayed in our pursuit. As they had no idea of the ceremonials of civilised life, we were all addressed and spoken of by the titles we used to each other: they assured Mr. Train they thought '*George*' a very fine fellow, and in cases of emergency were continually encouraging me with '*now George - make haste – don't you see - now – now*' - etc etc in the most familiar style, but so simply and naturally that it would have been barbarous to check them. My brother's name puzzled them at first, for I can imagine they perceived a degree of familiarity in '*Dick*' which they could not so easily venture on, as in the full and respectable name of George. He was not so quick with his gun as an older man would have been, and this rendered energy of expression more requisite; so after urging him once or twice with the generalism 'sir' – as 'now sir – now – now' in one extremely urgent case when Rock Pigeons, Scarfs, Black Guillemottes and Cormorants were rushing past on all sides, the instigation came in a parenthetic way, thus 'now sir – now – make haste sir! (What's your name sir?) – oh sir! oh!' Dick banged down a Cormorant, told them his name was Atkinson and got nothing but 'Kison' from them ever after.

I never experienced anything finer (in its way) than our invasion of these caverns, if silence is kept a boat can generally row within them, before the great mass of fowl takes fright. Our plan used generally to be, that when we got within 50 yards of the mouth of the cave, a noise should be made to startle the birds, that those which flew past might afford good shots to the gunners in the boat; and as my rifle would have been perfectly useless in their sort of shooting, the noise we made to alarm them, was usually a shot from it, at the yellow head of some old Scarf near the mouth of the cave; whether killed or not, down he and his companions (a good many of them at least) tumbled into the water, and the unwounded ones dived beneath our boat, a hundred yards out to sea. The pigeons however, and Guillemottes, take the opportunity of flying past very rapidly. A few Scarfs would still remain on the ledges of the rock within the cave, uttering the most doleful croakings; rendered very difficult to distinguish from the dark recesses they select. After the first shot or two they often remain stupidly poking about their yellow heads from side to side and mingling their deep note with the echoing lash of the waves in the furthest recesses of the cavern, and (when we heard them) with the constant reports of our and encourage-ment multiplied a thousand times by the echoes among the rocks, it formed a scene, partaking very much of the sublime, and which can never I think, be forgotten by any who partook of it.

The Rock Pigeon is the most difficult to procure of the inhabitants of these caves; they are very shy and leave the place with their dashing rapid flight, often when the boat is out of shot, but at any rate at the first noise made: their nests as I before observed, are rather difficult of access and during this day we did not get one.

The Scarf, *Green Cormorant*, make their nests nearer the mouth of these 'halls of shells' often on ledges above the entrance, and generally where the rock hangs over the water, situations selected I should think to afford their young immediate access to it at first leaving the nest, and themselves, as they exemplified to us, a ready and effective means of escape at all times. The nests, though generally difficult to get to, are easily seen, for they are of considerable bulk (5 inches deep and 12 or 14 in diameter) and built of black seaweed placed on ledges of rock, white with their dung. They lay 3 or 4 longish white eggs, rather less than an ordinary hen's, and characterised by the chalky matter on the shell, peculiar to the Cormorants. Most of the nest contained young birds when we were there.

The other dwellers of these caves, the Black Guillemotte is an independent sort of fellow, coming forth from his concealment at the first alarm, or just as it suits him: his flight is rapid and straight, and he dives pretty well.

Otters are common throughout the Hebrides, they frequent parts of the shore, inaccessible holes among the rocks present a secure retreat; from these they are sometimes driven by terriers, (those on Skye being particularly adapted for the purpose) and make good sport, as they bite severely and are not bashful about it.

We landed at the Fox-hunter's Cottage, near to which is a splendid waterfall, formed by a rivulet running from a lake a couple of miles to SE of the Storr. I think it must be at least 120 feet in fall, and springs from the rock in a bold and peculiar manner. Mr.Train got a sketch of it as we disembarked from Holm island. This last landing from our return from the caves was at 5 o'clock, we then climbed the hill above the Fox-hunter's to the comparatively level on which the mountain called the Storr stands: this we found a bad place as it is 7 or 8 miles to Portree, and being new to us, tired us pretty well by ten o'clock when we got back to Portree. Coming home in the evening a

golden plover abused Crab's confidence by pretending lameness and leading a long chase over the hills. And here let me observe that within my
experience, nothing makes so satisfactory a mark for rifle, as this bird,
when you are near its young; after dashing past you once or twice, it skims
swiftly over the heather and alights on some small eminence, at the distance of 60 or 70 yards, exposing its black breast, motionless and round,
and calling your attention by a shrill plaintive whistle. Level a good deal
below him, and bring the rifle slowly and steadily up till you cover the
head, and instantly draw the trigger - with a little practice, you will find
that death pretty generally ensues - that is to say if your rifle is good and
judiciously loaded; mine carries a ball of 80 to the pound, I use ¾ drachm
of powder as an average charge, which from experiment, I find to shoot
correctly and point blank at 70 yards: the American measure is simple
enough; the bullet is laid on the extended palm of the hand, and powder
gently poured upon it till it is covered, this is a point blank charge for
every distance under 100 yards, they say, and they have a right to know as
they excel in all the world in the use of this beautiful weapon. One thing
in the furniture of it however had often struck me as very imperfect; the
breach sight[35] - it is usually in good guns made with flaps for 3 distances
on the barrel, thus

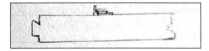

Diagram of Breach Sight (a)

the one represented up, for 100 yards, the next for 150 and the longest for
200; but should any intermediate distance be required, it becomes almost
guess work - you are told the target you are to shoot at, or you are aware
the animal you are about to aim at, is 120 or 130 yards off: what can you
do? You must either use the low sight and aim high, or the sight for 150
yards and aim low! Either is bad – the way in which I remedied this is
simple enough, and from experience I have had of it, superior to the old
plan in many ways, it is merely an inclined plane placed longitudinally on
the barrel where the breach sight is to be, containing a dove-tailed groove,
throughout its length in which an ordinary sight is fitted to slide

Breach Sight (b)

so that when at the lowest part of the slide it is arranged for 100 yards,
when in the middle for 150 and when on the most elevated part for 200,
giving in gradation, all the intermediate distances.

☞ **Tuesday, 24th May** ✿ ✿ ✿
Wet, dressed flies and went fishing near Portree, Skye.

IT RAINED today till 12, so Dick and I dressed flies till then, after which we set off to fish in some small lochs we passed yesterday at the foot of Storr; the nearest of them is about 4 miles from Portree, and the other which is larger and does not contain much fish, a mile further on. The latter discharges itself into the sea in a fine cascade at the Fox-hunter's Cottage, which is well worth a visit. I am not quite sure that this is the fall which McCulloch[36] describes as 300 feet high, but I think it must, as in sailing along the coast a day or two after, no other fall of any magnitude presented itself: if it is however, he is egregiously in the wrong, as it is not nearly so high (about 120 feet) and differs considerable from his account. I have always thought him a man who seems to sacrifice correctness to the pleasure of saying a good thing; this I believe has been proved in many places where his abuse of Scottish accommodation has been facetiously unbounded.

The smallest and most southern of the lochs above mentioned, discharges itself into the north side of Portree bay, and the stream by which it does so, forms the shortest and easiest guide to these lochs and the Storr at the same time, as we discovered by repeated experience. Our fishing today was disastrous enough as we broke our two rod tops, and only got 3 dozen fish: the quality of them however compensated in some measure for the lack of numbers; they were all good fish, averaging ½ pound and pink-fleshed. Lighted a fire under a rock to endeavour to cook our fish and keep ourselves warm, for it had rained and made us rather chill; but after many attempts it burnt so badly that we set off without accomplishing it, and I got home hungry enough by 10. Mr. Train stayed at home to finish some sketches.

☞ **Wednesday, 25th May** ❀ ❀ ❀
Exciting expedition to the Storr with its incredible rocks and views.

SET OFF at 11 to visit the Storr,[37] Dick taking his rod with intention of remaining at the loch till our return: calculated this would be three hours from parting, but were much mistaken, as it took us nearly 6: it is a tedious walk to the top of the mountain called the Storr from the lochs, and to descend by the other side (N) and return by the curious pinnacled rock at its east base, will be found to occupy about that time even though the travellers be better mountaineers than Mr. Train, or more inspired with the principle of 'getting on' than George Atkinson. It is however so much finer and so different from any other mountain scenery I have seen, that I should recommend to any friend who peruses this record of it, to make a point of seeing it, though he go from Glasgow to do so. The view from the summit is in the first place very extensive, and in beauty or rather diversity and interest yields not to that from Ben Lomond or Goatfell on Arran. To the west is seen distinctly the whole range of the Long Island from the Butt of Lewis to the south Isles of Barra; to the east and north-east the coast of Inverness-shire with its unexplored mountains and lochs, and the intervening islands of Rasay, Rona and Scalpa: and to the south the whole of Skye lies before you like a map, displaying in the most satisfactory and intelligible manner, its curious intersection by branches of the sea, so that it is affirmed no part of the island is more than 4 miles from it. Mr Train's rambling had nearly come to an abrupt conclusion today in our ascent of the Storr; near the summit of the east face up whose grassy perpendicular (nearly so, at least) we had climbed with some difficulty; masses of herbage had slid away from the action of the rain descending in torrents from the hills and had left exposed narrow gravelly ravines on the steep side of the mountain which from the insecure footing they afforded and the dizzy height of their situation, constituted the most formidable difficulty in the ascent. I never thought about it and crossed one of these gullies near the summit without hesitation or consideration and in two or three jumps attained the comparatively level ground on the top, where I threw myself in breathless fatigue on the green bank of a little rivulet: after enjoying this for a few minutes, I began to feel alarmed at the non-appearance of Mr. Train who though generally a little in the rear, had had full time to station himself beside me. At length I jumped up and commenced retracing my steps with some rapidity; and I certainly found him in an awkward and amusing situation enough; in attempting to cross one of these gullies, he had after cautiously assuring himself of the stability and responsibility of a resting place for his foot, proceeded to cross it by swinging himself upon a point of rock about the middle; unfortunately however for his arrangements, the projection on which his dependence chiefly lay, most inopportunely commenced a series of vibrations which entirely discomposed him, and after experiencing no consolation from the unpremeditated departure of his sketch book, which danced down the mountain side with enormous bounds, he resigned himself to his ridiculous fate and was sticking in the middle when I arrived to his relief.

The view from the top of the chaos of rocks below is singularly grand, though their height is lost from being so much above them; and to look down one of the tremendous gaps in the face of the precipice, a rather nervous operation, which should by no means be omitted, as except an out of the way place at St Kilda, I know nothing like it. We enjoyed the different scenery for half an hour, and then proceeded northward to return

The Storr from a loch on the south-east

by the singular rocks at the base of the mountain; this, in consequence of Mr. Train's want of skill in climbing and the difficulty of the descent, occupied a long time, and we had to go so much further round than we anticipated, that on another visit, I should return from the summit by the south side to visit the rocks below. When however we got among them and between the most striking steeple shaped rock, and the cliffs of the mountain, we were richly repaid for our walk: of course it is quite out of the power of language to describe it, but it would be very stupid to say nothing about it, I may as well, like many who indulge in that imagination exciting commonplace, proceed forthwith to do so. In the first place (and for the occasion I think the flight of imagination is exceedingly reasonable and comprehensible) I can conceive nothing with which to assimilate these rocks and the surrounding scenery, but the ancient burial place of a race of giants! The massive and irregular side of the mountain suggesting the remains of some vast edifice, and the strange fantastically shaped upright rocks, scattered round its base, the rude memorials of Gigantic dead.(not intended for poetry). Tremendous masses of rocks of the most grotesque form close the view on every side; the rugged basaltic precipice of the mountain, black as night frowns on one side and imparts its gloomy shadow to this extraordinary spot; the winds eddying above howl among the rocks, but interrupt not the stagnant stillness below; and the only records of life are the shrill piercing notes of the Eagle and the deep hoarse tones of the Ravens in the chasms of the mountain. It is difficult to prevent a feeling of awe in the contemplation of this strange place and the animal spirits become subdued under its influence; conversation is discontinued by degrees, and an uncontrollable sense of insignificance

comes on the beholder. You feel bewildered with the imposing sublimity of the scene and experience a kind of relief in quitting it, sensible as you do so that it is the most extraordinary scene you ever beheld; you long for the painter's talent, yet you feel that you durst scarcely represent such improbable scenery, and you are impressed at the same time with the impossibility of describing it, from the absence of ought else to liken or compare it to.

We left at length this wonderful place, and calling for Mr. Train's sketchbook proceeded to join Dick who had caught 5 dozen fine trout, and then proceeded home tired enough to supper at 10.

☞ **Thursday, 26th May** 🏵 🏵 🏵
  Meet Sunderland Tommy[38] *- Storm bound on the Island of Rona.*

I N OUR VOYAGE to Portree in the *'Maid of Isla'* last week, a gentleman who eventually proved to be Col. McNeil[39], an uncle of McGillivray told us that his nephew Donald, on our introduction to whom we relied for so much assistance, had taken his passage to Rowdill in Harris, by the sloop *'Rhoderick of Greenock'*, which had not sailed when we left that place. This vexed us a good deal and we almost gave up any hope of seeing him; this morning, however, the *'Rhoderick'* came into Portree Bay, and I proceeded on board and delivered my introduction to McGillivray in bed: he came to breakfast with us at Jameson's, and as the sloop was to remain a day at Portree and then go round to Stornoway in Lewis, we hired a small boat and 2 men to proceed to Rowdill: for this we were to pay a couple of guineas, when, if we had had the wit, or our boatmen the honesty, to start from Loch Snizort, an inlet on the west side of Skye, running up to within 5 miles of Portree, the cost in time and money would have been about half.

Before starting this morning the landlord came in and said a boy wanted to speak to me; I was somewhat astonished but desired Jameson to shew him in: upon this being done, an ugly red-haired wide mouthed varlet of 13 presented himself and accosted me in a broad Sunderland dialect; stating that 3 years ago he went as cabin boy on board a vessel to Dublin where he had the misfortune to be left behind being on his first voyage; that under the vague idea of getting nearer home, he had come in a vessel to Portree where he had been for 3 years, ignorant of all relating to his friends or home as they must be of him; had been received into the house of a kind-hearted fisherman at Portree who had housed him ever since, and who afterwards gave him an excellent character. This little narrative he concluded by asking me if I knew his mother! Of course I thought it requisite to ask her name; it was Atkinson he said and she lived in the High Street, Sunderland. I told him I did not know his friends, but on my return would make a point of informing them of his situation and his wish to come home. Poor Tom cried, and was very thankful which he evinced by several little attentions during our voyage of which he was a companion, his patron's boat being the one we had engaged.

It may be as well to observe here that on my return home I wrote to his aunt by his desire and waited impatiently to hear from her; after a lapse of a fortnight without doing so I took the opportunity of a visit to Boldon to go to Sunderland where with much difficulty I found his aunt and after a most pathetic scene suggested such arrangements as I thought would restore Tommy to them shortly; this is the second good thing I ever did.

We got on board at 12.30 and had the satisfaction of leaving the bay and finding the wind quite contrary, so after tossing about till between 7 or 8 we were compelled to put into Rona for the night: it is a small island 5 miles long and about 1 broad, separated from the north of Rasa, of which it is almost a continuation, by a narrow channel. The small harbour we put into, is on the SW side and is a favourite refuge for small craft if bad weather, as like many other similar places among these islands, it is completely landlocked: there is however no public house, and most uncomfortably we fared; our boatman knew the inhabitants of the most promising looking house and we were introduced to them, and promised all they could provide by the inmates, a stout melancholy woman with 5 or 6 smoky daughters.

Isle of Rona

While they roasted some potatoes for us (Mr. Train says they did not roast us any potatoes, so I hasten to rectify so important a mistake), we rowed in a boat to an island on which we had observed seafowl at the entrance of the loch, and got a dozen of eggs of the Herring Gull, and a few of the Oyster Catcher, which, I knew from experience to be better than nothing: with these we returned to our hostess, and finding the potatoes not yet done, proceeded to make an inspection of the island.

This I should have been sorry not to have seen as it is unlike any place I ever saw. I do not mean to say it is worth a special visit, for except its desolation and strange mournfulness of character, I should not know how to particularise it; but these qualities were so sensibly perceived by us all, that for months after we used the term '*Rona-ish*' to convey an idea of loneliness and mournful seclusion. The rocks rise in round masses from the heather grey and solemn, and the island is a series of hills and valleys of this material containing no vegetation but the heather and that only in its lower elevation. It is the very place for Fingal and his heroes, and would cure a man of misanthropy in a wonderful brief period.

On our return we were miserably uncomfortable: our peat fire smoked to a degree and there was no animal food but the eggs we had got, so with some whiskey and biscuits we made a late dinner and as we were to rise betimes in the morning, went to bed.

The eagle builds on the S of this island. During the morning Mr. Train was a good deal indisposed and as usual, especially when in that condition, exceedingly amusing; he got a capital likeness of our boatman – helmsman I should say – Murdoch McDonald[40] who managed our boat beautifully, just looking as he is represented, when a squall of wind was blowing which made him rather anxious; but it was the next day between the north of Skye and Harris.

☞ **Friday, 27th May** 🏴 🏴 🏴

A Rough voyage from Rona to Rowdill, Harris - useful contacts

OUR BOATMAN called us at 3 and we got to sea by 4: there was no wind but a heavy swell from the remains of yesterday's squall: I took an oar for a couple of hours and we rowed towards the Point of Sunish (Hunish, the northern extremity of Skye), Train amusing himself and us by singing heroic songs etc to dispel sea sickness: when within 5 miles of it we got a fine northerly breeze which put us along merrily, a good deal to the increase of Train's vivacity, who whistled and sang, told stories, made remarks, till it became very squally when he laid himself on a seat, wrapped as to his head in a plaid, and making a final request that we would take care of his hat, spoke but little. Sooth to say we were very uncomfortable, for the sea broke over us very much and wet us deplorably. McGillivray took the helm and did not manage her with the dexterity of Murdoch McDonald so that we had even more wet than there was occasion for. We had however a famous run from Sunish Point to Rowdill, a distance of 25 miles which we did within 3 hours. On our way we passed close to McDonald's Tables, a group of flat topped precipitous islands 6 or 7 miles to the W of Sunish Head; and to the north we could just make out the Shiant Isles, which lie between Sunish and Stornoway, and are a most favourite breeding place of sea fowl.

At 3.30 we landed at Rowdill[41], a complicated little harbour with two entrances on the SE side of Harris, our steering point from Sunish, being a mountain called Roneval immediately to the north of it, a complete mass of white stones among which the Ptarmigan breeds. There is a Cathedral at Rowdill the capital of the island, but like many Scotch churches it is sadly out of repair: the drapery from the pulpit lying on the floor among wheel barrows and washing tubs; and the benches set against the walls to attain the nests of Starlings which breed there. There is nothing of much interest within the Cathedral, but one or two tombs of the McLeods, who have been for ages the proprietors of this island, and now, pity to say, it is in the market, and in consequence of the small value of the kelp[42] now, is not likely to produce any thing like the value it held 20 years since. I was told that then its value was above £200,000 but that the Trustees now would not hesitate in accepting £60,000 or £70,000 for it. Much of this kind of information I got from our old friend Col. McNeil, McGillivray's uncle, who landing with us at Portree had contented himself with a shorter sojourn, and going over land to Dunvegan had taken the

Rowdill Cathedral

packet thence to Rowdill. Here we found him, poor man, dawdling about and telling everyone he had been taking 'some strong medicine', and looking as if it was not unlikely to take him some day, so great was his apparent debility and exhaustion: but it was so heightened by his awkward lankiness of person, that I hope his case is not so desperate. He was on his way to Pabbay to recruit after having injured his constitution by service in the West Indies, where he knew my father well, and spoke most kindly of him; since then he has taken it into his head that he has discovered or can discover the perpetual motion, and this is his foible: we were told of it in the steamboat, and I tried to introduce the subject, but he seemed shy and distrustful of my seriousness so I gave it up. In this country all the inhabitants seem known to each other and this being so was of advantage to us, as I know he urged the people to be kind and attentive to us, and suggested to John McDonald some days after, to take a blanket in the boat to St Kilda.

If any admonitions of his could have tended to allay the independence of our host John McLeod, I am sure his intercession would have been most advantageous, as though amusing at first, it was a decided bore when the novelty was gone. He received us somewhat surlily at first, but appeared to get reconciled to us: not however till he had inspected us thoroughly, which for the convenience of more uninterrupted observation, he took the opportunity of doing when we were at dinner, coming in and seating himself for the purpose, or walking about with his hands in his pockets.

He was to have quitted his house tomorrow, but Col. McLeod wrote to the Factor and he is allowed to stay a few days longer for our convenience.

McGillivray seems to know and be known by all on the island: all the old wives have some case to consult the Doctor on, and as this is done in Gaelic I conceived it no breach of decorum to stand by and notice the character – external at least, of the people. I cannot conceive anyone more likely to be of use to us: St Kilda will be easily attained as the Tacksman goes about this time on his half yearly visit.

McLeod, or as he is always called 'Harris', intended building a house in the Glen to the N of the town of Rowdill, and planted a part of it preparatory to so doing, but though a most desirable thing for the inhabitants he was prevented by the involved state of his affairs, and it is not now likely to take place. Along this Glen we walked before dinner, deviating to the right to look at a small loch where I shot a sandpiper and Dick tried unsuccessfully to fish: dined on Codfish and potatoes, which we relished amazingly after yesterday's Fare and today's sail.

McGillivray and I shot a couple of Rock Pigeons in some caves N of the town.

Northton Hill

☞ **Saturday, 28th May** ❀ ❀ ❀
   Procrastination - a frustrating day, exploring and shooting.

WE HAD ARRANGED to be up this morning at 8 but owing to
McGillivray's sauntering Scottish system it was nearly 10. Why on
earth people cannot at once do a thing when it is to be done, I cannot
divine: to me nothing is more unsatisfactory than with a limited period at
my disposal to feel dependent on such triflers: it has been my fate on
more than one occasion to suffer from this failing, so I may be excused the
philippic[43]: at McG's suggestion we set off to visit a small island where
numerous sea fowl breed: it is 9 miles from Rowdill and only accessible at
low water for an hour; we went a mile out of our way to call on Mr.
Bethun[44], the minister's son at Scaristy, who knew the island well, and is a
truculent athletic looking fellow, and with his glazed hat would be a desirable man for Parker[45] or any other smuggler painting man. In crossing
Northton Hill[46] – a pretty high mountain by the by – on the north side of
which the island lies, we fell in with some golden plovers, two of which I
shot with my rifle: this took us some time, and I was a good deal vexed
when after allowing us to saunter this way McG – very coolly told us we
should be too late for the tide, and it was no use going on. However Dick
and I pushed on with Mr Bethun, both for the chance of getting on to it,

and to see if it would be worth a visit on another occasion: it proved too far off for the first and decidedly unworthy of a special visit. Upon this hill there is an Eyrie, I should think from its neighbourhood to the sea, of the Common Eagle, and we returned by the NW side of the mountain for the chance of a shot. We saw both the old ones though much too far off for the offensive measures: one of them came sweeping over the hill where Train and McG were lying, at a distance of not more than 20 yards, but McG's gun snapped and the Eagle sailed away unscathed!

Fell in with a good many snipes and sandpipers on our way home and shot a quantity, though a dog of McG's plagued us sadly by running and mouthing all we shot, so that though I killed only to inspect and send home for preserving, we could not keep a bird whole. Home tired at 10 – tea – single glass of Toddy as usual, and bed.

☞ **Sunday, 29th May** 🌸 🌸 🌸
Climbed Roneval, took bearings and saw St Kilda.

A S THERE IS no service at Rowdill, and no English duty at Scaristy, we devoted the morning to climbing Roneval[47] (Danish name I'm sure) in search of the nest of the Ptarmigan: as I said before it lies a mile NE of Rowdill, and is not very remarkable on any account: the elevation cannot be more than 3,000ft: the view is very fine from its summit, giving a most comprehensive prospect of the Long Island, but particularly of the Sound of Harris with its multitude of small islands and the flat part of Harris between Rowdill and the N part of the island called the forest. This flat country is full of small lochs, I counted above 90 from Roneval, and is bleak and desolate almost as Rona. In the morning before, and the evening after the sun, St Kilda and Borera are distinctly visible, in fact at all times if the weather be clear: but the time of day I mention is in general most favourable to vision, particularly at sea. Today we could just make them out, and I took the opportunity by means of a pocket compass of obtaining their bearing from Roneval, as well as that of Hashkir, a rocky island about ⅓ of the distance to them; Cleisheirri, the highest mountain in the forest: the Shiant Isles and any other remarkable object which is visible. And here I may be allowed to recommend this easy process to all tourists: nothing in the first place, so effectually recalls the geography of a country, after a lapse of years, as memoranda taken on the spot of the relative bearings of all remarkable objects from the highest hill you ascend and it may be that the information you so acquire is the means of finding your way among extensive moors, or at sea where the knowledge of your guide or pilot is at fault. It eventually proved so to us.

There are some excellent springs on Roneval of which the natives are very proud: they are only superlative, though in comparison to the other water on the Long Island, which is in general bad, from the deep peat of which most of the islands consist: Harris being an exception from its more mountainous character.

Bearings from Roneval.
'*Hashkir*' WNW; '*Cleisheirri*' 4,000ft high NExE; '*Northton*' NNW
'*Pabbay*' NWxW; '*St Kilda*' a little N of the same line;
'*Flannan Isles*' N; '*Rowdill*' SW; '*Coshlatter*' NW; '*Shiant Isles*' E;
'*Sunish Heads*' ESExS; '*McDonald's Tables*' a little south at the same.

Our search for Ptarmigan was unsuccessful, so we returned to dinner at 6. Our landlord who is fond of conversation, asked me today how I liked our yesterday's dinner – Codfish and potatoes as before mentioned – I said the fish was excellent, the potatoes good, and the preparation of sour cream, which I omitted to mention as our second course, delicious. This I told him on the principle of trying to feel pleased with everything which if well acted up to, saves a deal of vexation and dissatisfaction in going through the world and the Western Islands: and I thought it rather a matter of policy to put our independent host in as good a humour as possible, that, to say nothing of the chance of his turning us out, if offended, he might be induced to use us kindly and feed us well. He seemed pleased at my answer, not I found in consequence of our felicity in the remembrance of yesterday's dinner alone, but because he was going to give us '*a much better one today*'. From this moment we conceived great hopes of him, and he certainly improved vastly, for except that he would have his own way, and wore his wig awry, he grew to be a capital landlord, and took a wonderful fancy to us all. Dick greatly insinuated himself into the good graces of the community at Rowdill, and the old crones used to clap him on the back and in their lack of more appropriate English, call him '*pretty boy*'.

I have some difficulty in hauling our friend Mr. Train from his bed; the fatigue we undergo is more felt by him than by the rest of us, and he is usually the last in all our movements: as I could not get him up this morning I took his likeness as he lay in bed, in part revenge for his caricaturing me with the tooth-ache: and must have him depicted under the miseries of sea sickness, and then my cup of revenge will be full.

Mr. Bethun promised to dine with us today, but did not come, which I fear is a consequence of the increasing bad health of his father who has been unwell.

☞ **Monday, 30th May** ❀ ❀ ❀

Swimming for eggs, visit Eagle's Eyrie, leave for St Kilda at 9 pm.

ANOTHER LATE START – McG[48] – dilatoriness is a perfect nuisance, and then when we were off, every other man is sick and wants advice for himself, and the rest for their wives or children. It was between 10 and 11 before we set off this morning, our intention being to visit a freshwater loch in which a large diver is frequently seen, and is supposed to breed. They call it L. Longuvat, it is the largest on the island, being 7 or 8 miles in length by 2 or 3 in width; is situated 5 or 6 miles N of Rowdill and is full of fish, the salmon being rented by the Doctor and minister. This day's ramble promised much sport, as McGillivray spake largely of the animal productions of the district we were to visit, and we prepared ourselves accordingly; Dick taking a fowling piece and his fishing things, and I my rifle. Our way lay along *the* road – the only one in the island - about 4 miles till a fishing village called Coshlatter occurs, containing by-the-by the only mill in the island, when we struck off to the NE along the side of a loch connected by a deep burn with Longuvat.

The loch contains a good many rocky islands, particularly at the W end which are frequented by numbers of sea fowl, but owing to the shallow water in which they are situated, their nests are visited frequently by neighbouring boys, as they have discovered that sea fowl eggs are excellent eating. At the E end however there is an island situated in deep water, which they cannot attain, as swimming seems little understood among them; and on this island McG – had made up his mind that the Diver we were in search of would have its nest: so I stripped and, much to the dismay of Donald Ross a shepherd we met on the moors, commenced swimming to it.

As I rather pique myself on the plan I adopted to bring any eggs I might get safe to the shore, I may as well explain that I intended to do so, on a water proof bag procured in Newcastle for the purpose, and selected as containing deep ridges in which I speculated the eggs would lie, while I pulled the whole concern along with my teeth. However, in my passage over today, I found it so addicted to turning over that in my next swim for eggs, I took my rifle case – likewise water proof though with the advantage of holes to drink out of; for while in Skye about the Storr, where no good drinking water occurs down by the lochs, Train and I used to fill it for Dick's benefit and bring it to

him from the hills: this bag I afterwards used and found it to answer
exceedingly well for bringing eggs from small islands. I landed on the
island and found it covered with very thick rushes, or sedges, among the
roots of which there were many tracks of some animal, sometimes ending
in the plundered nests of a bird which I conceive from the fragments of
the eggs I saw to be the Red-breasted Merganser. These tracks were very
deep taking me up to the middle; nevertheless I explored them all and was
enjoying a gleam of sunshine when Donald Ross shouted to me that it was
no use looking any longer as the island was full of 'Otter beasts' which
would destroy the eggs of anything breeding there; at this intimation I put
myself quietly into the water again and swam ashore for I had no notion of
intruding on their privacy. Dick caught a good dish of fish though they
were only small, as the other end is supposed to contain the best.

After this, being informed of an Eagle's nest on the NE side of Roneval,
we returned that way, and as they, being tired, would round the hill to go
home and get dinner ready, Ross took me up to the nest: it was most easily situated in point of access, and I have no doubt from the astonishment
and terror of my guide when I climbed it that many other represented as
unattainable are only so in the awkwardness and want of resolution of the
natives – I've climbed a Raven's nest on Whanney crags worth a dozen of it
for neckishness. It proved to have been robbed or forsaken before my visit,
so after standing a moment or two within it, I climbed into the last year's
tenement and then we went home to dinner. These nests would fill a cart
and were composed almost entirely of heather, though I think there was
some seaweed intermixed.

As I before observed, good water is scanty on the Long Island, occurring only on the hills and then in small quantities: in drinking it, it is
therefore indispensably necessary to throw a handful of grass on the
spring and drink through it, a most excellent plan when water is turbid
or infested by insects, and one we learned from McG – who told us it is
universally in use among the shepherds.

While crossing Roneval, we sought for some time for the nests of the
Ptarmigan, which Ross described as so like that of the Golden Plover, that
I have no doubt he had mistaken the latter for it: our search was unsuc-
cessful and we got to Rowdill at 7.

Found McG – would not be able to go with us to St Kilda, as there is
some situation now vacant in N Uist, for which he intends to offer himself:
he recommends our seizing the opportunity of an easterly wind which is
now blowing and get away tomorrow morning. However it is a good piece
of temporal economy to sail during the night if the weather be fine, so we
got a boat 18 feet in the keel belonging to John McDonald of Coshlatter,

who with two others constituted our crew, and embarked[49] at 9 for the island of St. Kilda. So little enterprise have the good people of Harris that they could not at all enter into our feelings of going on a rather uncertain voyage from curiosity about the inhabitants and productions of a small island, and from the sensation our departure created I was almost inclined to conceive our undertaking one of more difficulty than we had arranged for; however, away we went with a light breeze at first, but which towards 12 got fresher and promised us an expeditious voyage.

Our boat, as I observed, was a small one considering the distance she had to go in the open sea, but the fact is the Atlantic comes so heavily into the bay at St. Kilda, if the wind has any south in it, that you must either go in a vessel large enough to ride with safety in any swell, or in a boat small enough to be hauled up on the beach while you remain there.

We chose the latter, and John's boat was about 3 tons burden, yawl built, and 18 feet in keel. By our kind friend Col. McNeil's suggestion he had taken two or three blankets and a pillow or two, besides five bottles of whiskey, a cask of water, and (which we did not then know of) a bag of oatmeal; of course we had cold meat and oatcake for immediate consumption. We had the after part of the boat filled with straw for sleeping on, and a fire in an iron pot forward. Thus provided we went merrily on our way to St. Kilda, or Hirta as they call it, an island which by many has been

St Kilda from the east with Soa, Stac Lea, Stackanarmin and Borera

described as all but unattainable, and attended with so many dangers and difficulties to reach that our departure was looked on as a rare and memorable circumstance by the natives of Harris. However we gathered more encouragement from John McDonald whose two assistants had been there before, and we had considered fairly before we set sail the kind of authorities on which it had been pronounced dangerous, and had come to the conclusion that, though of necessity there must be a risk attending sailing 70 or 80 miles in an open boat, where there is nothing to look forward to in the event of being driven from our course, within a considerable distance (America), still the difficulty has been much exaggerated by our leading authority, McCulloch, who in his letters says it is needless to go with a fair wind, as it raises a dangerous swell in the bay of landing on the SE side of the islands. This is all very likely, but we had an easterly wind and ran it in 13 hours, landing comfortably and tolerably easily at the bay aforesaid at 10 in the morning of Tuesday, 31st May.

2. St Kilda at Last

May 31st – June 2nd

The People and Way of Life, Breeding Birds
Description of the Islands, Climb Conachar
Visit Borera to see Gannets, Watch men climb Stack Biorach
Explore Soa, Admire Fowling Skills of the Men

Tuesday 31st May 🌼 🌼 🌼

> *Landing at St Kilda, a great reception, meet the Minister and
> People*

THE BREEZE HAD slackened when we got within a mile of the island
and, our approach being observed, the whole population anxiously on
the look out; for it was the time of the half yearly visit of the Tacksman,
and our boat was supposed to contain him and the supplies of Tobacco,
Knives etc, which he brings.

About 10 in the morning we reached the head of the bay, and with the
assistance of the natives jumped on shore, which at the landing place
consists of rather large slippery masses of rock: the sails and moveables of
the boat then followed and then the boat herself, for they haul up all small
craft immediately on its arrival, men women and children lending a hand
to the rope cheered on by a particular cry from one of their party, the
words of which meaning *'here with her altogether'*, were *'Hoy sho wallosho,
wallosho'*.[50]

Our two junior boatmen, who had cleaned themselves and smartened
up, previous to landing, were exceedingly well received and no wonder, for
one in particular, Ian McCloud was a handsome lad with the merriest face
I ever saw, and amused us with singing, and joking with his companions,
all the way over.(I got the *'Saint Kilda Wedding'* from him). We were
received by the minister Mr. McKenzie[51] on the rocks, and proceeded with
him to his house, which with the church was built about a year before and
stands close by the landing. He introduced us to his wife who is a Glasgow

Village of St Kilda

lady and has not one word of Gaelic. She has just been a twelvemonth on
the island, and it is nine since she had exchanged a word with any one
but her husband, and the Tacksman[52] (who was here for a day or two six
months since) if he had English, though it is just as likely he had not; so I
am quite inclined to believe she was glad to see us. What a cosy place to
spend the first year of married life, under her circumstances. We foolishly
neglected to bring them any newspapers, which we might have judged
would be most acceptable, and were ourselves so threadbare of recent
intelligence that we could only give them a general idea of political
circumstances, and a short recital of the most spirited murders and
accidents. By the by, their first question, or rather one which was asked in
Gaelic (for only one man on the island has *any* English) of our boatmen,
while preparing to land, was '*if there was any war?*'

The Inhabitants – *100 souls, their dress and health*

Our first remark was on the extremely good looks of the inhabitants of
this lonely little spot: they are rather small in person but neatly made, and
both fair and dark complexions, but almost unexceptionally they exhibit
the most beautiful teeth imaginable, which tend to set off their intelligent

countenances to great advantage. The dress of the men is much the same as that worn by the fishermen of our poorer and more remote fishing villages, coarse blue jacket and trousers and a woollen shirt with or without shoes and stockings: that of the women a loose gown of the same material drawn in at the waist. All their clothes they make themselves, each man weaving, tanning, shoemaking etc. etc. for himself alone; and taking that into consideration the goodness of their costume is rather astonishing. Their shoes they make from sheepskin tanned with the root of tormentil, which abounds on the island, sewed together with strips of the same, and sometimes soled with a lot of sea fowl feathers, though generally only with the thickest part of the skin.

The fair sex predominate on the island, so that there are a good many specimens of ladies of a certain age here as elsewhere. The whole population amounts to a little more than 100 souls, and is, and has been, about the same for centuries which may perhaps be accounted for by the circumstances that from want of surgical attendance a good many of the women die in childbed.

They are however in general so healthy that except in these and a few other cases they scarcely feel the absence of such assistance: while we were there an old woman was suffering from dropsy, but it was an almost unprecedented case: Mr. McKenzie told us agues and fevers were the most formidable diseases they had to contend with, and their temperance was of such advantage that the latter were more easily managed and subdued by their simple means than diseases of the same kind under more civilised circumstances.

He had been informed that the itch prevailed among them to a shocking extent, and came prepared to contend with it, with a large stock of the most approved specifics, sulphur etc.; he was however much gratified to find it almost unknown, and never in such virulence as he had known it on the mainland.

Of course their surgical knowledge is confined enough, one of the men has a lancet and bleeds them occasionally, and in cases of fracture and dislocation, he splices and replaces to the best of his ability. Some shipwrecked sailors who had been with them for six weeks one winter produced a great sensation in their winter stores and supply of tobacco, and before leaving they provided an opportunity for their surgical attainments, in the fractured arm of one of their party. They gave us a capital account of the successful result, for the man was almost in full use of his limb when he left the island.

Moral simplicity and integrity, unsophisticated, kind and hospitable

Nothing could happen more unfortunately for the moral simplicity and integrity of the inhabitants than such a visitation. However the evils which might have been anticipated by their intercourse were avoided from the moment the seamen landed, from the disgust their undisguised profligacy awakened in the minds of their entertainers. It would indeed have been a pity if their hospitality had brought on them an acquaintance with the social vices, and been the means of corrupting the most innocent and unsophisticated people in the universe.

For the St. Kildans are in a curiously primitive state of integrity and simplicity; murder, of course, from the impossibility of escape and the absence of the usual causes of incitement, is unknown in their traditions; and dishonesty from similar causes very nearly so; a case of adultery has never been known among them; and as no fermented or spirituous liquor is made on the island, and they only receive a trifling half yearly supply from the Tacksman, they are of necessity sober.

In addition to these negative virtues, they are kind and hospitable in the highest degree; observe the most scrupulous regard for truth; and are obliging and attentive to strangers to a most pleasing extent. They are celebrated for the goodness of their singing, and their cheeses; – the island, for its lonely situation in the Atlantic and the myriads of sea-fowl which resort there to breed, and which constitute the food, the staple commodity, and almost entirely, the circulating medium of the island.

Island Government meet on the roof of a house, Naval Activities

Their government is strictly a republic for, though subject to Great Britain, they have no official person among them; and as they are only visited twice a year for a few days by the Tacksman, who is referred to as a sort of umpire or settler of disputes, their knowledge of our laws must be very trifling, and of little use or importance in their system of economy. Everything of importance is managed and arranged by a common assembly of the male population, convened on the roof of a house somewhat larger than the rest, in the middle of the village[53] * I say everything of importance – of course they meddle not with the emancipation of the Catholics, the disfranchisement of rotten boroughs or the Newcastle and Carlisle

---

*I should observe that the rafters of the houses rise from the inner side of a broad low wall, which leaves the thickness of the wall as a seat, or shelf to place household utensils on . . ... They sit and portion out the rock to climbers, examine into the state of ropes which have lain for the winter, and settle any disputes which may have arisen among their number; anything of more weighty import being left for the decision of the tacksman on his visit.

44

Railroad Bill – but all the interests of their own community are arranged in council; the fowlers have their separate districts of rock allotted to them, and the naval economy of the state is considered and discussed.

Their naval Railroad establishment is extensive - they have a single, awkward, heavy ship's boat of maybe 2 or 3 tons burthen, and she belongs to the community at large so that all employment of her comes under the consideration of the assembled people. She rows with 3 oars aside and has a square mainsail of a most curiously varied fabric of wool, made by themselves, and serves them in fine weather to go to Borera in.

Visiting Borera for a few days, stay in the Stal House

This island lies five miles to the north of St. Kilda, and as it possesses no shore low enough to allow hauling up the boat, they land those of the party who cultivate the fowling department, and leave them till they conceive sufficient time has elapsed to have ensured the capture of the desirable quantity of fowl, when if weather permit, they return and bring away their companions. This usually occupies three or four days, but they have often been detained three weeks, as they are wretched sailors and the sea is often heavy out there.

During their sojourn on Borera they occupy a curious old edifice, like one of their own houses, situated on the south west side of the island, called the Stal house. It is supposed to have been the residence selected by some recluse and consists of an oval room, 10 or 12 feet by 6 or 7, with sleeping apartments opening from the sides, like rabbit holes. This is the only semblance of a habitation on the island, and is likely to remain so, as the supply of water is far from abundant, and there are few places sufficiently sheltered for dwelling houses.

Fowling for the Sea Bird Harvest, Ropes Tested, Working in twos or threes on the Cliffs

From their dependency on the capture of sea fowl for their support, all their energies of body and mind are centred in that subject, and scarcely any of their regulations extend to anything else. From the period of the arrival of the fowl in the month of March, till their departure in November, it is one continued scene of activity and destruction: every method is adopted to procure their feathered visitants, and next to a sense of astonishment at the immense quantity of fowl, is a similar feeling that their numbers remain undiminished, under the ceaseless attacks of every kind which are made upon them.

The season commences by a general examination of the ropes and climbing gear which appear good enough for more service: this for a few years past has been made a point of particular scrutiny, and is witnessed by the whole population and it arose from the melancholy death of one of their lads a few years since, who went to rob a falcon nest with a rope which had not been tried, and which, breaking, precipitated him many hundred feet into the sea. On examining the rope afterwards, it was found so rotten that a man could easily break it between his hands. This however is not a common cause of destruction to them, as very little reliance is placed upon the rope in climbing, particularly on a rope of more than two or three fathoms, its use being more to steady and balance the adventurer, than to sustain his weight.

They generally climb in pairs, though in the descent of their highest cliffs a third man is employed, who descends with them as low as they can attain by the assistance of the short 8 fathom ropes they each of them carry, and then, fixing the end of the long one – about 25 fathoms – to some convenient projection of the rocks, stations himself beside it, to see that it retains its firmness and security, or to move it in any direction his companions below may direct.

Vegetation is so profuse on these islands that every ledge of rock is covered with herbage, and it is chiefly in these situations that the fowl deposit their eggs, and the daring skill of the islanders is exerted. The profusion of herbage on every surface - horizontal at least - of the rock, has rather an odd effect in looking upwards and downwards at the precipices. In the former case nothing can appear more barren and impassable, a bleak front of awful extent and elevation presenting itself; while from above it seems so green and smooth that you can scarcely persuade yourself it is not the sloping steep of a grassy mountainside.

Climbing Skills - in places, hand over hand like a monkey

In traversing this tremendous front, those who are intent on the active duty of fowling, are connected by one of the ropes which (as I said before) they each carry. This is not so much to sustain either of them in case of slipping as to leave their hands perfectly at liberty to assist them in their progress. The one who has agreed to lead the descent ties one end of the rope under both arms, round his waist, and his companion ties the other end over one shoulder and under the other arm: thus they clamber among the rocks, assisting each other when close together by touches and assistances so slightly perceptible, that to a stranger their reason for doing so, is quite unintelligible. At the same time when it is considered how the strength of a hair will determine the balance of matters of great bulk, it will easily be seen how the slightest touches, applied in the time and manner their experience points out as most effective, will tend more to their safety on the face of the cliff than any mechanical contrivance or individual boldness and dexterity.

The one who is highest on the cliff takes care to keep the connecting rope as tight as possible, both to prevent the dangling of it from impeding his companion, and also to relieve him of his own weight to a certain degree. His own rope he keeps coiled on his arm to use when occasion requires: this is not often – I think only in descending perpendicular faces of rock which afford no footing to climb by. Then indeed their mode of proceeding is beautifully ingenious and effective: the second man commences by fastening the spare rope round his own waist and, fixing himself in some recess of the rock lays hold of that which is attached to his companion's waist, as near to it as possible, ready to lower away as soon as he leaves the last place of footing. The leader at the same time seizes the other rope as close as he can to his supporter's body, and then leaving the ledge of rock he stood on, they both lower away together by the different ropes, so that in a most simple manner the strength of two men is applied to raise or sustain the weight of one, who in reality only lifts half of his own weight. Before we were fully aware how this was accomplished we were exceedingly puzzled to understand how men could ascend hand over hand by a rope with as much apparent ease as a monkey: to do which at all requires a much greater degree of muscular exertion than most men possess.

The long rope is sometimes used to lower a fowler to situations where their ordinary modes of fowling could not place them; and then two or more of his companions are required to sustain him and lower him to the desirable situations.

Fowling Rod with a Horse Hair Noose and a Gannet's Quill

The only destructive weapon they employ against the fowl is a clumsily made rod of 12 or 13 feet in length, and something like a very strong fishing rod. On the end of this is a strong horse-hair noose about 5 inches in diameter stiffened at its junction to the rod with slips of the quill of the gannet. With this seemingly insufficient instrument they catch nine tenths of the sea birds obtained in the course of the year, and the dexterity with which they use it is the only matter of equal astonishment to a stranger with the ridiculous simplicity and folly of the birds themselves – the guillemottes especially.

The whole front of the rock is abundant in small shelves and ledges which, till within 80 or 100 feet of the water, are covered with herbage on which the fulmar lays her egg. On the lower ledges the Razor Bill and Guillemotte breed and congregate in immense numbers – so much so that they sit huddled together in close, compact bodies wherever a projection affords them room to alight. In descending to the lower and more frequented ledges, it was amusing to see the puzzled, disconcerted look of a shelf of these foolish birds, when the fowler in his progress displaced a lot of them to obtain himself a footing. With the exception of those he kicked from the rock, a feeling of amazement seemed the prevailing one, and not until he had stooped and captured one or two in each hand did they seem to think it worth while to tumble themselves from the rock. The birds as they are taken, receive a double contortion of the neck, and are deposited on any convenient ledge of rock till the day's work is done. In using the rod, which is done whenever they can secure a footing within reach of their game, the noose is first distended, and then the rod taken at first by a small end, and then thrust through the hands till it encircles the heads of one or two of the fowl, which are unceremoniously enough dragged from the rock and dispatched as above-mentioned. In this manner 20 or 30 Guillemottes are often captured from a single ledge of rock, very few of them making any more active endeavour to escape than by moving their heads from side to side as the noose approaches, or sometimes preventing its embrace by keeping it aloof with their bills; as they diminish they certainly evince a little more distrust and apprehension, some of them taking the trouble to shuffle away to the furthest extremity of the shelf, and a few, even quitting it under the threatening aspect of things in general.

Villainous Smells – Fulmar Oil, Offal, Carcasses, Manure – Nothing Wasted

This is the common mode of capturing most kinds of fowl, particularly the Guillemotte, Fulmar and Solan Goose. The two latter - the fulmar particularly is much more wary than the bird whose capture I have described. He is however to be met with in much more accessible places, and being accounted by them the most delicate eating, they pay an especial degree of attention to his capture, and his oil, which he spurts out when taken, forms a component part of a peculiarly unsatisfactory smell, discoverable when in company with the natives, and which, before the manse was built (a year since), when strangers were compelled to house with them (the natives), invariably attached itself to them for 5 or 6 weeks.

To account for the remaining components of this delicate perfume I should observe that the manure they employ for the growth of a small quantity of barley raised on the island is the offal and refuse of sea fowl and other filth, carefully preserved in their houses throughout the year, and mixed with the thatch of their cottages, which, as they are destitute of chimneys, is intimately impregnated with smoke from their constant turf fires.

Add to this the scent of their hoards of sea fowl feathers and carcasses and the consequences of naturally uncleanly habits, and I think a faint notion of the *tout ensemble* of this '*compound of villainous smells*' may be formed. We were assured by our friends in Harris that we should be nosed by a whole neighbourhood on our return to England.

Guillemottes caught on nesting ledges at night – using a decoy

The mode of capturing the guillemotte on its first arrival is singular enough, and is almost as illustrative of the stupidity of the bird as the one above described. The fowler, having provided himself with a dead bird, or skin of a last year's guillemotte, stations himself at dusk on a ledge where they have been used to congregate, and, sitting perfectly motionless, places the dead bird with its white breast conspicuously exposed, before him. The birds returning to roost in the evening, fancying they behold a companion already settled in a convenient situation, come pouring in by scores and if the fowler escapes being wounded by their extended bills in their impetuous flight, his harvest is generally a good compensation for this trouble.

Puffins – Huge Numbers on the grassy slopes – dig their own burrows, lay single egg

Puffins[54] do not, generally speaking, affect such inaccessible places, the sloping side of any of the islands, or the mixture of rock and grass at the top of the precipices affording them either natural holes and crannies to deposit their eggs in, or a loose soft soil fit for their excavations. These, by the by, are so like rabbit holes that on the Fern Islands (*Farne Islands. Ed.*) they are supposed to be deserted ones, adopted by these birds; however, as this little animal does not exist on St. Kilda, the industrious puffin must receive the proper credit, and whoever has had a live one in his hands will testify that they possess wonderfully sharp claws at the extremity of their webbed toes, and can use them right vigorously.

Soa and Borera are more abundant in them than St. Kilda, though at the tops of the cliffs on the north west of that island, and on the promontory, the Doun, which bounds the bay of St. Kilda on the west, they are found in great numbers. In rainy weather they are most numerously to be seen about the islands, as they then fly to and fro incessantly, and do not go to sea to fish. They are likewise driven from that element in stormy weather, but keep themselves within their holes. It must be curious to see them when most abundant, for though the weather was particularly fine when we were there, there appeared to be no end of them, giving one more the idea of an immense flock of midges than anything else, as they skimmed noiselessly past and covered every projection with their numbers. They are not quite so stupid as the guillemottes and are seldom caught with the noose, but by reaching the arm into their holes and taking them where they sit. Some little skill is necessary in doing this, as they bite and scratch severely if, before they recover from the surprise of the first assault, they be not seized by the head and expeditiously pulled out; when with this murderous intention their privacy is invaded, they sometimes utter most dolorous groans, and if it will admit of it - retire to the furthest recesses of their holes.

Little Crab, a pet terrier of Dick's, was much amused in their capture at which he soon became expert, for he is so small, that the larger holes easily admitted him, and the bites he at first received only made him more determined.

A curious circumstance in the history of the puffin, which is well ascertained here, is that if it be plucked of the feathers of the body, leaving only those of the wings which are requisite for flight, the new plumage will be entirely white. This is something like the skin of a horse where the hair has been rubbed off, producing white hair. With regard to the puffin, it is well known among the Kildeans, though they could not point one out to us which had undergone this operation.

This bird lays only one egg, almost as large as a hen's, but tapering more towards the narrow end. It is white, with almost imperceptible blotches of a darker shade, and with the exception of that of the fulmar is more esteemed than any egg they have.

The hole in which it is deposited, if constructed for the purpose, is the size of a small rabbit hole and extends about the length of a man's arm. With such holes the south slopes of Soa and Borera abound, and the birds sit in thousands on the rocks and stones projecting from the grass.

We often knocked 2 or 3 at a time from their station with stones, and for a time they certainly seemed disconcerted and *hors de combat*, rolling down the steep declivity in company with the stones we hurled at them; but by the time the latter were performing some magnificent bounds preparatory to plunging in ocean's bosom, these little fat fellows always contrived to take wing and skim away merrily with the rest.

On the east side of Soa large stones are heaped together in magnificent confusion, forming caverns large enough to shelter the natives when they sometimes spend a day or two on this island in fowling. In the more remote nooks and corners of these caverns the puffin often accumulates and arranges the little quantity of grass which forms his nest, and, still further in, the Stormy Petrel, whose egg is consequently difficult to obtain.

The Gaelic name for the puffin is 'bouger'. His feathers form a considerable proportionate part of those collected on the island, and with the exception of the gannets on the northern group of Borera and its rocks, he is more numerous than any fowl on the islands.

Razor Bill – less abundant than Guillemotte and Puffin, single egg on ledge or in cavern

The Razor Bill, or as they call him, the *'falk'* ranks more nearly with the guillemotte in appearance and habits, and would have been made mention of after the notice of that bird, but that it would be a pity to molest, and infringe on, the total absence of method or regularity which characterises 'the journal'. Though exceedingly abundant, his tribe bears no comparison with the Guillemotte or Puffin, between which he seems a connecting link as well in form and general appearance, as in habits and disposition. He breeds sometimes on ledges of rock like the Guillemotte (though not in such numerous assemblies), and sometimes in the caverns on the east of Soa, with the Puffin depositing his single egg on the flat surface of some tabular rock, many feet underground; thus he is sometimes associated with the Guillemottes, while reposing on the lower ledges of the vast precipices I have mentioned, and sometimes sits in company with the Puffins on the large stony projections of Soa. He does not dive so well as the Guillemotte, though better than the Puffin, and in like manner takes a middle station in point of cunning and shrewdness.

His egg is very like the Guillemotte's, but does not taper quite so much, and

Rhoderick MacLeod

is generally of a dirty yellowish white, blotched and streaked with brown and reddish yellow marks, whereas that of the Guillemotte is

Woman and child

very often green in ground colour, with black or very dark brown markings: but no egg varies so much in appearance as the Guillemotte's, and I have seen specimens curiously streaked, almost entirely brown, or in one or two cases pure white.

In the ascent of the Thumb rock, one of the boys procured an egg of the Gillemotte, of double the usual size, which they occasionally met with: it is only an accidental double-yoked one and varies considerably from the Great Auk's which I have seen in Mr. Yarrell's[55] collection, and which in greater roundness of form proclaims its connection with the Razor Bill.

Fulmar - vast numbers, esteemed eating, oil collected from young and used medicinally

The next sea bird I shall mention is almost peculiar to the island; with the exception of a few among the precipices of the south isles of Barra, and some of the Shetland Isles, they are almost unknown as birds which breed in Great Britain: here Fulmars are in vast numbers, and are constantly to be seen flying heavily to and fro in front of the precipices containing their nests. Their food does not seem to be well ascertained, but from the abundance of the oily secretion which they project through their nostrils, there can be no doubt that it is chiefly animal. All the petrels, however, are exceedingly fond of the leaf of the sorrel which grows in abundance among the cliffs, and their nests generally contain some, freshly gathered. Their throats too will be found to hold some of it in a masticated state, and the oil to be a good deal tinged with it in many cases. The colour of this oil, in what the Kildeans consider its purest state, is nearly that of amber, and is used by them medicinally as an almost universal specifics. It is procured chiefly from the young birds in the end of June, about which time they are almost able to leave the nests, and are exceedingly fat. The fowling rod is used against them, and as the noose is relaxed from the throat of the captured bird, a wooden bowl is presented to receive the oil, which he commences squirting forth with great zeal; having concluded which, his neck is twisted and he is laid up for winter beef.

The north west side of St Kilda (properly so called) abounds most with this bird, and as it is the shyest of the sea fowl, not only laying but one egg, but also deserting that on the slightest pretext, the Kildeans refrain from fowling on that part of the island till the season I have named.

In point of eating, this bird is in more esteem, from the egg to maturity, than any other they have: I do not think it is larger than the Kittiwake, but its egg is larger than the Gannet's, much of the same form, but of a more delicate and fragile texture and of a whiter colour. Like the rest of the petrels, it lays but one, and the characteristics are, as with its congeners, great size in proportion to the bird, extreme frailty, and pure whiteness of colour, deposited on the grassy ledges of the precipice in the case of this bird, and as I shall hereafter describe, with the others.

Manx Petrel - uncommon, found on Soa and Doun - nests among the
puffins

The Manx petrel, or 'scrabe', is by no means common; less so, indeed,
than any fowl on the islands (tolerably common in Shetland, where the
Fulmar is unknown), and as I am not aware of its breeding anywhere else
in Britain I was glad to have it in my power to ascertain satisfactorily the
particulars of its domestic arrangements.

Why it has been called the Manx petrel I cannot conceive, as on my
visiting the Isle of Man a few years since, a pretty diligent investigation
proved to me that it was not known on the Calf, as my old friend Bewick
mentions; but as we find the present day changing gradually from those
which have gone before, and in nothing more strikingly than in the
increasing scarcity of nature's wild denizens, we may fairly conclude the
bird we speak of to have been so abundant on the Isle of Man, some years
since, as to induce some naturalist to bestow on it the trivial name I have
scribbled half a page about.

Bewick's figure of the bird is exceedingly good, and he had a most
wretched stuffed specimen to draw from, so I was delighted to find him
so successful.

The Scrabe breeds indiscriminately among the puffins on Soa, and the
island or promontory of Doun; but is so uncommon that only a few are
caught in the season, as their holes are somewhat longer than the regula-
tion length of the Puffins, which is just an arm's length in, and it is not
therefore worth the while of the natives to get them. It is scarcely possible
to distinguish his residence externally from the Puffin's, though they
told us to try those holes, which from a stony entrance were rather more
difficult of access, though larger in general appearance. After poking
for a whole day in this manner to the great annoyance of the puffins, we
found only two nests, on one of which, found by Dick I shall form my
description.

It was in the after-mentioned colony of puffins in the east side of Soa,
where my worthy brother, the minister, and I, had been (assisted by a
dozen of the natives) endeavouring to find a nest of this bird. No mercy
was shown to the puffins which occurred during our search, as their eggs
are capital eating, and they possess a tempting stock of excellent feathers.
Therefore as we accumulated four or five eggs, we brought them to a
large basket for general stock. I was standing beside this basket when
my brother put in a lot of half a dozen eggs, and observed, as he placed
the last in, that it was a large one. From one which I had seen at the
minister's, I said at once it was the egg of the Manx Petrels and very
fortunately my brother not only knew the hole he got it from, but gave an

interesting account of the biting propensities of the owner of the tenement, which, after withstanding all his solicitations to come forth, had retired to the penetralia of its domicile, whence we forthwith proceeded to dislodge it.

After some little trouble we were richly repaid by drawing forth an old Scrabe; his hole was about 3 ½ feet in and his nest consisted of as much dry grass as would cover a hat crown, most inartificially arranged. It contained a single egg and several fresh leaves of sorrel; there was likewise some in the throat of the bird. Neither this nor the stormy petrel possesses such a large proportion of oil as the Fulmar, nor do they effect it so violently when captured. The egg is a little larger than that of the puffin, of a rather more oval form and a more fleshy white colour; our assistants got us another one, and the minister gave us a third which he had in the house.

We never saw this bird on the wing, but from his more slender form I should conceive his activity would be greater than the Fulmar's, whose flight is rather like the Kittiwake's but more sluggish, and characterised by a peculiar jerk, something like that of a butterfly on a cold day in autumn, or a dragonfly over a sedge bed. And to continue a digression about the fulmar, in flying he makes use of no cry but when driven from his nest, and then their concert resembles the cry of the Sandwich Tern, though graver in tone.

Stormy Petrel and Leach's Fork-tailed Petrel – both nesting

The last of this genus, the Stormy Petrel, in Gaelic 'Assilag', is more abundant than the one described, though much more difficult to procure, from the inaccessible nature of his habitation, which is in the smallest chinks and crannies among the large masses of stone on the east of Soa. Here he entertains himself by singing in a voice like that of a starling, and thus betrays his retreat to those who will be at the trouble to get him out. On St Kilda, however, he is not numerous, and from the rugged nature of the soil, much more difficult to get than on Pabbay (an island between Harris and North Uist) where he is comparatively abundant.

Mr Bullock[56] found the Fork-tailed Petrel or *P. Leachii* on St Kilda, and I have no doubt, like the *Cygnus Bewickii* which had been confounded with the common wild swan, that the Fork-tailed Petrel is nearly as common as the Stormy Petrel. We only procured one egg of this bird; which is now in the Museum. In form, texture and colour it is similar to those before described and is almost as large as a blackbird's, though the bird is only as large as a sand martin. The flight of this bird is something like that of a single swallow, as one has seen them not going very quick, on a boisterous cold day.

Solan Goose – specially adapted, fish for herring, many birds caught by Kildeans at night

The solan goose, called from his keen eye '*soulear*' (or the looker) breeds only on Borera; not one pair building on St Kilda or Soa, while the rocks of the more northern island swarm with them. But they are very fanciful; the Bass Rock, Ailsa Craig, South isles of Barra and the Shiant isles, sending forth all, till we come to the more northern points of Foula, North Rona, etc.: however, they are more numerous here than anywhere else and are worth going far to see.

This bird is easily known at a distance by its size and the straightness of its flight, and by the position of its wings which are further back than in any other light-coloured sea bird. It is a highly interesting sight to see them fishing among a shoal of herring, when there are many of them their flight is so rapid as to resemble a fall of snow, and to observe the descent of an individual reminds one of the whirling descent of a slate to the water; and it is a matter of admiration that the forcible concussion with which he precipitates himself should not either stun or disable him but a provision has been made for his safety which has only lately been observed: between the body of the bird and his skin, a quantity of air may be received through curiously contrived openings, which would not only prevent the unyielding parts from sustaining the first shock, but afford a degree of buoyancy apparently intended to facilitate his return to the surface.

The upper mandible of the gannet is in a certain degree moveable by a joint near its base, to enable it either to capture more easily, or retain more securely, fish of such bulk as would be otherwise unmanageable.

The egg is larger than a hen's and longer in proportion to its bulk: a greenish white, covered as all the eggs of this Genus of birds are, with a thin white chalky coat, so thin in parts as to expose the greener tinge of the ground colour, and almost an eighth of an inch thick in others. One would almost imagine this coating to have been in a partially soft state when laid, as the egg often bears the marks of straws or grass on its surfaces; this coating bears the appearance as well as the consistency of chalk, and may be cut with a knife or scratched with a finger nail.

The nest is composed of grass plucked from the hills on windy days when they can not go out to fish, in evidence of which occupation, the turf near their nests during the breeding season exhibits numerous little bare patches, whence the grass has been plucked for this purpose.

The gannet is more numerous than any other fowl among the islands, and breeds in incredible numbers on Borera and the adjacent rocks, at every elevation on the barren shelves of rock from within a few feet of the summit to twenty or thirty from the water, and in many places so close together as to render the rock perfectly white from the effects of their dung, and their own compact masses as they sit.

This is peculiarly the case with Stack Lea on the south west side of Borera, which is visible at a great distance and is perfectly white, standing from the water like a ship under sails and Captain Basil Hall[57] in his *'Fragments of Voyages and Travels'* gives a similar account of Rockall, an uninhabited rock 174 miles to the west of St Kilda, on which he landed with a boat's crew, and nearly remained there longer than he wished owing to a fog. Of this rock the minister made some mention to us, having received his information from the natives, who had heard it from some vessel which had touched at St Kilda.

The gannet does not allow other fowl to breed among his ledges of rock, but drives them elsewhere. The mode of capture of this bird is the same as that of the guillemotte, with the fowling rod, but they catch him likewise at night in great numbers by cautiously approaching and securing the one which is always stationed as sentinel. If this be executed without awakening the rest, immense numbers are easily taken, which partially repays the natives for the eminent risk they run in traversing these cliffs by night.

Green Cormorant – many breeding in the caverns

The Cormorant I did not observe among the fowl, but the scarf or green cormorant – *'Scarbh'* as he is here called – constantly breeding in the caverns with which the islands abound, and like the puffin when intruded on, uttering croakings of a most dolorous character. The only nest we thought it worth while to deprive of its eggs was situated in a curious horizontal fissure of rock on Borera, and to attain it we were obliged to push one of the islanders like a ramrod into a slippery hole, and withdraw him in the same way. He and his ways are too well known to need description, as are also the remaining birds of the island, which I shall therefore shortly detail, and then proceed after my long digression to the more active details of our expedition.

Black Guillemotte - not common, nests in holes in the rocks

The Black Guillemotte, *'geara 'breachd'*, is not common on St Kilda, only about three pairs breeding there; one of these had placed its nest in a round hole in a rock in the Bay, to which we pulled in the boat and caught the old one on her eggs; they lay three, and as there were only two here, they were quite fresh.

This bird differs from the common Guillemotte in the number of its eggs and the situation of its nest, more than in their appearance; for their shape, though their size is not so straight is very similar, and the texture of the shell also; but the markings are more varied in colour and partake more of the appearance of the egg of the Sandwich Tern which they resemble than of any other.

Kittiwake – only a few small colonies, some inside the caverns

The Kittiwake, '*rudag*', is not nearly so numerous as on our Northumbrian shores, in fact, I only saw one or two small colonies on the east side of the bay, and they are too insignificant to awaken the cupidity of the climbers, even were the situations they select for their nests more accessible. It is, however, exactly in the most difficult situations that they place them, often where the cliff beetles over and renders it equally impossible to attain them from above or from below. By-the-by, a few pairs breed in the roofs of almost every cavern we were in, where of course they are safe.

Oyster Catcher - not very common

The Oyster Catcher, '*trilachan*', breeds about the bay, but is not very numerous.

Great Black backed Gull - One pair only

A single pair of the Great Black backed Gull, '*farpach*', form their nest annually on Stack Donne, a small diamond shaped rock between St Kilda and Soa, and are the only ones about the islands.

Herring Gull – a few nests

The Herring Gull, '*faol'ionn*', has a few nests on a bay about the north west side of St Kilda, associating himself with a few Oyster Catchers affecting the same situation.

Great Auk – very scarce, not breeding

The Great Auk, '*gairfaol*', is very scarce, coming only once in ten or a dozen years and never breeding there.

Peregrine Falcon – Two pairs nest

A Falcon which the minister, I know not on what authority, called the Goshawk, has two eyries on the islands; one on the east side of St Kilda, in

Young Peregrine Falcon, Borera in the distance

descending to which as I have mentioned before, a lad a few years since broke his neck, and another on a small cliff on the west side of Borera from whence we procured two young ones, a drawing of one at 3 months old graces these pages. I intended to have taken some pains in noticing their progressive changes of plumage, which, even though they be but the Peregrine Falcon, as I shrewdly suspect, would have been interesting; they have however saved me the trouble, as one escaped in September and the other in October.

Starling – breeding

The Starling abounds, breeding inland in holes of the ground or among stones; they call him *'Truidg'*.

Kitty Wren – breeding

The Kitty Wren we also saw shirking about among the large stones. And this, I think, concludes the ornithological zoology of the island, and enables me to resume the more generally interesting portion of my journal.

The Islands Described [58]

The general appearance of St Kilda, in approaching it from the east, is striking, particularly with the addition of Borera and its satellite Stack Lea, which strikes the eye even before the more bulky mass of St Kilda becomes visible. Borera is situated 5 miles to the NNE of it, with Stack-an-armin on its west and Stack Lea on its south west side; independent masses of rock of nearly half the height of Borera itself (1450 feet, McCulloch says 1380) rising from the sea at the distance of a musket shot from it, and presenting an extraordinary spectacle from the amazing number of gannets which nestle on them, and in the immediate vicinity of which the minister earnestly dissuaded us from using our fire arms, as, when startled, they fly over the boat in immense numbers and render the situation of a good coat or hat undesirably hazardous.

On the west side of St Kilda, separated from it by a channel of about a 100 yards wide, is Soa, a comparatively grassy island about a mile in diameter, and of an inferior elevation to St Kilda or Borera, which are nearly the same – 1450 feet: in the NE side of the channel which divides Soa and St Kilda there is a lofty isolated rock called Soa Stack, inhabited by a few Guillemottes and Fulmars, and rendered rather curious from a cavernous arch which it presents, large enough to allow the passage of a boat.Rather more to the south, in the middle of the channel, is the celebrated Thumb Rock, called by them Stack Biorach, and not, as Martin in his excellent description of St Kilda names it, Stack Donne, translating Donne *'dangerous'* when its true meaning is simply *'bad'* or *'unproductive'*; imparting a name to a small, insignificant, but most easily accessible rock, a little further to the south in the same channel, on which no fowl but a single pair of the Great Black-backed gull rear their young.

Stack Biorach he rightly enough describes (under the name of Stack Donne), as being an extraordinary column of two or three hundred feet, rising perpendicularly from the sea, and though abounding more than any rock in the islands in Guillemottes, seldom climbed, from its exceedingly dangerous character, in one part of the ascent (at a height of only 30 or 40 feet certainly) requiring the fowler who leads the ascent to suspend his whole body on a joint of the thumb while he swings himself into a nook of rock where he can assist in hauling up his companions.

From this it derives its name of the Thumb Rock, and so dangerous is the ascent considered that it was four years since it had been attempted, and a high degree of celebrity attaches itself to those who have at any time achieved it.

The dimensions of the islands, I think, are: St Kilda, five miles by two and a half; Borera, nearly round, one and a half in diameter; and Soa,

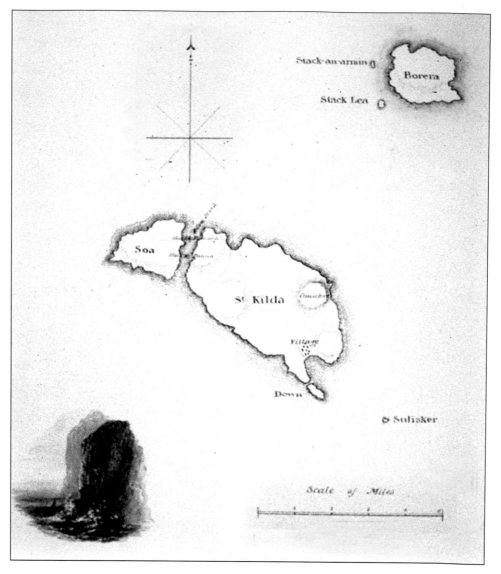

Sketch map of St Kilda

rather triangular, somewhat less. The west side of the bay of St Kilda is called the Doun or Down, which however is accessible at low water. Its elevation is trifling, and though abounding in Puffins, and rather a favourite resort of the Scrabe, it is more remarkable for being perforated in the middle by a lofty arch, and containing on its south extremity the remains of an old castle of some kind, though the minister could not furnish us with any details concerning it.

About two miles to the north east of the bay another barren rock called Sulisker or *'the rock of the ship'* is situated. These form the entire group of islands usually called St Kilda, and of which so little is known to the world in general that they are seldom even laid down in maps of Great Britain.

On the main island, water is exceedingly abundant and of fine quality, and they have particular names and attributes for every well on the island, calling one the 'well of youth' from an idea that its waters – which, by-the-by, are so scanty as scarcely ever to be seen – are detersive to old age. Another, a splendid well near the NW bay, is called the 'well of virtues' or *'good qualities'* and many more which I do not remember. Borera and Soa have each only one ill-supplied spring, and the barren rocks, none.

Small cattle thrive on the island, and with a proportion of their milk mixed with that of the sheep, the natives make a small but excellent cheese, which they pay, with sea fowl feathers, as rent.

Their ponies, about twenty in number, are likewise small and of no very eminent service except in bringing turf from the hills.

Of sheep they have a considerable number, like the above-mentioned quadrupeds of a small size, but affording delicious mutton. On Soa they often assume a dun colour, or even striped and spotted varieties of fleece, which gives them an odd, wild appearance, and this is not diminished by a length of leg and lightness of general appearance which suggest very much the idea of animals reverting to a state of nature.

The value of a pony is about 25/-; of a cow, about the same; of a sheep 2/6 or 3/-; and of a lamb 9d. or 1/-.

Goats they have none, for though they tried them and found them to thrive apace, yet they interfered with the sea-fowl in the breeding season and were exterminated in consequence; for they could not be prevented from rambling along the ledges where the Fulmar breeds, by an extended rope of straw stuck with feathers, which they use to deter the sheep.

I think the dogs complete the quadrupeds of the island, and are about equal in number to the human populations; they are a most mongrel set, and I am inclined to think, of no advantage in capturing fowl. It has been said they indicate to their masters the holes in which any of the subterraneans have taken refuge. When I observe that with regard to the Puffin, every hole in their colonies is pretty sure to have an occupant, this will be thought needless; and if he only gets the Scrabe, the scarcity and worthlessness of that bird would render canine assistance at any rate valueless. So I think it is not much more than a traveller's story. In point of breed they seem to partake equally of one universal cross of Coally, Terrier, Dutch Pug, Lurcher, and yellow old wife's dog.

Such is St Kilda and so passionately attached to it are its inhabitants that it is a notorious circumstance that they seldom leave the island, and only one or two men from it are settled throughout Scotland.

Their firing is composed entirely of turf pared from the hills, and sometimes of portions of wreck cast ashore on the island, though from the precipitous nature of their shores this is very seldom the case.

From March, when their feathered visitants make their appearance, till November when they all disappear, their food consists of the birds and their eggs in a fresh state; and during this period they employ themselves in drying and laying up in oven-like stone buildings with which the hills are covered, the stock of fowl which serves them through the winter. In addition to this they grow a small quantity of excellent barley near the village, which tends to some little variety of fare. Yet even thus, in long winters, or more properly when the interval between the departure and arrival of the fowl has been long, they have been reduced to eat seaweed from the rocks to sustain life.

As I before observed, a comfortable manse and Church have been built near the village, and to the minister, Mr. McKenzie and his lady, we were much indebted during our sojourn for every attention and hospitality; with the tractable and unsophisticated materials he has to work on, his task must be a pleasing and gratifying one, and most sincerely do I hope he may be of benefit to his little flock both in a spiritual and temporal view.

The people are very particular in not too closely intermarrying, which in a community so small is a matter of some importance. I did not inquire the particulars of the ceremony, but the minister told us that from their method of climbing among the cliffs, each one following in the rear of the other, their marriage processions present the same singular arrangement: the bridegroom walking first, followed by the bride, and they in similar manner by the inferior performers.

The Journal resumed – and now for our Journal again

☞ **Tuesday, 31st May** ⚜ ⚜ ⚜

Continued – Climbed Conacher

ON LANDING about 11 o'clock on Tuesday 31st May as aforesaid, the minister met us on the rocks and took us to a most acceptable cup of tea, after which we walked with him to the top of *Conachar, the highest hill on the island, which descends perpendicularly to the sea on the N side, and forms, I believe, the highest precipice in Great Britain. (McCulloch says it is so, if not exceeded by Foula, which he did not measure.) We were accompanied by two of the natives, who descended the cliff a little way and procured us eggs of the Fulmar and Puffin. Unfortunately a heavy mist was on St Kilda, which prevented us enjoying the magnificent prospect we should otherwise have had.

During this walk, the minister gave us a most interesting account of the morals of the inhabitants, which, with other matters of information then and afterwards derived from him, I have already availed myself of. Home to dinner at 6, and after some chat with Mrs McKenzie, to bed at ten.

☞ Wednesday, 1st June 🏵 🏵 🏵

Visit Borera to see Gannets, Peregrines, back to Conacher

After breakfast, away in the native boat before-mentioned, with twelve of its owners, to Borera[59]; and here we had an opportunity of remarking on their miserable ignorance of naval tactics, which renders them the most awkward, timid sailors I ever met with. They pull six oars at a time, two men sitting on the same bench, but as their oars are inconceivably heavy and clumsy, and they ingeniously contrive never to dip two of them together, the progress of the boat is attended by a continued splash, except when the rowers are being relieved by their six companions. Then there is no cause to complain of unnecessary agitation of the water, for they gossip and chat and idle about until you long to see them splashing again. Moreover, their timidity induces them to keep close to the rocks, coasting every little bay and headland in a most tiresome way. However we arrived at Borera in due time and landed on the east side.

As I before remarked, this island is more universally precipitous than St Kilda, and to a timid or awkward person would be really difficult to land on. But the Kildeans, though so clumsy in the ordinary management of a boat, are very dextrous in landing or embarking on or from a rocky shore, where the long, heavy swell of the Atlantic keeps the boat rising and falling by the side of the cliff a height of 14 or 15 feet, even when the sea appears quite calm. The boat is placed with her broadside to the rock and kept from striking by a man in the head and in the stern, with each a long pole for the purpose. One of their barefooted climbers stands ready in the middle, with a coil of rope on his arm, and seizing an opportunity, springs on the rock and establishes himself on some rough projection. He then hauls on the rope, the other end of which, I should have observed, is held by someone in the boat, or attached to it, and, giving way when the boat falls, tightens the rope at its rising. Another companion joins him, and, standing 3 or 4 feet from him, employs another rope in a similar manner, so that together they form a firm and safe gangway or railing for an inexpert person to spring to land by.

When this is attained, however, a most arduous ascent of the precipice is to be accomplished, which is here of the height of 600 or 700 feet, and quite difficult enough for most indifferent climbers though unembarrassed by any load: and we were told the women often ascend and descend this with a sheep or a couple of lambs in their arms.

Crossed the island to look at the Gannets on its NW side, which is a most extraordinary sight; but one of the chasms of the precipice they frequent forms what I conceive to be the most striking object on the island. It is in a part where the elevation is greatest, and though the size of the square gap it forms is immense, it here looks like a large chimney, and is unexceptionally one of the most sublime things I ever saw.

We then proceeded to a small inland cliff on the W side of the island, where the Falcon breeds, and had soon the satisfaction of being put in possession of two young birds by a couple of lads who accompanied us. The old birds I hope reared in a satisfactory manner the two remaining youngsters which the lads told us occupied the nest.

On our return to St Kilda, we rowed to the bottom of the cliff formed by the hill of Conachar, to receive the fowl captured by a party who had been there since the morning; and here we had an opportunity of seeing in perfection their feats of climbing, on the loftiest precipice in Great Britain.

On this occasion two young lads of 16 or 17 occupied our chief attention, as they had descended to within 50 or 60 feet of where our boat lay, and were noosing away at the Guillemottes on all sides with infinite success: chattering away with our boatmen in the intervals of their sport, and chucking bundles of dead birds from the nooks they had placed them in with more coolness than most men would look over a high bridge.

At the same time other sets of climbers were similarly engaged on other parts of the rock, and nothing tends more to convey an idea of the immensity of the scene to one unaccustomed to it than the difficulty he experiences in distinguishing them from their comparative insignificance. We took home this day half a boat load of birds, and enjoyed in perfection the smell of Fulmar oil. Got home late, dined and tea'd almost simultaneously, grumbled confidentially to each other on our somewhat indifferent fare and went to bed.

Fowling for guillemots at the foot of Conachar

☞ **Thursday, 2nd June** ✿ ✿ ✿

Watch two men climb Stack Biorach[60] for a little Tobacco, then explore Soa and in the evening leave St Kilda

UP AT EIGHT and breakfast immediately.

The minister told us a deputation of natives had waited on us to say, if we would give them some tobacco they would take us to the Thumb Rock and display their utmost skill and dexterity for our gratification. Now, our stock of this valuable commodity had only amounted to about 3/- worth, and by the minister's advice we gave them about half of it in compensation for their trouble yesterday. Not that under ordinary circumstances we should not have given them a liberal pecuniary compensation, but their idea of the value of money is so vague that Mr. McKenzie thought they would be more pleased with tobacco than with any reasonable sum of money. We were rather sorry to find, therefore, from our own boatman John McDonald, that they had been dissatisfied, and determined this morning to make it perfectly understood how much we intended to give. So we joined them on the beach, and by the aid of John Ferguson, the only one who has any English, told them what tobacco we had, they should receive. They exclaimed, very fairly, against it being too little, but what could we do? Money would not satisfy them, and we were making up our minds to take our own boat and row about, when they acceded to our proposition, put their boat into the sea, and away we went to Biorach.

I may observe here that the minister told us in the evening that they fancied we had more tobacco, but that, as it was, they were better satisfied with their remuneration than they had once been when a gentleman who came in his yacht and lay in the bay for a fortnight for the purpose of exploring the islands, but without eventually seeing a tenth part of what we saw, gave them three guineas for their day's labour.

All this being arranged, we served out a glass of whiskey apiece, which made them our most devoted servants for that day, and pulled away by the E side of the island to our place of destination. I never saw any place apparently more inaccessible than this rock; of which a pretty faithful sketch is annexed with Soa stack on the right and Stack an-armin in the centre at a distance of 5 miles: the part of the rock where the thumb is used is on the left side a little below the slightly prominent part of the rock, the landing being effected rather to the left of the centre of the rock, as it is here represented, and a spiral course then adopted. A high degree of celebrity awaits those who have climbed it, as it is considered infinitely the most difficult rock they have, and its ascent is never made but for some weighty consideration in general, to gratify the proprietor or

Stack Biorach, Stackanarmin and Soa Stack

his friends, but in this case to obtain a little tobacco of which they then happened to be destitute.

As we drew near the rock I found that the hearts of some of the crew began to fail and the rapidity of their rowing and talking to wax faint. The minister, who always went with us, saw it too, but said he should be astonished if they failed in their engagement. At length we fairly lay alongside the rock, and the crew folded their arms and looked at each other. How it would end, we could not divine, and John McDonald shook his head and looked rather glad of a chance of their not attempting it. Well, we waited in this solemn state of contemplation half an hour, then one oar dipped and made a kind of involuntary pull towards Soa, and then another, till we were going on more unanimously than we had ever yet done, when a fine lad of 18 jumped up and exclaimed it should never be said by the strangers that they were inferior to their fathers in skill and courage, and that if anyone would accompany him, he would lead the way. He was immediately joined by another lad of the same age, and the boat was again brought to the foot of the rock.

Rhoderick McDonald (his companion's name was John McDonald) then tied his end of the rope round his waist, the other end of which was retained by his friends in the boat, and succeeded in obtaining a footing on the foot of the rock. The boat then pulled a few strokes off, both to observe his progress and to be clear of him if he should fall at the corner, which has happened once or twice, though the consequence is only a good ducking, as he is immediately hauled on board by the rope attached to him. In this case the climber succeeded in passing the dangerous point, and then in a manner I have elsewhere described, assisted in hoisting up his companion.

We watched them in their ascent, and picked up the fowl they threw to us, captured in their way, and having seen them fairly established at the top and their operations commenced among the mass of Guillemottes there assembled, proceeded to land on the SE of Soa. Like the other landings among the islands this is not particularly easy, though in general Soa is not nearly as precipitous as the two other islands.

After walking round it, I returned to the east side to assist in finding a Scrabe in its nest, to which we devoted a great part of the day. Dick found one nest and one of the natives another; and through one of the latter we procured an egg of the Stormy Petrel on the same occasion. The east and south sides of this island constitute the largest colony of Puffins, and consist of a steep grassy slope mingled with masses of stone.

After dining on some cold lamb, and longing very much for a glass of Porter, or anything of a nutritive and encouraging tendency, we joined the boat and picked up the two courageous fellows at Stack Biorach, who had caught a vast quantity of fowl, and then proceeded to coast home along the north side of St Kilda. This, from the fatigue of the rowers and their undeviating system of following the winding of the shore, promised to be so tedious that we got them to land us in the bay on the NW side, and, accompanied by the minister and John McDonald, walked over the hills home.

I rather imagine our three boatmen had not fared very sumptuously while at St Kilda, for John came alongside in ascending the hill and said *'We must be off tomorrow, sir.'* *'Why so, John?'* *'Why, sir, you see, if an easterly wind was to come on, we might be kept here a long time.'* In short, after trying to laugh him out of it, and still finding him very desirous to be off, we determined to go that night after tea. Accordingly about eleven, with the assistance of the natives, we got our boat into the water and our stores on board for the voyage. Previously to bidding the minister *adieu*, I enquired what was the Gaelic for *'Goodbye'*, as I wished to salute the islanders at parting. He told us *'Slan leave ullah'*[61], and afterwards, when jumping into the boat, I shook hands with some of our old friends and made my parting in the best pronunciation I could muster.

There wanted but this to produce a display of feeling which was the most gratifying I ever remember to have witnessed. A general murmur ran through the assembled population, which ended almost in a shout, and concluded by our shaking hands with almost everyone on the island. This ceremony being gone through, we set sail and under the influence of a slight westerly breeze, got about 2 miles from the bay, when it fell a dead calm. After listening for half an hour to the lazy flap of the sails as our little boat rolled in the long, deep swell, our men took them in and commenced rowing, as they evinced great dread of being driven from their course, and seemed most eager to continue on their way, even at the tedious rate at which two of them, with a pair of awkward oars, impelled the boat.

Dick and I cared little the while for passing events, for the night was beautifully clear and mild, and so light throughout that we could easily consult our watches. Moreover, we lay snugly wrapped in straw and blankets and soon resigned ourselves to sleep.

3. Return from St Kilda

June 3rd – 23rd

Rowing from St Kilda – through the night – Bernera — Rowdill
Climbing Roneval (Harris), Looking for Mr. Train
Visit McCrae's of Hushinish, Gashkir, Glen Ulladil and McCloud's Cave
Boatman trouble, Factor at Luskintyre, on to Rowdill
Harris to Kilmuir Kirk (Skye) — Portree – Storr
Marooned on Rasa, Stay with Sir John McCrae, Smugglers at Sligachan
McKinnons of Corry, explore Curruisk
Steamboat from Broadford (Skye) – Tarbert – Kyles of Bute – Glasgow
Coach from Edinburgh to Newcastle

☞ **Friday, 3rd June** 🎏 🎏 🎏
   Leaving[62] *St Kilda – through the night, hoping to reach Hashkir*

OUR BOATMEN continued rowing through the night, and when we awoke and breakfasted on oatcake, whiskey and water at 8 o'clock, there seemed every chance of their labours being unrelieved by wind; the sun had risen some time and I never remember a more cloudless and beautiful day; we amused ourselves by blowing and packing the curious eggs we had procured, feeding the two young Falcons which accompanied the head of the boat, on some fowls brought for the purpose; and occasionally by relieving the men at the oars for an hour or two. We likewise fired shots at the shoals of Dogfish which surrounded us, and some of which were constantly displaying their backs above the surface, but as may be imagined, unsuccessfully. We dined on oatcakes and St Kilda cheese, of which by-the-by, I brought away a stone (28lbs) consisting of 10 small cheeses and washed it down with water, for our whiskey was low, and our poor fellows now stood in need of all we could spare them. Our hope was to attain Hashkir[63] that night and sleep on shore to give the men a rest, but all their exertions only brought us to within 3 miles of the rock, when night fell, so I made them occupy their beds, and Dick and I kept watch, the boat lying idle on the waves.

It was a disappointment not to have reached Hashkir which is a barren rock about one third of the way from Rowdill to St Kilda, for it abounds in seals, and as well as the fun of shooting two or three, we thought a seal or two in the boat would repay our men for their long pull. But there was no help for it.

Saturday, 4th June 🕸 🕸 🕸

Caught in the mist, saved by G.C.A.'s compass and bearings.

AT ABOUT 2 in the morning a light breath of wind came stealing over the sea from the NE point, and in a few minutes came so steady that I stirred up John, who slept sound in spite of a considerable degree of fear, and we soon had the sails set. I have often observed that just before sunrise or after sunset, objects are most distinctly to be seen at great distances, and this morning the hills of the Long Island presented their varying outline very plainly. Of the hills we saw, it now became an interesting question which was Roneval; John could not tell, for it appeared he had never been himself at St Kilda, so that though his two assistants had, they had made no observations of the striking mountains of Harris on their return, and could not now assist us.

Fortunately my memorandum book contained notes of the bearings of the remarkable objects from Roneval and among the rest, of Hashkir, near which we now lay; so I pointed out this steering mark to John, by the end of the small compass I carried, and had deposited myself again among the straw, when a thick mist came suddenly on, and not only had Roneval disappeared from us, but even the rocks of Hashkir which we had now approached pretty near. John's knee as he sat steering the boat was in contact with my head and I could feel it trembling violently, for which he was soon provided with a reason, by a providential break in the mist, which disclosed the breakers on Hashkir not 100 yards ahead. He was terribly frightened, and the mist closing in again immediately, he took a course which he imagined would clear us to the south of the rock; those who have not experienced the bewildering effect of a fog at sea, it will appear almost incredible that he should so thoroughly lose his reckoning as to steer in the exact contrary direction! Yet so it was in much less time than it has taken to tell of it, as fast in fact as the boat would come around! On looking at my compass and finding our course west, I asked where he fancied he was going? He was positive that we had run south of Hashkir, and would be in the Sound of Harris in two hours. I had the greatest difficulty in convincing him to the contrary, and persuading him to put the boat about, for he could not believe that the compass was right, as it was not like those he had seen in vessels where the index is suspended on the needle and traverses; so for half an hour I sat with it on my knee, turning it as the boat shifted her position, to keep the needle corresponding with the N and S of the index.

During this time we had run to the south of the rocks, and as the breeze was steady and John was half stupid with fatigue and fear, I made him lie down again, previously stationing the freshest of his men forward as a look out, and resign the helm to me. So I put the compass on my knee and kept the course which I conceived would bring us to the Sound. This might be at 5 o'clock. It continued very misty and at 8 my man forward shouted to me and pointed ahead where again I saw breakers through a hole in the mist. Upon this I applied my toe to John's shoulder, and informing him of the event resigned the tiller to him, assuring him we were now in the Sound for we had come along at a merry pace during my administration – he was as much frightened as ever, but most opportunely and providentially, the mist now rose and left us a clear look out – we found ourselves as I expected on the outside of the Sound, and as their knowledge of its intricacies was very tolerable, we had no more fears. By-the-by, had it not been for our really awkward situation, John's case would have been truly amusing, for he had not understood the compass and was continually asking *'Am I right now, sir?'* and other questions interlarded with ejaculations of fear and despair.

I found on landing he had given a more glowing account of my ability in bringing them out of the mist, and that one half of the island knew of it. Ian McLoud the youngest of our boatmen whose merriment and musical propensities had so amused us in going to St Kilda, had before leaving Rowdill to go to St Kilda, stored his sea chest with a quantity of oatmeal in a poke, and well it was for us that he did so, for our own stock for the return passage was an unthrifty one, and reduced us to his stock: there is, as I have elsewhere said, but one mill on Harris, so most of the meal is ground in the quern; and such it was which we now devoured with infinite relish; formed into scones by the fair hands of master McLoud, and baked on stones heated in the pan of peats constituting our fire; for idle men our fare was wholesome and not unpleasant: I fancied I never tasted such nice oatmeal: it was very coarse; many of the particles being half the size of the original grain, but whether from the absence of any condiment or from its own intrinsic excellence, it tasted wonderfully sweet and good.

I fancy our propensities must be more of a bibulous character for, not content with venting our abuse on the excellent St Kilda water, we imagined ourselves tired of whiskey too, and longed not in silence but most

vociferously for ale, porter, port, small beer or any common or ordinary
potation.

We soon drew near an island on which were men, women and houses as
Bernera and though only 5 miles from Rowdill, landed to beg some milk
for ourselves and whiskey for our boatmen, both which (to us) luxuries we
procured and came on board to revel in. A gallon of milk was a great
lounge certainly to us all, for we were such in want of animal food, and
soon dined on this fortunate apology for it. Bernera and Pabba are the
largest islands in the Sound of Harris; they lie about 5 or 6 miles from
Rowdill and are more numerously inhabited than an equal portion of
Harris.

Bernera is about 1 ½ miles in diameter – but I only speak of these two
islands from recollection, so I may be a little wrong - and lies a short
distance to the south of Pabba; it is celebrated only I believe for its shell
fish, of fragments of whose shells we found the beach composed: the most
delicate is the Razor fish, which they catch by rapidly inserting two
fingers obliquely into the sand so as to press against his shell and prevent
rapid descent he would otherwise make: he is then roasted and they every-
where consider him superior to any other shell fish.

Pabba is about the same size, but much higher, consisting in fact of a
mountain of considerable elevation: and is one of the only places in the
Long Island where smuggling is carried on, and now contains 4 stills. But
all the Long Island whiskey is considered so bad by the Skye and Inverness
people, that they hold it in great dis-esteem and have a particular name
for it which I do not remember, though it is a similar expression to swipes,
comparatively with table beer.

The St Kilda Tacksman usually takes a boat from Pabba when he pays
his biennial visits, both from it being a few miles nearer, and independent
of the difficult rocky navigation of the Sound, and because the people of
Pabba boats and men are better adapted for the purpose - moreover it is
the near next habitable point to St Kilda, being within 60 miles of it.

Much to our satisfaction our journey now drew nigh to a close, for on
leaving Bernera we held on with a steady breeze and soon found ourselves
in Rowdill harbour.

On landing we found old McLeod (our landlord) in more bustle and
confusion than ever, though rather gladdish to see us than otherwise.
Our other friends greeted us with thousands of congratulations, as they
seem to consider our expedition in the same light as the people on the
continent do the ascent of Mont Blanc.

As McLeod was so near to moving we were obliged to sleep on the floor,
and there was no furniture in the room, and the house door open all night

and the key hanging on the outside of the door, so our 'put up' was rather deficient in elegance, and our slumbers being much discomposed by McLeod's squalling children, made us rather regretful of the necessity we found of devoting the next day to comparative rest, and recruiting our powers of body, after our spare diet since we left Rowdill for our voyage.

On our first arrival, having (as usual) tumbled all our things out of their respective bags etc on the floor of our bedroom, I said to McLeod as we were leaving the house a few minutes after for a ramble, '*I suppose our things are quite safe in your house?*' '*Oh yes,*' he answered with some indignation, '*I will answer for everything but tobacco.*' Remembering a stock of fine cigars were exposed upstairs, I immediately proceeded to lock them up; my care was too tardy however, for not one was to be found, and though I remonstrated rather energetically, I could only recover a small portion of them.

The most provoking loss was that of a number of rifle bullets which the children had run off with, and which, as I could get no lead, might have proved a serious loss if we had had much use for that weapon at St Kilda.

When Dick (our paymaster throughout) came to his settling transactions with our host the scene used to be very rich. '*Well Mr. McLeod, will you let us have your bill?*' '*Why, sir, I don't think there's much occasion for one! You've had so much whiskey*' – that he could tell – and '*You've been here so many days – will such a sum be too much?*' – Dick, for our own satisfaction used to make him particularise a little and between them they used to get something like a bill made out – Our expenses were whimsically small.

On the whole McLeod was a very decent fellow, and took such pains to make us comfortable, – pity our acceptation of that word should differ so much! – and evinced such a kindly feeling at parting with us, that we readily forgot the little discomforts we experienced in his house.

☞ Sunday, 5th June ✿ ✿ ✿

Climbed Roneval looking for Ptarmigan.

TRAIN, in the meantime, had left Rowdill on the day after our departure for St Kilda to visit the north part of Harris, called the Forest: both because this part of the island (which is by-the-by to the north of the isthmus and might therefore be supposed to form part of Lewis) contains some magnificent scenery, to tempt him on the one hand; and because his sufferings at sea, and the inducements to accompany us, were not of a kind to hold out much temptation, on the other hand: he therefore journeyed by easy stages towards the forest, tarrying a day or two at Mr. Bethun's[64], the minister at Scaristy, and then for a similar period at the Factor's at Luskintyre, 8 or 9 miles nearer the forest: his next move was from thence over Loch Tarbert in a boat to a brother of Sir John McCrae's living on the borders of the forest and Hushinish.[65]

About 14 years since his father had taken a lease of the forest as a sheep farm and now Mr. McCrae was living in a small shooting box on the side of Loch Tarbert, and making the best of an unprofitable bargain.

Our determination was to go on Monday, after some little rest, from our fatigues, to join Mr Train, and after seeing a little of the interesting district which he had gone to see, to return and see something more of the magnificent scenery of Skye.

Today we ascended Roneval after breakfast, to look once more for the nest of the Ptarmigan; and in this performance we became aware of the insufficiency of our late oatmeal diet, for it was with considerable labour we accomplished it, and returned to dinner completely tired by 6 – hen and hashed mutton was our lot – then followed some little preparation for the morrow's journey – and then our single glass of toddy and bed.

☛ Monday, 6th June ✿ ✿ ✿
Possibility of visiting the Flannan Isles. Looking for Mr Train.

CONSIGNED our hawks till our return to the care of a lad in Rowdill; and then with a boy to guide us and carry our bag, set off to look for Train – kept to the road till we came to the mill at Coshlatter and then turned to the right up the burn to Loch Longuvat, along the west side of which we kept in a NNE direction. We saw some Golden Plover on the moors, two of which I shot with my rifle for the hawks. We rested a while by the side of Longuvat, and having nothing to eat, Dick and I swam to the islands in the west of it and got a lot of sea fowl eggs, which we mixed with the whiskey we had, and were wondrously comforted thereby: this is the Loch I had before navigated in a like manner for the same end.

At 5 we arrived at the sands on the opposite side of a branch of Loch Tarbert from the Factor's, after a walk of 16 or 18 miles: we were very tired and hungry, and commenced a most vociferous outcry for the boat: there seemed to be no symptom of any thing of the kind and we were thinking

Scene from the sands of Luskintyre

seriously of walking 5 miles round by the head of the Loch, when we found some fishermen who put us over.

Our situation on the sand, for the hour and a half we waited in hope, was sufficiently unsatisfactory; and we whiled it away as well as we could by eating cockles, criticising the correctness of the drawing of sundry impressions of naked feet on the sands.

We were all this time in sight of Mr. Stewart's (the Factor's) house and could see the inhabitants in their several occupations about it. By the aid of our friends the fishermen we however reached it about seven, and met the factor on the sand coming to meet us just as little 'Crab' was amusing himself by pinching the neck of a Spanish Goose, a flock of which the Factor had been at some pains to rear, this was untoward, but his hospitality prevailed over his indignation, and we were most kindly received into his little house which is not 20 yards from the Loch. Here the only members of his family whom we saw, was Miss Stewart, a young lady of 19 who in the absence of her mother performed the honours to us, in a most engaging way; our satisfaction was infinite to enter a house with carpets and coal fires; and when we experienced in addition port wine and soft bottomed chairs, blacking and white sugar; wheat bread, intelligible conversation and scented soap, it is almost impossible to express the feeling of complacent benignity which came over us.

Young Stewart had been over the Loch with Mr. Train, who left them that morning, and he returned before bed time. He was a fine looking young fellow of 20 or 21 and greeted us most cordially.

In enquiring of them about the natural curiosities of the neighbour-hood, they gave an account of a wonderful monster which had been repeatedly seen in Loch Lachsdale (Laxadale), a lake a few miles to the north of the isthmus. Its size must be immense, and its description very much like those we have of Kraken: the resemblance consisting in its bulk, and its likeness when floating on the surface to a row of huge casks, in the intervals of which a boat could row; this similarity of this story to those related of the Kraken of the Norwegian coast, as well as the general belief prevailing concerning it, form the only curious points in the detail. Young Stewart promised to accompany us on the morrow in search of Train, whose amusing qualities had gained him the goodwill of all he had met; and we almost entertained the idea of going to the NW of Lewis, to Gallen Head, and thence procuring a boat to the Flannan Isles.[66] This group, often called the *Seven Hunters*, we had wished to visit in McDonald's boat on our return from St Kilda, but could not persuade that worthy to under-take the voyage, after our ridiculous adventures in our former one; and eventually we were compelled to lay aside the idea entirely, for the prospect of getting a boat at Gallen Head seemed very doubtful and we wished to devote some more time to the splendid scenery of Skye.

☞ **Tuesday, 7th June** ❈ ❈ ❈
   McCrae's[67] of Hushinish, eventually tracked down Mr. Train.

BREAKFAST at 9, and at 10 took Mr Stewart's boat over the Loch about 4 miles to Hushinish. On our arrival there we found that Mr McCrae and our friend Train had walked forth to inspect some farming operations carrying on among the hills; we accordingly begged a drink of milk at his shooting box and went in quest of them. Eventually we all returned together to dinner at 5, and he persuaded us, instead of going to the Flannans to spend the next day in an excursion to a small island called Gashkir, which lies 8 or 9 miles out from Harris, and is celebrated as a favourite resort of seals. He paid about 2 ½d per acre for his land which he said was too much: his farm comprises nearly all the forest and abounds in game of all kinds – or rather in moor game and Red Deer for there are no partridge on the island; and black game and pheasants being fond of wood are equally unknown. Two English noblemen rented the shooting on Lewis last year for £100, and killed immense quantities of grouse, but found rea-son to dislike their bargain, as they could do nothing with it, being so entirely out of the world. Deer shooting commences in the end of August, and continues through the winter: Mr McCrae could not tell us how many

Mr McCrae's House at Hushinish, Harris

the island contained, but said they were increasing in numbers. Leave is easily obtained from the Factor to shoot them during the season, and in fact we were told if we met with them to take a shot by all means. Our host gave us some capital London porter to dinner, than which I can't pretend to say, I ever enjoyed anything more. He piqued himself much on his whiskey, which came from Strathglass, the only district where smuggling continues to be carried on to any extent: it certainly was most fascinating stuff, and was served out in such a characteristic bottle, that we did not get to bed till '*some wee hour*' in the morning.

☞ Wednesday, 8th June ❀ ❀ ❀

Wednesday, 8th June – Landed on Gashkir, soaking,
visited another Seal Island.

UP BEFORE BREAKFAST – I mean an hour before – and had a delicious bathe, tending not a little to the demolition of potatoes and herring, cold kid, cheese, oatcake and whiskey, which formed our breakfast. Then got on board a six oar boat we had engaged to take us to Gashkir[68] Mr Train was rather poorly and made a terrible row in the boat, carrying his whimsicalities to such an extent that our men (scarcely one of whom understood English) were in fits of laughter, though he was sitting in the

head of the boat, their backs were to him and they had
nothing therefore but sound to go by. In compassion to
his sufferings, we proposed to put him ashore at a place
4 or 5 miles along shore from Mr McCrae's, but he
would not hear of it, and afterwards reverted to it, as
one of the most unfeeling schemes ever devised.

It proved a long row to Gashkir; 5 or 6 miles along the
shores of Harris and at least as many more from the
nearest point of that island, directly out to sea. It is curious from containing 2 or 3 small freshwater Lochs in the
middle of the island, where seals breed; it is customary to go in August
and kill the old ones before they can escape to the sea, in which they on
one occasion got 130, though last year's capture amounted only to 10. On
approaching it we had the mortification to see a sloop land her boat, and
the crew rambling all over the island. This was being in bad luck, as in all
probability, no one had set foot on it since last August, and we had made
up our minds to be merciful and only kill three!

We found the fellows leaving the rock as we landed, with a quantity of
eggs of Great Black-backed and Herring Gull, and a few of the Oyster
Catcher; they denied even having seen any seals, though we suspected
their object was to catch these animals, if our approach had not alarmed
them; for trespass of this kind is rather severely treated by the Factor at
Stornoway, when complaint is made. It is only fair that it should be so, as
the tenant in this case derives nothing from the island but seals. The
island of Gashkir is about ¼ of a mile in diameter, low and rocky; the
landing place is in a creek to the south and except in a heavy sea, easy
enough.

We amused ourselves with seeking eggs, lunching and rifle shooting: in
the two former, succeeding wonderfully, though Mr Train and I only, made
anything of the latter.(Bearings from Gashkir, Gallen Head NE; Flannan
Isles N +½W; Cleisheirn SE, Tarbert SSE about 18 miles.)

Having remained on it a couple of hours, we got into the boat and
commenced our return, landing as we passed on some rocks a little to
the south where we fancied the seals might have withdrawn: and in this
supposition we were right; though we could not effect a landing imper-
ceived by them, so that where we did do so, they were all in the sea, eyeing
us curiously: our only plan therefore was to lie among the rocks and fire at
those which rose near. I fancied I must have struck one or two with my
rifle, which I had now become accustomed to, and could use pretty rapidly,
but we did not succeed in procuring one: however, some weeks after our
return, Dick had a letter from Mr. McCrae, by a kelp vessel, and he men-

Flannen Isles from the island of Gashkir

tioned that the day after we left him, a very large one was washed on shore, shot through the head by my bullet.

The landing, or rather re-embarking here, was much more difficult than at Gashkir, and was a somewhat ludicrous affair, particularly as our friend Mr. Stewart fancied, or pretended to fancy us, too awkward to accomplish it unassisted. I made a spring and was getting on very well, when as I reached the gunnel with my foot, he rushed at me and nearly knocked me overboard, throwing me, as it was with my side on the gunnel in an unsatisfactory way enough. My entry was not nearly so brilliant as Mr Train's, though, for after letting the swell catch on the rock and souse him very plentifully, he made a bounce, and like me was in a fairish way of getting on board, when Stewart caught him in his arms, and between Mr Train's original impetus and his desire to display his strength, that gentleman performed a complete summerset *(somersault – Ed.)*, and finished his career at length in the bottom of the boat.

During our stay on this rock, our worthy host got a most complete ducking: the moment he got out of the boat, he climbed over the other side of the island, and seeing an unmerse seal sink at his appearance, he crept rapidly near to the water's edge, and sheltered himself behind a large rock to await its rising again; being busied in examining his priming he did not perceive that he had got within reach of the surge, and the first idea he received on the subject was imparted by the breaking of the long Atlantic swell, over the rock behind which he had concealed himself.

I cannot conceive anything finer in its way than paying a visit to a place of this description, where nature's creatures are never disturbed by man, and where surprise and curiosity, supply the place of fear. There is more-over something solemn in the noiseless, mysterious, appearance and disap-pearance of these same seals; no hurry or discomposure is evinced, but the same majestic bearing. Some, which we saw here, were so large that I conceive they must have been the *phoco barbate*. Mr McGillivray, in an account of the Hebrides published in *Cheek's Journal*, says they are found on Hashkir, and this island is so similar to it, in seclusion and appearance, that I have little doubt of their being here also.

The Flannan Isles are visible from Gashkir, bearing by my compass N+¼W. We found it a long and tedious day's work altogether and did not get home till 11 – to bed with amazing satisfaction.

Our host is a famous fellow: a young brother of Sir John McCrae's. He has settled himself here to make the best of a bad bargain, in the shape of a long lease of part of the island, entered into by his father in better times. Young Stewart, rather ill-naturedly described him as a silent well meaning man, intending to carry the impression that he was stupid: how-ever, the character could bear no comparison in point of worth and estimability.

☞ Thursday, 9th June ✿ ✿ ✿
Glen Ulladil, McCloud's Cave, Lost Whiskey Flask, Red Grouse.

McCULLOCH'S remark on the difficulty of making an early start, is more well grounded than some others he has made; we found it constantly the case, and this morning it was near 11 before Mr Train and I got off with a man called Cain Morrison for a guide to visit one of the most extraordinary scenes in the forest – Glen Ulladil:[69] this consists of a mountain side, perfectly precipitous from its summit to the plain on which it stands, and a very imposing grand mass of rock it is, but it should have been visited before seeing the Storr in Skye or the rocks at St Kilda. Near it on the south west side, is a cave which afforded shelter, in Charles Stewart's time, to McCloud of Berneray[70] for some weeks, while parties who were aware of his being somewhere in the neighbourhood, passed often within view of his retreat: but it is nearby at the summit of the mountain and quite imperceptible till you are within a few feet of it: it is moreover so critical of access that, barring firearms, a dozen good fellows might defend it against an army. Our worthy guide had no idea of dragging himself up to show us it, but pointing out the situation from below he said he would remain till our return. There is a well of goodish water within it, so that with a supply of provisions, and the good will of shepherds, who

Rock in Glen Uladil, Harris

were the only creatures aware of the existence of such a place, McCloud
might have lain long concealed.

On our descent we applied to our guide for a mouthful of whiskey, of
the flask containing which he had charge; but the villain had lost it – at
least he said so, and we did without. After making sketches of the rock
which is more remarkable for overhanging the perpendicular, than for

McLeod's Cave in Glen Uladale

immensity, we turned homewards to pick up Dick at some Lochs he had remained to fish at: just before joining him, Crab set up an old Red Cock – the only Grouse we saw during our rambles among the islands, which made so much more noise than there seemed occasion for, that I levelled my rifle, and rather unexpectedly, brought him down.

Dick had caught 5 or 6 dozen small trout with which we arrived at home at 7. After dinner we amused ourselves with jumping shy-

ing stones, seeing the Goats milked etc. and then having supped on oatmeal porritch and herrings retired to our repose. Young Stewart though intending to have accompanied us to the Flannan Isles, had we gone, pleaded important business at home, and went back this morning. I offered Cain Morrison half a crown if he could find the flask which he said he lost this morning, as it was a very nice one, and I strongly suspected he knew where it was.

Cain Morrison

☞ **Friday, 10th June** ✿ ✿ ✿
Leave Hushinish – Boatmen! Reach Factor's House at
Luskintyre.[71]

AFTER BREAKFAST Cain brought the flask and got his half crown. We determined to set out towards Rowdill today, and in spite of a very delicate nicely urged inducement to stay, in the prospect of some good fishing work our host promised us, we took his boat and three men at two o'clock to get as far as the Factor's on our way south. Our worthy friend Cain was one, the only one of them who had any English: his knaveries though sometimes provoking were amusing and ingenious enough: as only two could row at a time he took the last turn and dozed away on one of the thofts *(thwarts Ed.)* there was a little breeze and I told him to make them put the sail up: this however would have involved him in the hoisting of it, and he accordingly said something in Gaelic to the other men, and then turning to me asked if I knew what they said. *'No'*, I answered, *'What do they say?'* His look was admirable as he informed me of some reason which he wished us believe they had assigned for not doing so. But after rowing for some time one of them tired, and master Cain must take his place: in two minutes without orders, up went the sail and Cain deposited himself again on the bench: on reaching the shore at some distance from the factor's they put the boat on shore entirely disre-

garding our request to be rowed as near the house as possible; for here again our worthy guide and interpreter exchanged some Gaelic with his companions, and explained that Mr. McCrae had desired them to take us no further. So we shouldered our bag and walked about a mile to Luskintyre. On our arrival here, we were vexed to find that both Mr. Stewart and his son were from home and no one to receive or entertain us but our old friend Miss Stewart: this threatened to interfere with our intention of remaining all night there, as it seemed rather incorrect to stay and not even see one of our own sex: however Miss Stewart's simple quiet way of insisting on it, put our scruples to flight, and we enjoyed a most pleasant evening.

After dinner, which was made ready for six, and at which she presided, she took a single glass of wine, chatted with easy frankness for half an hour, and left us till we should ring for tea: at that she returned to us, and after ordering us toddy wished us good night and went to bed. It is quite

impossible to convey an idea of the quiet simplicity with which she behaved, and the impression it produced on us; and yet she had never, I'll be bound to say, even heard of good breeding: but the easy unembarrassed way in which she conducted herself, was a beautiful illustration how closely allied are the most elaborately refined manners with the most inartificially simple and natural - premising always that there be a sufficient quantum of good feeling and good sense, on the part of the latter to compensate for artificial propriety and decorum on the other.

☞ Saturday, 11th June ✺ ✺ ✺
Sketching each other! Heading south to Rowdill

BREAKFAST at 9, our fair hostess presiding, and after a most cordial expression of regret that we could not prolong our stay, we set off at 12 intending to spend the night at Scaristy where Mr. Bethun the minister lives. Loaded the food at the Factor's, where Mr. Train thought Dick looked so picturesque that he made him stand until he succeeded in sketching him: I thought the opportunity a good one, and stealing quietly behind Mr. Train, put him down as he was unconsciously standing. I had determined to have him depicted in misery in retaliation for his unfeeling conduct when I had the toothache at Oban, and I had an opportunity of doing so in coming from shooting (no) seals at Gashkir. He had enveloped his head in a plaid and there was a pinkish tint about his nose, which told of seasickness and distress.

We called at Mr Bethun's at 3.30 and I fear he is very seriously unwell, or they would not have allowed us to depart: dined there and walked on with Big Donald to carry our bag to Rowdill, calling in passing at John McDonald's to tell him to row round against midnight with his boat to Rowdill. On getting to that place, there being now no place of entertainment, we called at the Doctor's (Clarke) to ask for something to eat. *'Oh yes, come in,'* said he, opening the door and answering our request, *'we'll give you a boiled herring or something.'* So in we went, and while some tea was in course of make down stairs, we sat stupefying over the thrice told tale of

St Kilda which has caused quite a sensation in Harris; and I got into a scrape about the people of Stornoway by some questions I asked and in fact things were not going comfortably when the door opened, and I do think the prettiest woman I ever saw in my life made her appearance. To her the Doctor introduced us to his lady and added rather spitefully that her native place was Stornoway. She talked very broken, though prettily spoken English, and wanted us very much to stay: however we bade them adieu at 12, and embarked once more in McDonald's boat with our hawks, cheeses, sketch books etc. etc.

☞ **Sunday, 12th June** ❀ ❀ ❀

Rowdill (Harris) by boat to Kilmuir Kirk (Skye), on foot to Portree

OUR INTENTION had been to sail to the head of Loch Snizort which is within 5 miles of Portree and walk over, but the SE wind blew so strong down the Loch that we landed at Kilmuir Kirk to the north of it, 24 miles from Portree. This was at 12, and finding it difficult to get anyone to carry our bag, we left it there and with the hawks in the corner of a plaid, set off. We had had nothing to eat that morning but oatcake and whiskey so we soon felt the effects of walking, and it was nearly three before we got to Uig, a small fishing village on a branch of Loch Snizort, 8 miles from Kilmuir Kirk. The road is very uninteresting and the population scanty: few as they were, though, I fear we scandalised them much as we met them trudging to the Kirk. For the hawks were almost certain to commence screaming and struggling in the plaid, at every group we came to, and travelling with guns and fishing rod, looked terribly raffish. Had some eggs and bacon at Uig and sent a man back for our bag. It is a long 24 miles to Portree and it was 9 when we got there. It was amusing to find that our fame had preceded us and numerous were the questions about St Kilda proposed to us. They consider the Kildeans to speak a bad Gaelic and wondered we did not perceive it! As also that we were so sweet[72] after being there.

Our travels I suppose had imparted a degree of consequence to us, for Jameson[73] was most assiduous in his attention, and presented indications of activity in serving us, which were manifested even in the jerking of his coat tails. Capital tea and then to bed.

☞ **Monday, 13th June** ✻ ✻ ✻

An Eerie Day on the Storr, Mr. Train Entertains!

W E DETERMINED to spend this day in another visit to the Storr, which had increased in value much, from the comparative insignificance of all else we had seen (except St Kilda). Dick took his rod and off we set: on arriving at the south loch, a mist entirely concealing the mountain, so we watched Dick's success, and Mr. Train sketched Crab as he lay sleeping on the grass; however the rocks seemed at times much clearer than at others, so we left Dick and commenced the ascent encouraged by transient glimpses of the extraordinary mass of rocks before us: but it was a vile day for the purpose: a thick driving mist sat close by the summit and entirely circumscribed our view of what we wished to sketch. I climbed to the top of a sort of rocky castle and stuck myself in a crevice to keep dry: Train

The Storr, Skye

88

Rocks at the Storr

preferred rambling in a little fairy valley below me, so smooth that it seemed a mockery of all around us. As I have before observed, that gentleman is most whimsically amusing when in distress, and he now shivered and ranted, sang heroic songs and martial bravuras, whether the *Keel Row* and *Bonny Pit Laddie*, imitated divers instruments of music and illustrated the style of walking etc of odd people known to us both amidst the screams of Eagles and croakings of the Ravens in the echoing rocks above us. I have seen many incongruous associations, but never I think, anything much more absurd than our situation that day. During an interval of mist I got one sketch of the pinnacle which is so conspicuous from Portree, and then finding the mist damper than ever, we left our station and scrambled down the mountain to meet Dick: met him coming up to us – hunted some young wild ducks in a pond, and then down from the region of the mist to the burn which ends in the fall at the Fox-hunter's cottage mentioned before: its distance from the most northern of the lochs is about two and a half or three miles, good fishing all the way. Within half a mile there is a smaller fall, though under other circumstances it might be worthy of notice, it is so completely eclipsed by its fellow that it must remain in insignificance. Sent home a letter this morning in a Shearwater skin per Steamboat.

☞ **Tuesday, 14th June** ✿ ✿ ✿
Rainy Day - Bits and Pieces

RAINY, so stayed at home to finish sketches, mend fishing rod and dress flies. At Jameson's request, wrote a Eulogy on the Storr, which Train copied in a legible hand on a map hanging in the room. Whether it may induce anyone to visit it I don't know - perhaps it is too like one of parson's puffs but it should be known to travellers, as of many who had been at Jameson's, only one had gone to see the Storr – I believe it was a Colonel Murray, and only a week or two before our visit. A quiet uneventful day.

☞ **Wednesday, 15th June** ✿ ✿ ✿
Leave Portree for Corry, diverted to Rasa, Stay with Sir John

WE HAD determined today to proceed to Corry and see a little of the civilised society of the islands, but it rained hard, and we stayed to conclude some of our sketches. In the course of the morning Mr. Train and I being out, a worthy of the village walked into the room where Dick was investigating fishing tackle and prefacing by a disquisition on the difficulty he experienced in procuring good colours, modestly requested our sketching box as a memorial of us, and suggested that it would be no loss to us as we could replace it at any time. Dick took it very quietly, regretted they did not belong to him, but he had no doubt the gentleman whose they were would be much gratified by his acceptance of them, and begged he would call again. Whether Dick's extreme civility led the man to believe himself hoaxed, I don't know, but he never made his appearance again.

At 6, although it blew rather fresh, we got the same boat which took us to Rowdill, and putting our things on board, set sail for Corry. The gusts of wind which sweep from the hills in navigating these narrow seas, are so violent and sudden that it would be madness to fix the sheet, except in finest weather, for in a moment the boat is all but gunwale under, and then if you do not mind you stand a chance of losing your things etc. In coming out of Portree Bay, as I had formed a somewhat poor opinion of our boatman's skill, for he had sailed with us to Rowdill when Murdoch managed the boat so well, and as I had an idea I could do somewhat better, I took the helm. The boat was wretchedly equipped this time, and our anticipation of making a good and rapid passage, by no means

Cliff near Portree

glowing, when we saw important articles of rigging got up impromptu
from the twine and scraps of cord they had in their pockets: however we
managed to hoist sail and as the wind was pretty much in our teeth stood
over towards the island Rasa[74] which lies for 7 or 8 miles parallel to Skye,
and between which two islands there seemed every prospect of our having
to make a multitude of tacks, as our craft did not go by any means near
the wind. On nearing Rasa, it seemed such slow, stupid work sailing, that
we landed and walked on, instructing our boatmen to pick us up on their
last tack.

This gave us an opportunity of seeing a little of Rasa, which as I before
observed is almost a continuation of Rona, and very similar in character,
though as we only skirted its west shore it did not appear so desolate and
mournful; for throughout the islands, the habitations are confined almost
entirely to the sea shores. Our walk had not continued more than a couple
of miles when we perceived our boat in a miserable predicament: owing to
the failure of some part of their rigging, the crew were endeavouring to
recover the sail which was flying like a pennon from the mast head. I
believe they were eventually compelled to unstep the mast, and whether
their supply of string was scanty, and required knotting to make out the
requisite length, or from their own clumsiness, it was long before they
continued their course. We in the meanwhile were getting hungry, and
finding on enquiry, that a place of entertainment would not be likely to

Cottages on the island of Rasa

Rasa House

occur, turned over in our minds the propriety of calling at Rasa House where we remembered our old fellow passenger, Sir John McCrae, to have landed, and beg something to eat. It was now near ten o'clock, and excepting some biscuit before leaving Jameson's, we had not had anything, so we were not dissatisfied soon after the formation of the above eleemosynary[75] determination, to come in view of Rasa House[76]; a handsome modern stone building, reputed one of the best houses – indeed with the exception of Lord McDonald's, the best house on the island. We approached the front of the house, and were somewhat disconcerted to find that there was no bell: while we were puzzling how to proceed, Sir John who had seen us bothering about the front, came out and received us with a most cordial welcome, laughing heartily at our petition. When we explained to him our plan for proceeding to Corry, or Broadford, for they are close together, he would not hear of such a thing, but gave orders, that our boat should be signalled, our property landed and the men sent back: we remonstrated hypocritically, discharged our boatmen, and resigned ourselves to our disagreeable situation.

We now determined, at his suggestion, to visit Brochel Castle, a ruin situation on an isolated rock on the east side of the island, 4 or 5 miles from Rasa House, this was for the morrow.

The house which is about equal to Acton House near Felton, is situated in the centre of a small bay on the SW side of the island: it is a modern structure built since Johnston's visit in 1773: trees have been planted round it and have grown very well, some of them having attained the bulk of a man's body; a colony of Rooks are in possession of them, and are just now very much occupied with their young.

After tea, which was the refreshment, aided by cold meat, collops, herrings, eggs etc, which we were presented with, Sir John produced some whiskey – Strathglass of course – decidedly the finest I ever tasted: it is quite a hobby with him, and he assured us, that although his brother's was very fine, it was not so good as his!

Sir John MacRae

A criticism of this liquor being of proper strength to drink in the morning as a whet, or in fact at any time, raw, is when the bottle containing it, is violently shaken, it should retain on its surface a quantity of small bubbles: if either too strong or too weak, these will not remain. In making hot punch, put in the spirit first, and the water as hot as possible afterwards. For cold punch the water first and the spirit slowly into it.

These interesting portions of information we received from Mr McCrae at Hushinish, one morning when he tried to persuade us to take a dram – 'morning' he called it, from the 'Corporal Nymi'-ish' looking bottle represented on Sir John's left hand.

In the evening Train amused our host exceedingly by some of his musical divertissements, and Sir John in return played to us the Bagpipes, on which he is an excellent amateur performer. It is charming to find ourselves in a good house again, and feel otherwise in a gentlemanly way. Rasa House belongs to McLeod of Rasa who is a young man in the army and lets Sir John the house, and part of the island in his absence. Its present occupant wants us to stay a week, but that is impossible, even if the island did hold out objects worthy of so long a visit: this is not however the case, as there is little worth seeing upon it.

Thursday, 16th June
Rainy Day on Rasa - Sketching Rasa House and Glamaig

THE MORNING proved rainy, so after breakfast we adjourned to the rookery with my rifle to procure food for the two hawks, now grown fine fierce looking fellows. This is the only fair, or creditable way of rook shooting, as some little nicety is really necessary to knock them off with a

View of Glamaig on Skye from Rasa House, by G.C.A.

94

single ball; I am sorry that we all succeeded better than our host in doing so, for he was very anxious on the subject. The day continuing rainy we retired to the house to finish drawings etc, and afterwards during a cessation of the wet, got a view from the terrace in front of the house of a striking mountain on Skye just opposite called Glamaig. Mr. Train also got a drawing of the house from the same situation whilst I was busy with Glamaig. Sir John looked over my shoulder to beg me to introduce his little yacht, the *Elizabeth* which rode at anchor a little out of the line of the sketch I was taking. He instructed me to make her appear *'a beautiful wicked looking thing'*, a term of nautical fondness and admiration which would be rather puzzling to a person unacquainted with the little elegances of naval language.

Rasa is celebrated for its pipers,[77] sending forth more good ones than any other part of Scotland. McKay is just now the celebrated name; three very fine players of that family from Rasa being now pipers to the Duke of Sussex, Lord Gwyder and the Duke of Gordon.

Rasa is mountainous though not very high in any part: the population is about 1,500, and the island about 10 miles long by 3 or 4 in width. It contains a good deal of moor-game, some Black and a few Partridges – a few Roe Deer, others etc., and lots of Corncrakes.

Friday, 17th June 🏵 🏵 🏵
Rasa to Sconsor, Whiskey Smugglers at Sligachan.

AFTER BREAKFAST and getting a likeness of our kind host, we got into a boat at 11 to proceed to cross the strait to Sconsor[78] on Skye, whence it would be easy to procure a conveyance to Corry. The channel, scarcely a mile broad is very much exposed to violent gusts of wind from the mountains, and is rather dangerous to navigate without caution.

Arrived at Sconsor at 3, intending to go on during the night to Broadford and spend the intermediate time in seeing Glen Corruisk, which Sir John told us was only 6 or 7 miles off: however we found the distance was considered by the natives much more, and as it was considerably later than we had intended, when we got to Sconsor, we gave up the idea of seeing Corruisk from the north side, in which I am inclined to think we erred, for the Coolin hills over which you climb to attain it must present some magnificent scenery when you are in the midst of them. I have no doubt, like the Storr, they contain prodigious scenes of unexplored grandeur, and regret very much, I could not devote a day or two to them.

After our landing at Sconsor, we rambled forth to see the country and

Coolin Hills from Sligachan

make the most of our time till night. We followed the south side of the Loch Sconsor to Sligachan,[79] a small hamlet 2 miles up the country, and then a severish rain commencing, we took shelter in a little whiskey shop. There were three powerful, intelligent looking fellows about the door, and on Sir Walter Scott's excellent principle of endeavouring to derive something new from everyone, we attempted some little affability with these men, but entirely without success, as we received nothing but monosyllabic answers, to enquiries on matter which we conceived they must be well acquainted with. As a last resource we made them come in and ordered them some whiskey; after this had made a round among them, it was quite evident, a degree of reserve was wearing off, and after sundry interchanges of looks one of them went to a bed in the corner and produced from it a barrel of whiskey; the tale is soon told; they were smugglers[80] from Strathglass, and had with them some splendid stuff. I made arrangements for taking some to England with us, and was fairly in for a smuggling transaction, but our three friends, who had engaged to bring us to Sconsor by midnight, had before we left, made such cordial

96

application to the wooden cup out of which they drank that I can easily understand their excuse.

One of our own party was likewise affected by the same cause, and did not regain his composure till next day: two of the party proceeded up the small rivulet to try for a salmon, in which it abounds at times, and the individual above mentioned, awaited their return on a small hillock near the scene of his misfortune. The endeavour at salmon fishing was unsuccessful and we got back to Sconsor at 11 – tea and bed at 11.

Smugglers in their shop at Sligachan

☞ **Saturday, 18th June** 🏵 🏵 🏵
    Sconsor, Broadford, and visit the McKinnons of Corry.

I N SPITE OF most earnest remonstrance from the one of the party, we rose at 4 and proceeded on board our boat of yesterday which we had engaged to proceed with us to Broadford: I think the distance is about 12 miles – speaking from memory - and in the course of it we had some of the best shots at seals we have enjoyed among the islands, though unproductive of any inconvenience to them. Mr. Train was rather pensive and talked of his prospects in after life; with regard to which, I assured him I thought it depended only on a requisite degree of application and perseverance on his part, to render them of the most glowing description.

Whether my look conveyed any disbelief in his possession of these qualities, or his oft repeated determination to exert and display them, did not produce a sufficiently evident effect in my countenance, I know not, but his professions were most promising and he deprecated exceedingly the look I wore, saying I *'looked as if I could see into futurity.'*

We got to Broadford at 9 after coasting the shore of Skye all the way: this part of the island is very inferior in grandeur to the NE side, being lower and more level; and there are few or no sea fowl, but abundance of shellfish in the shallow water between Skye and Scalpa.

GCA Washing

We presented our introduction at Mrs. McKinnon's[81] after breakfast and being invited to dine at 4.30 spent the intermediate time in seeing a little of the neighbourhood: in this there is nothing curious, and leaving Dick to catch trout in a small rivulet, which empties itself into the sea here, Mr. Train and I had another bout of sketching, or rather, though I have always termed our indoor occupation 'sketching' my employment was much more generally scribbling down the events which had occurred as we proceeded.

Our party at dinner consisted of Mrs. McKinnon, two unmarried daughters, a son and daughter-in-law, all nice people, most comfortably settled in the snug little house at Corry. In the middle of dinner, a long stalked old fashioned wine glass with the McKinnon Arms, reversed by 'Kingsburgh' the place of residence of another branch of the family, was introduced and handed full of whiskey to each at table: Prince Charles had drunk from it, while concealed in Skye, it is now most religiously preserved as an invaluable relic by our friends at Corry. Some other family had a pair of old shoes he had worn, but they are nearly extinct now from the many morsels shaved off by curious visitors.

Prince Charles' cup

After dinner we had some music and were delighted with some of the Gaelic songs, sung to us by the ladies. One *Vari dhoun* we admired so much that Mrs. McKinnon wrote us the words, and I continued to note down the air as they sang it, and is pended hereto, in company with the *St Kilda Wedding*, a song enthusiastically performed by Ian McLeod in our voyage to that island.

It was amusing to perceive how much they dislike McCulloch: two gentlemen who came in the evening and with whom I had some chat on the subject expressed themselves in a manner which would hold out few inducements to a second visit, it appears he stated facts which were positively contradicted, by-the-by he was at this very house.

The former of these is I believe a love song, and the words are pretty correct. The other is a celebrated St Kilda Song which Ian McLeod sung in going to St Kilda, but of which I only remember the chorus part.

☞ Sunday, 19th June ✿ ✿ ✿
Exploring Corruisk

GOT INTO A cart after breakfast and away 5 miles west to Loch Schlapan, which must be crossed on the way to Corruisk,[82] our today's destination. The Spar Cave[83] is on the side of this Loch, a few miles (4) to the west of the ford: we did not go to see it, for we heard in consequence of frequent visits to it, the beautiful white Stalactite of which it is composed had been blackened by smoke, and terribly broken by people who went to see it. The distance of Corruisk from the ford on Loch Schlapan, where we left our cart is 7 miles over a hilly road, presenting nothing very fine till nearly the end when some mountain scenery on the right excites some admiration; this is just before the ascent of the mountain which bounds Corruisk on the south of the summit of which we attained about 10 o'clock. The day had been previously misty and unpromising, but now cleared away and afforded an admirable opportunity for beholding the magnificent view before us: Corruisk, *or the Glen of the Water* is a narrow, and deeply precipitous valley occupied by an apparently small Loch, which is however a deceitful effect produced by the stupendous scenery adjacent.

For McCulloch in his *'Highlands and Western Islands'*, declares that under a similar impression he set off from one of its extremities to walk round it, and then became aware of a deceptive effect of the gigantic scene before him. The mountains which bound this Glen on the north are

Huge Stone – Corruisk

Corruisk from the south

the Coolin Hills, and they form a most striking feature of the place; from
the irregularity of their outline I have no doubt that they must contain
among them rocks almost as fine as the Storr, and I regretted much that
we could not devote a few days to exploring them. On all sides of Corruisk
the mountains descend in an almost unbroken slope of rock, and it is
difficult to conceive anything more desolately grand than this glen.
However I think the visit to it should be made from Sconsor, which
would bring one upon it from the summit of the Coolins. These hills
contain the only Red Deer remaining on Skye, and they are not abundant:
Goats which had been pastured among them have become wild and are
now obliged to be hunted or shot when wanted. Corruisk should certainly
be visited at any rate – I thought I was disappointed at it at first, but
like a fine picture, it has dwelt strongly on my mind, and improves on
consideration. The fact is my anticipations were founded on McCulloch's
really fine description of it, in comparison with which he scarcely
mentions any other scene, so that when I remembered he was at the
foot of the Storr I ought to have been acquainted with its grandeur yet
scarcely noticed them, I prepared myself for something unreasonable.
Nevertheless, I still think the Storr finer! We made one or two sketches
and got home at 10.

Sea-sick passengers

☞ **Monday, 20th June** ✿ ✿ ✿
Steam boat from Broadford on Skye, interesting companions

MacLean of Coll

UP AT 6.30 to join the steam boat from Portree, which takes just 3 hours to accomplish the 24 miles between Portree and Broadford. The sail through the Kyles is very fine, as I dare say I mentioned before, and as we had a stiff head wind, we had plenty of time for its contemplation. During our tour we had once or twice stumbled on strangers whimsically like friends at home, and today one of three gentlemen who had been at Broadford to visit the cave and Corruisk and with whom we had associated while on board the steamer presented such a likeness to our friend Mr Collinson that we almost simultaneously made an exclamation of the name. At Tobermoray I was about to send a letter which Isaac had procured to McLean of Coll,[84] as his house was near the town, but was told by the captain that he was going with us to Glasgow: accordingly he came on board, and I presented myself and the letter and we mutually regretted that it had not been in our power to visit him at his house. He was very kind – about forty – and promised to get me eggs of the eagle next year. The Arctic Gull breeds on a loch near his house.

Another dignitary whom we had on board was McNeil of Canna,[85] a comfortable clerical looking person in black, to whom McLean introduced us, in consequence of which a most pressing invitation to visit him on any future opportunity, ensued, which I should unhesitatingly avail myself of, for it is quite impossible to describe the difference of their general invitation from the often unmeaning place of civilised life.

☞ Tuesday, 21th June ❀ ❀ ❀
Tarbert through the Kyles of Bute to Glasgow

A T 10 THE STEAM boat landed us at the head of west Loch Tarbert, and over the neck of land a mile in width, our things were conveyed in a cart: there is a considerable village at the east end, where as it would be some time before the Glasgow steamer was ready we dined. It was too rainy to see much, so we confined our rambles to an old castle on an eminence to the south of the town, and in about 3 hours put ourselves and chattels on board the *Superb* for Glasgow. She made rapid work of it, being one of the swiftest steamers going, being able to do 11 knots in the hour.

Symptoms of populousness and civilisation became now more frequent as we advanced; we soon reached the narrow channel between Bute and the mainland, called the Kyles of Bute, which resembles in character more the features on an inland lake than an arm of the sea.

The mountainous island of Arran, little known, but magnificent in some of its scenes, is seen to the south just before entering the Kyles, but does not in this point of view present the appearance of a

warrior's helmed head, as it is said to do from the East.
After passing Bute, at whose little neat black and white
looking town of Rothsay, we called for passengers, the
navigation is that of the Clyde, than which I know few
similar scenes finer.

Since leaving Tarbert, our passengers have
gradually increased in number, though they are
getting so much more worldly in style and appearance
that the contrast is stronger than I expected to find
it, in coming from the unsophisticated islanders to the
neighbourhood of cities and men: to have been among
them, is as invigorating and refreshing to the feelings
and faculties of the mind, as a plunge in the wide sea is
to the members of the body: and the similitude holds good
still further, inasmuch as they are both elements foreign to our natural
destination.

Somewhere in the Kyles of Bute, two gentlemen and a lady joined us,
with whom we enjoyed a good deal of chat, which going on matters now
going on in the world, was interesting to those who had absolutely lost
sight of it for a time. One of the gentlemen amused us considerably, he
was very tall and well made; dressed in a lightish blue coat and tight
nankeen remainders,[86] crowned by a broad rimmed white hat: but the air
of refined old school punctiliousness which seemed blended with every
movement, was the strong characteristic, and induced us to catch a
likeness of him for our sketch book, which by-the-by was then only
intended as private remembrances for ourselves and many of
whose contents should not have been introduced here, but that
in the existence of this more perfect record of our wanderings
and the little events connected with them, the original transient memoranda are likely to be neglected and lost, and there
is nothing ill-natured or reprehensible in our motives for depict-
ing those who are associated in our minds with particular
circumstances of our rambles. On our arrival in Glasgow we
ascertained by their cutting us out of the best room at McLean's,
that their name was Royd, and that they came from Liverpool.
This was a light to us, as Dick immediately remembered that we had con-
nections of that name there: this was absurd enough.

Mr Royd

As I said the best room was occupied at McLean's, and we were not
quite so comfortable as in passing through before: I believe I was in a hor-
rible bad humour, however we got our tea and went to bed.

☞ **Wednesday, 22th June** ✿ ✿ ✿
       Glasgow, Dick heads for Liverpool, others to Edinburgh

DICK AND I got our accounts settled this morning and find them lower than I had anticipated, which would not have been the case, had we sojourned more than we did in Skye, or any other land of accommodation; but in Harris, which I believe only contains one inn, we met with such inevitable civility and hospitality that our expenses were whimsically trifling. After almost missing the *Liverpool* in which he had taken his place for that town, Dick left us at 12. Mr Train and I took places in the 4 o'clock Edinburgh coach and dining at 2, forgot the St Kilda cheeses and joined it with our hawks and other luggage. The coach was very full and our journey to Edinburgh destitute of comfort or incident; got to our journey's end at 9 and put up at Scott's Star Hotel in Princes Street from whence a coach goes to Newcastle at 5.30 in the morning.

☞ **Thursday, 22th June** ✿ ✿ ✿
       Coach from Edinburgh to Newcastle

MOUNTED Newcastle coach at 5.30 which contained nothing worthy of notice – breakfasted uncomfortably enough at Lauder and dined at Wooler cottage and arrived in Newcastle at 9, concluding our journey after an absence of between 5 and 6 weeks, spent by us all in the most delightful manner, and during which we found ourselves in the most fortunate manner, favoured by circumstances which at first seemed to threaten the destruction of our schemes, and by weather so fine that wherever we went they told the same tale of not having seen the like for several years.

CONCLUSION

IN CONCLUSION, I do not hesitate to say that the scenery of Skye is far superior in grandeur to anything I ever saw, and the accommodation on that island so fair – particularly at Broadford and Portree, that the inducements to visit it, may satisfactorily be yielded to. I think a month or six weeks devoted to exploring it, would well repay any tourist, and I have no doubt, like the neglected Storr, there are many points of extreme grandeur and sublimity totally unknown. The Roads are good and except that English is not much spoken, I can see no let or hindrance to the unembarrassed progress of the traveller.

With regard to Harris, it is not worth a visit from the ordinary tourist: excepting the mountainous district called the Forest, it is generally low, barren and rocky: interspersed with multitudes of small lakes, 90 or more of which I counted from Roneval, a mountain near the capital of the island, Rowdill. The mountains in the forest are fine, but not at all equal to the Coollin Hills of Skye, as may be conceived from a glance at the sketch of one of their finest scenes, a precipitous mountain in Glen Uladale.

St Kilda, except to the ornithologist is not worthy of a journey, for though even sublimer and more uncommon than any of the scenes in Skye, the difficulty of attaining to it – though generally very much exaggerated – renders a special visit scarcely worth while.

And now My Dear Madam or Sir, if you have perused, or skimmed over these leaves, with ought of satisfaction or information, my purpose in writing them is completely answered. Should you by my instrumentality be induced to visit the Hebrides, I think the objects which would occur, would scarcely fail to impress themselves strongly on your recollection, and call up feelings of admiration and care for the Maker of a world so wonderful.

That the reader, if he visit them, may be as vividly impressed with these feelings as the writer of these pages, is the sincere wish of

Geo C. Atkinson

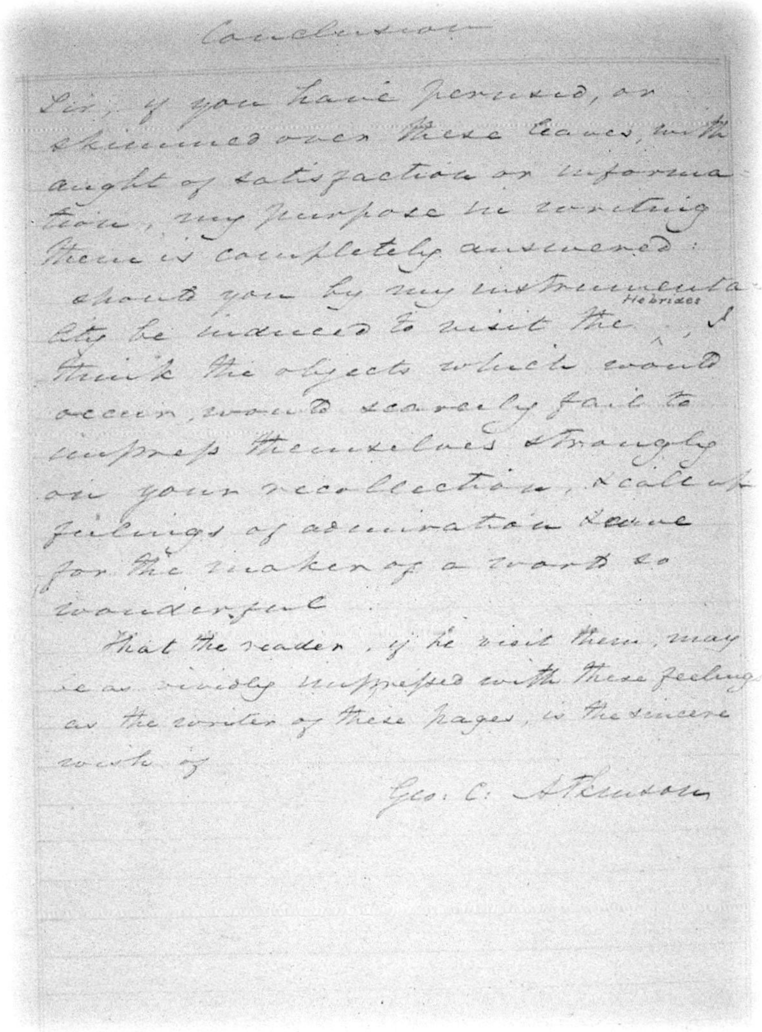

GCA hand-writing from the last page of his 1831 Journal

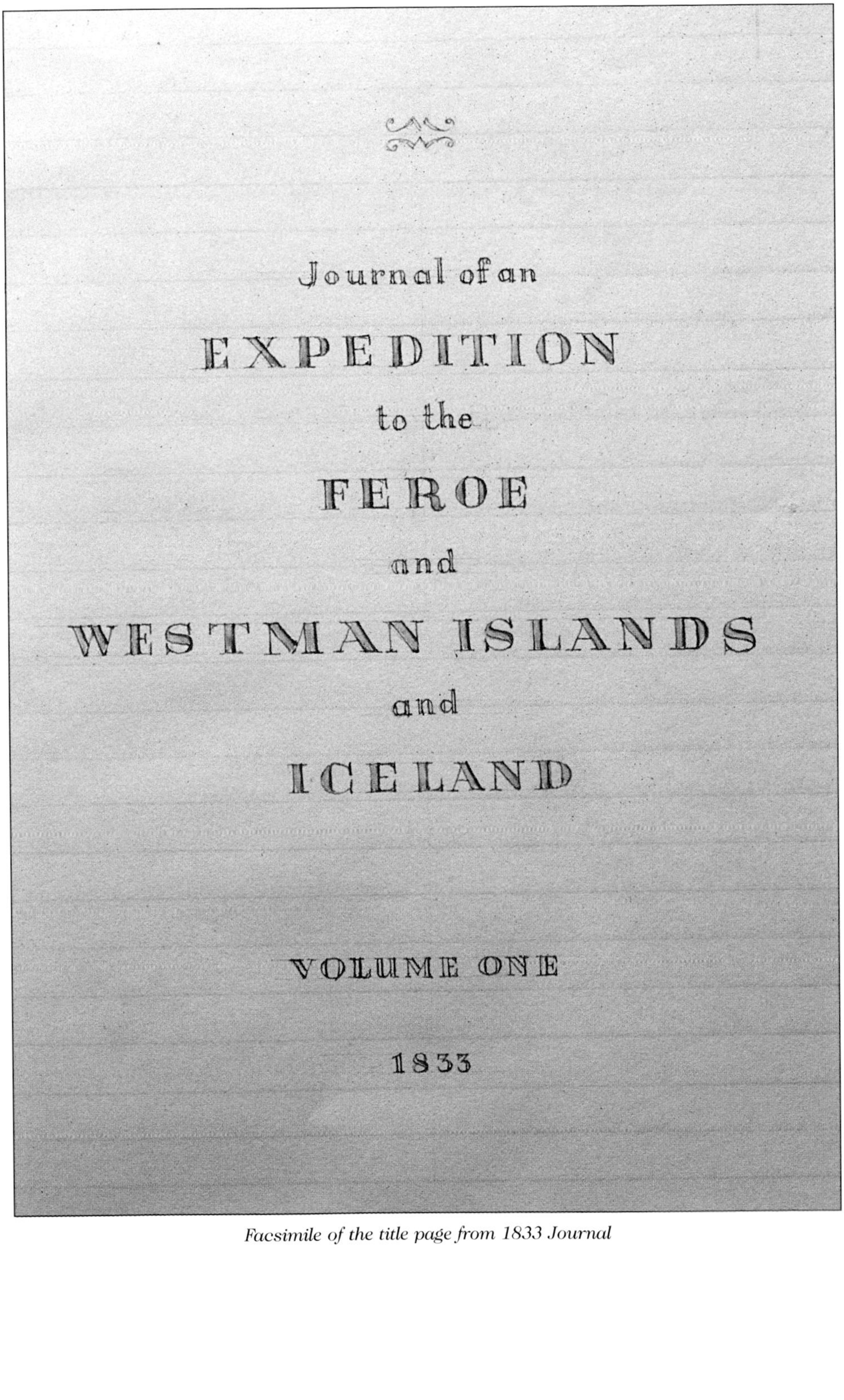

Journal of an

EXPEDITION

to the

FEROE

and

WESTMAN ISLANDS

and

ICELAND

VOLUME ONE

1833

Facsimile of the title page from 1833 Journal

Rocks at the Butt of Lewis by G. R. Richardson

Extracts

Relating to the time in Glasgow,
Portree on Skye, the Shiant Islands and
the Isle of Lewis

'I longed to see the isles that gem
Old Oceans purple Diadem'

Dedication

I dedicate these volumes, without hesitation, to friends who have derived
amusement from the perusal of my former Journals, and therefore in a
certain degree, been the cause of my continuing to trust my travelling
details to their good nature and indulgence.

Friday, 10th May 🕸 🕸 🕸
Setting Off Party

IMPRIMIS – Our Party consisted of William Cookson, myself, Proctor, and
two dogs, Cato and Teapot: the former of the quadrupeds a handsome,
lazy, useless setter, which Cookson had determined to present to some
important dignitary in Iceland: and the latter, a brown pugnacious poodle,
exceedingly conceited of his tail, which he carried so rigidly erect as to
resemble the handle of the useful implement whose name he bore. Proctor
was a remarkably decent fellow from near Durham, whom I had long
known as a bit of a naturalist and a preserver of animals, and whom we
prevailed upon to go with us, to prepare any skins of rare birds etc. which
we might procure, and to make himself generally useful to us.

Cookson's father had engaged a vessel for us, to be ready in Stornoway
in Lewis on the 20th and to remain in our employ at the charge of a guinea
a day for an indefinite period. She was reported to be an excellent sea boat
and was provided with a sufficient crew, and provisions for four or five
months. We were to provide ourselves with everything but the ordinary
bread, meat, water etc., of the vessel for which we paid a sum of 10
shillings apiece a week, and her tonnage was 54.

As our expedition held out much promise of sport in the shooting way, we took a couple of rifles and 3 fowling pieces, and a due amount of ammunition. The usual companion of Ramblers; sketch books, note books, a few mathematical instruments, and a chess board with our ordinary luggage, a box of books, and some geological tools, completed our equipment.

The Ramblers met on board the *Ardincaple* steamer at the quay (Newcastle), at 6am: and in the course of a couple of hours crossed the bar and got to sea. The day was cloudy, wind N.N.E., and the passengers peculiarly uninteresting; most of them horribly sick and unbecoming . . . Owing to the head wind, we did not reach Newhaven till twelve at night, and instead of finding a boat ready to put us on shore immediately, which ought to have been provided by the owners, we were compelled after much lapse of time and patience, to employ a boat from the shore at a rapacious charge, which turned us over to a set of porters on the quay, even more expert at imposition, and these again delivered us up to a coachman, who beat them all. It may fairly be imagined that we were out of humour when we arrived at two in the morning at the Crown in Prince's Street. As for poor Proctor, either looking at Cookson who was very seedy, or the general cold and discomfort of the day, gave him the Influenza, and it required several days of doctoring and nursing to bring him all right again.

☞ **Saturday, 11th May** ✿ ✿ ✿
Shopping in Edinburgh and stage coach to Glasgow.

A FTER BUYING a small telescope, a compass, etc., at Adie's, we proceeded at 11 o'clock by a heavy coach to Glasgow, and put up at the Buck's Head, a house by no means comfortable, where they gave us some very decent Claret. They charged us 10/- a bottle for it.

☞ **Sunday, 12th May** ✿ ✿ ✿
Glasgow, visit Professor William Hooker

I T OCCURRED to me, by the merest chance, in thinking if I knew anyone in Glasgow, that Mr. Trevelyan had given me an introduction some years since to Dr. Hooker,[87] the Professor of Botany, which in the absence of that gentleman, I had presented to his father, who showed me much attention at the time. Now of the three or four English books on Iceland, that I had been able to lay my hands on, none had interested me half so much as Dr.

Hooker's, and I had taken a number of memoranda from it, without for a moment considering anything of its author. An exclamation of pleasure, therefore, broke on me, when Cookson interrupted a chain of thought where Dr. Hooker formed the top link, and his valuable publications on the science he professes, with all the beauties and wonders it presents, were following each other rapidly through my mind, by referring to some statement in Dr. Hooker's *'Iceland'*. The recollection that I knew, or might know that gentleman, of course assumed a most important character, and we called at his house before church today, were admitted, and on my stating that I had had the pleasure of formerly bearing a letter to him, were received in the most gratifying manner, and accompanied him to church. In the course of the afternoon, we dined with him, and obtained much information of a most desirable character, which he communicated in a most amusing way, and intermingled with so much anecdote and general information, that our intended journey became invested with new interest at every word . . .

At five we waited on our friend again, who amused us a good deal by a detail of domestic miseries incidental to the absence of his lady from home, which among other inconveniences precluded his access to that part of his habitation, yclept[00] the cellar; nonetheless, we were very comfortable, and highly pleased with the kindness and attention of Dr. Hooker. He seemed to regret much that we had not procured letters of introduction, through Danish merchants in Copenhagen to people in Iceland; and that any he might give us would be almost useless, from the changes that must have taken place since 1809 when he visited the Island, but he promised us the best he could give us, and also the loan of three or four valuable books which we had not yet seen on Iceland . . . he insisted on our taking with us.

In the course of the evening, he introduced us to his friend, Dr. Schouler,[89] who came in to tea, and who exclusive of much general scientific information, is considered one of the first naturalists in Scotland. Dr. Hooker kindly sent for him, thinking he would be able to inform us on various points of natural history which would be likely to occur to us in the course of our expedition, and a good many of my memoranda on that subject were grounded on the conversations we had then and the next morning. As for the Doctor himself – I mean Hooker – no trouble seemed too great for him to impose on himself in the furtherance of our plans, and we left him at 9 for our Hotel, with a strong feeling of gratitude for his kindness, and of thankfulness to our lucky stars that we had thought of calling on him.

☞ Monday, 13th May ✿ ✿ ✿
Visit Dr. Schouler, gift of a skin collected by Capt. Sabine

SOON AFTER breakfast, Dr Hooker's son called and took us to the Andersonian Institution, where Dr. Schouler holds a leading situation. There is a pretty fair Museum attached to it which contains among other things a number of Arctic birds procured by Captain Sabine.[90] Dr. Schouler had the kindness to give me a skin of one of them, the *Uria Brunnichii*, a bird only lately distinguished from the *Uria Troile* or Common Guille-motte, and which is found to be a native of our own shores. As Captain Sabine has the credit of having ascertained its distinctiveness, and this is one labelled by his own hand, it is doubly valuable as an intrinsically rare bird and as one of the original specimens on which the discovery was made.

In the course of the day we were chiefly occupied in laying in such sea stock, as we should not be likely to obtain in Stornoway of such good quality; *viz.*, tea, sugar, cheese, lemons, fish sauce etc., etc.

We also went down to the Broomie Law, a long, busy, crowded quay, like our own canny Quayside, to inspect the *Highland Chieftain*[91] which is destined to convey us to Stornoway. To me it was an old friend, as I had partaken of its accommodation and dis-accommodation in visiting some of the Hebrides two years since, and I hinted to Cookson that his eye seemed engaged in looking for it among vessels of too magnificent an aspect – I was scanning the second and third rates. I ought to explain that as she takes the short cut to the Islands through the Crinan Canal, instead of round the Mull of Kintyre, she must of necessity be so small as to pass the locks of the canal . . . One consequence of her smallness is that she has no sleeping room, but lands her passengers every night at different stations for that purpose – a misery or not according to taste.

☞ Tuesday, 14th May ✿ ✿ ✿
Farewell to Hooker – heading for Tobermorey

THE *Highland Chieftain* sailed at 12, so before that we had plenty to do calling on the Doctor for his introduction and final hints on Iceland, and packing up our things and getting them a'board.

His introduction was a circular addressed to any of his old friends whom we might find alive in Iceland, and specified us to be illustrious and magnificent as two plain individuals could possibly be represented; for he told us they are particularly struck with anything like a title, or with eminence and celebrity of any kind. He walked with us to the Broomie Law, gave us an introduction to Lady Stewart McKenzie, the relict, it will be remembered of Sir Samuel Hood, and we parted . . .

There seemed to be very few cabin passengers; only one, a stout gentleman of the name of McIver went further than Greenock: a brother of the owner of the little sloop we are to proceed from Stornoway in, and a confirmed bore of the old school: hearty, good-natured and persecuting us with long legends of his family and their pursuits; much given in confidentialities with the people on board, and to drink whisky when *we* paid for it.

After leaving Glasgow there were three ladies on board bound for Portree, the eldest of whom, infinitely to my amusement, accosted me by name and said she remembered seeing me two years since at Portree where I stayed a week. She introduced herself therefore as a sort of acquaintance, as a sister of McCloud of Rasa, and begged me to call if at any time my ramblings should bring me again to Portree; for it had begun to blow fresh and she determined not to go.

Few finer river scenes are to be met with than that exhibited by the banks of the Clyde in sailing down. Beautiful wooded points opened on the view in rapid succession, and every now and then some little quiet nest-like residence is disclosed for a moment among the trees, sheltered by picturesque hills of considerable boldness. Then on the north side as the river widens to the sea, the scenery becomes somewhat less interesting till the beautiful Kyles of Bute are entered: The term Kyles (meaning a narrow of the sea) is here applied to the winding one between the Isle of Bute and the main land, and is very celebrated for its beauty which principally consists in the rich vegetation clothing the hills on both sides, and on the secludedness and quiet of the scene, as a stranger flits through it in that horrid affair, a dirty steamboat. Ours is villainously so, the day dull, chill, squally, and uncomfortable, and the Captain and people particularly civil and obliging.

We got to the east end of the Crinan Canal at 12.¼, and with some little difficulty got ashore, and the people at a house there roused up, and then to bed.

☞ **Wednesday, 15th May** ⚜ ⚜ ⚜
  Oban, Tobermorey and an important contact.

AS our stout friend Mr. McIver had slept in the cabin, as well as the Captain and mate, it was (on entering it this morning at 7), what we used to call it at Charterhouse, very frousty; and we gladly preferred walking along the banks of the canal as the steamboat worked slowly through, to its occupation. The country to the north of the Crinan Canal is barren and uninteresting, the view being confined at the east end, but stretching away over a large mass to some bluish hills in the background . . .

. . . After escaping from the Canal the voyage is pleasing and interesting in fine weather from the number of islands it discloses. First Jura and Scarba appear to the left with their intervening whirlpool of Corryvrechan, a place the dangers of which have been much exaggerated; then come the low islands of Luing, Seil and Kerera; the two former remarkable only for their slate quarries, and the latter for having in former times been one of the most celebrated places for smuggling in the Highlands. The Bay of Oban[92] succeeds to these, and is a very striking feature in the scenery of the Western Islands. Fancy a fine open bay, sufficiently sheltered by Kerera in front, to ensure safety to vessels which anchor in it; ornamented by a white picturesque mass of houses upon the shore in its centre, which contain among them a custom house, stamp, and post office, excise office and other official edifices of much importance; running out to the north is a fine woody point on which stands Dunally Castle! . . . Our vile, small undignified Steamer stopped here to renew its stock of coals, and we, hungry and dinnerless rambled on shore (and) the while(s) sketched blackguard children, and endeavoured in divers ways to elude the encroaches of appetite; till recalled to the boat by the most indefatigable ringing of a badly toned bell, and a long column of insurgent steam.

(Fizza! – Fizza! – Fizza! –) 'Jingle! – Jingle! – Jingle!– Come gentlemen, we've been waiting ten minutes!' So we bounced on board and away we went for the Sound of Mull.

This is another very fine part of the Island scenery of Scotland; scenery which resembles far more that of inland lake and river, than of real decided sea; but which the more I see of it, the more I am inclined to admire for the variety of nameless beauties it presents. This is my third visit to the scenery of today and not a mile of coast on either side of the Sound of Mull occurs, without convincing me that numerous little spots have entirely escaped me on former occasions.

At half past nine we reached Tobermorey, a prettily situated town on the north east of Mull. It lies at the extremity of a very fine bay, which would anchor the British fleet I should think, in point of capacity, and which is rendered very secure from the entrance to it being narrow and somewhat high, while the anchorage as far as regards bottom, I am informed, very favourable.

A mile to the south of the town is the comfortable quiet looking residence of Coll – or we should call him Mr. MacLean of Coll.[93] When

Dunolly Castle, Bay of Oban, by G. R. Richardson

last here we had an introduction to him, but owing to our time of absence running short, we had given up the idea of presenting it. Still we felt some little interest in a man who might have been a friend, so we enquired of two or three people about him, and at last, of a decent gamekeeper-like man in a black shooting jacket, who looked as if he was likely to know all the respectable people on Mull. *'Pray'*, said I, *'Do you know Coll?'* (It would have been considered rude to call him Mr. MacLean). *'Oh, very well, sir,'* said he, *'I am the man.'*

This fine Bay is still more secure from being sheltered by a long island the name of which I do not remember. After hunting about a little we at length succeeded in establishing ourselves at Mrs. Cuthbertson's lodgings,[94] had a glorious tea, and went to bed.

☞ **Thursday, 16th May** ❀ ❀ ❀
Portree, previous contacts from 1831 and Tommy.

COMMENCED by a false alarm from the ringing of a steamboat bell, which was intended only to awaken certain persons who had arrived last night on their way to Staffa, and taken up their abode promiscuously about the town; but unfortunately our discernment proved deficient, and down we came breathless, angry and very untidy at a most untimely hour, to jaw the Captain for going before the time he told us of yesterday. As soon as we were a little mollified, we lounged about until our time came, and then splashed on towards Skye.

This day's voyage – I mean between Tobermorey and Portree – is generally a tedious one from the number of intervening places at which it is necessary to call for the delivery of packages and people, and many of them places of very little beauty or interest. The island of Egg is however an exception, and its scenery is very fine, and there is a very interesting cave on its west side in which some centuries ago, the whole population of the island was smoked to death. They had displeased the men of Skye in some way, and retiring modestly to this cave on the approach of a large force from that island, they were detected and smoked as I said – their bones remaining even now. It was a disappointment to us that there was nothing to leave at Egg in passing, or our obliging Captain would have taken the boat round the other (west) side of it, and allowed us to land.

In the course of the afternoon we entered the channel between Skye and the main land, where there are some of the best scenes among the Hebrides: the mountains on both sides – the Inverness-shire side particularly, rising to a great height and receding in successive ranges in stupendous perspective. Imagine a tide running at a rate of ten miles an hour! It does so sometimes in this narrow channel, and then it is useless for anything to push against it. We were more fortunate than to arrive at the time when its course was against us, and went through at a great rate.

We soon reached Broadford, then passed within Rasa, and then entered Portree Bay, in as fine an evening as ever shone. This is quite a familiar district to me. There are the McKinnons[95] at Broadford and the famous fellow Sir John McRae[96] on Rasa (to whom I could not resist sending a note in passing to tell him that three Englishmen remembered his kindness): and last but equal to the others, the landlord of the Inn at Portree, Jameson.[97] Poor fellow, he remembered me in a moment and got into terrible long stories, as he caught me flitting about the house, about everybody I knew or that he thought I knew on the island: '*so and so was dead and so and so married*' etc. etc just as is usual elsewhere, and 'Tommy' was so comfortable! His mother had written as I had directed her and wanted Tommy to come home, but he had a good master and good situation and preferred remaining at Portree. Poor Sunderland Tommy![98] I remember thinking his a forlorn case when years since he came sobbing to Jamieson's and said to me in broad Sunderland, '*Please sir, I left home three years since when I was ten years old – on board a ship, sir; and I missed her, sir, at Dublin, and some person told me that I had better gang to Scotland it was on the way to England, sir – and when I came here they couldn't tell me the way to Sunderland, sir, and my name's Tommy Atkinson and I come from Sunderland. Oh, sir, do you know my mother?*' And then he burst into tears, which was injudicious as he was very ugly and did not cry becomingly. However, I found out his friends on my return, had a very severe crying scene with an aunt of his, and had the satisfaction of putting them in communication with Tommy whom they had long given up as lost.

I should liked to have seen the varlet but had not time that evening or the next morning.[*]

☞ **Friday, 17th May** 🕸 🕸 🕸
Portree - Shiant Islands and Stornoway, Lewis

WE STARTED soon – at 5, when it was clear morning, but afterwards grew thick, and eventually a heavy rain came, which continued until we reached Stornoway at 3.

The coast of Skye north of Portree is a very striking piece of rock scenery. It is very lofty and consists, I believe, entirely of Basalt, and is in

---

[*]Tommy has got home to his friends and called on me in October 1834.

many places curiously caverned out. About midway between Portree and the north point, at the distance of a mile inland, is an extraordinary rock called the 'Storr', which many of my readers will remember I raved a good deal about in my Hebridean Journal. Only fancy a pinnacle of rock about as lofty and bulky as the steeple of St Nicholas,[99] standing independently upon the side of a mountain of very considerable elevation! I declare it is the finest and most extraordinary production of nature in that line I ever saw. When in Portree before, I was persuaded by Jameison to write some high-flowing stuff about its wonders on the back of a map of Inverness hanging over the fireplace, and this he took care to exhibit to persons coming to Portree; for it was a fact, that no one used ever to go nearer to it than Portree – seven miles off – contenting themselves with wondering and admiring from thence; whereas the effect is beyond belief more grand on a near approach. Now, he says, people go often, and like it very much. Of course, after penning the description of it for him, I never thought of my composition, so that I was not a little amused a year after to find in a number of Lt. Col. Murray's[100] clever views in Scotland, which I was taking in, a very spirited drawing of the Storr with an accompanying description commencing with my eulogy of it, as the opinion, left in writing on the back of the map at Portree, by some tourists who had seen and admired, and which according to the gallant colonel, does not over rate its magnificence.

As soon as the point of Hunish – that is, the north point of the island of Skye – is passed, leaving a barren, rocky island called Rona on the right, a group of two or three very precipitous islands or rather rocks, open out on the left. On a former occasion I passed near them, and have reason to think they are too steep to land on. They are called McDonald's Tables[101] and are inhabited by certain sea fowl.

From Hunish we dashed on into the Minsh, as the comparatively open sea between the inner and outer Hebrides is called, and in a couple of hours came to the Shiant Islands[102] – three very lofty and desolate ones, 15 or 16 miles S.E. of Stornoway. It rained pretty hard and blew some, but our worthy captain, as the weather was nothing particular, steered the Steamer through the channel which divides them, and lowering his boat, landed us for an hour upon the northern of them, St. Mary's. As we rowed ashore two magnificent Eagles rose from the rocks, and I afterwards found that they had an eyrie on the precipice of the south side of the same island. Our boatman revelled away among the puffin nests . . .

We took a more enlarged survey of the island . . . It seems (like the two others) to be about 500 or 600 feet high, with a lofty cliff of Basalt on the north and west, and is inhabited by lots of sea fowl – chiefly Puffins and Guillemottes, but containing also a due proportion of Kittywakes and Razor Bills among its cliffs, and Oyster Catchers and Greater and Lesser Black-Backed Gulls on the grass of its summit. What more there might be. We had not an opportunity to see during our stay upon it.

The two other islands, apparently about the same size, lie nearly half a mile to the south. The most western of them, St. Culme, we had intended to visit in the boat to see a curious rocky arch which runs through one corner of it, but it had come on to blow rather briskly from the south east, which raised a short, choppy little sea between the islands that would have drenched us pretty well if we had not been saturated by a heavy rain when ashore. As it was we shipped some small matter of salt water and were glad to get aboard the steamer again.

About three we got to Stornoway and at five dined: then being informed that Mrs. Stewart McKenzie, relict it may be remembered, of that fine fellow, Admiral Sir Samuel Hood, was not in Lewis, we waited on Mr. Stewart, the Factor of the island, with an introduction given us by our kind friend Hooker, directed to her in the first place and, in her absence, to be delivered to Stewart. He proved an ungainly, awkward fellow . . . is very strict and severe to the poor people, and having an almost despotic power over them is exceedingly unpopular . . .

Lewis, which constitutes the most north-western point of Scotland, is generally low and uninteresting, except on its south end where it is joined to Harris by a narrow peninsula, called (like every similar situation in the western islands) *Tarbet* – or being interpreted, ' a boat carrying' from a common custom of carrying the smaller boats of the country over land, and at this point it rises into lofty and picturesque mountains of nearly 4,000 feet, I believe. These constitute the stronghold of the Red Deer in Lewis and Harris, which the Factor told us have increased much in number of late years, though how many there really are in the island neither he nor anyone else had the slightest notion of.

The island of Lewis, which to speak correctly, is not divided from Harris exactly at the peninsula, but a little to the north of it, contains, according to a magnificent map which had been drawn for Lord Seaforth[103] in 1809 (at an expense of £1,000, which was one half too little for the time and trouble it took) contains, I say, 274,274 Scotch acres, of which at that time 19.3.36 were in wood; 10,959.1.6 in arable and interjected pasture; 4,776.2.38 in fine pasture; 252,133.1.30 in moorish pasture and moss; and 6,385 . . . 38 in water – 274,274.2.28 in all.

The number of inhabitants is about 16,000, of whom 3,000 live in Stornoway. Harris contains about 4,000.

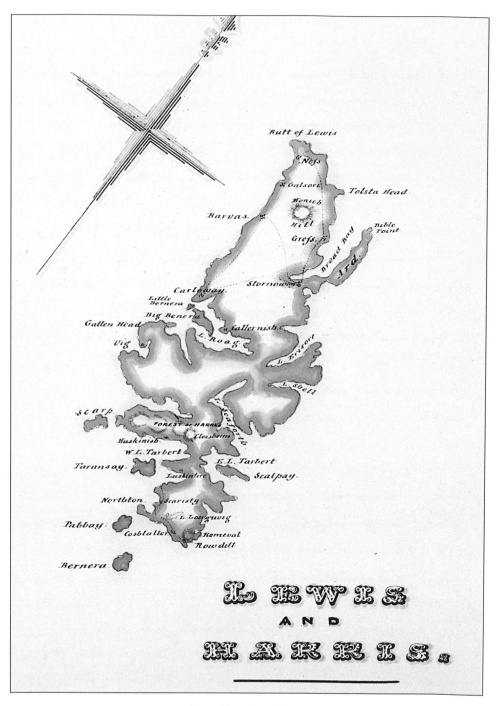

Map of Lewis and Harris

The town of Stornoway is situated on the margin of one of those numerous inlets which are likely to occur in island scenery, but which are particularly abundant among the islands and along the main land of the west of Scotland. The bay itself affords a good anchorage in all but easterly winds, and at its extremity there is a small harbour, accessible at high water, which would be safe at any time. It is an odd, whimsical, straggling looking town and runs for a mile (I dare say) into the country.

We landed and took up our residence in a house close by the quay, kept by some red-haired relations of the owners (Mr. McIver, owner of the Sloop *Peggy,*[104]) who managed to make us rather comfortable in spite of the miseries of raw-looking, carpetless and unpainted rooms, and much lack of ingenuity in their domestic arrangements – in which by the by, they only resemble every other house of entertainment I have seen among the Hebrides.

☞ **Saturday, 18th May** ✿ ✿ ✿
The Boat not ready for sailing – a little fishing

MISTER EVANDER (McIver) nephew of the owner, joined us this morning to walk to his father's house at Gresse, 8 miles along the north shore from Stornoway . . . determined to see as much as possible of Lewis, rather than be idle in Stornoway, for though it had been compacted that the *Peggy* should be ready for sea on the 20th, we were disgusted to find that it will be nearly a week before she could sail.

The Rivulets, which were to have afforded such excellent fishing, were almost too small to contain trout, and I was amused to find that the fine fishing is for the salmon smelts, as we call them here, which are to be caught in the shallow water to which (at its height) the tide has access. They are nice little fish and bite freely at a largish tinsely fly; this day, though, was far too windy for fishing or anything else, and in fact was the first of five Saturdays when it regularly blew a gale of wind. I absolutely couldn't keep my flies in the water, and hadn't those same sea trout been the most obliging, as well as unsophisticated little fish in the world, small would have been my chance of obtaining even the score which afterwards shewed at our dinner.

At length, roused from occupation by a hare cutting away up the hill opposite me, I relinquished my last stream at 4 or 5 o'clock, joined Cookson who had approached the house and was amiable – vying with old McIver, and then we all turned in. They kindly invited us to stay all night which we did.

☞ **Sunday, 19th May** ✿ ✿ ✿
The Legendary Tales, Methodists and Worship

YESTERDAY after dinner . . . Mr. McIver amused me with some legendary tales of the Western Isles, all of them curious and some of them interesting in an historical point of view.

Digression on the Methodists . . . The introduction of this overcharged degree of sanctity to the Hebrides took place 15 or 16 years since, and originated with an institution which was calculated in a simple form, and with moderate and judicious management, to do much good among the poor in reading the Bible and for some years it went on quietly and well. Nothing more was attempted, and all the advantages which so charitable and good measure was likely to produce were becoming gradually more apparent. Under the immediate guidance and inspection of the judicious men, who (it may be supposed) have the conduct of this society, there is no doubt that it works well now, and must continue to do so; But when the teachers – men qualified to instruct no further than in the simple reading of the scriptures, were sent forth to the more remote parts of the Highlands, where this bare qualification alone gave them a decided superiority over the common inhabitants; then they became puffed up – human nature couldn't stand it – and from teaching, they go on to explain(ing); from explaining to preaching; from preaching to disputing with the regular clergy . . .

It might have seemed unfair to enter into the foregoing attack on the Methodists in Lewis, and I should certainly have abstained from doing it, but we found while we were there that one of the most kind-hearted and excellent men on the island, the Reverend Mr. Cook of Ness, had been, nay it happened while we were there – that he was fairly compelled to leave the island in consequence of the ceaseless attacks of one of these men upon him.

What effect this state of things amongst the teachers of religion may have on the religion of the Island generally, I will not pretend to say; I hope a good one, and think on the whole it is so; at any rate there is a strong tone of seriousness perceptible in the conduct of the people and I am inclined to think that they are honest, sober and industrious from a similar disposing cause – religion – even though it be more from a desire to act consistently with the strictness they profess, than from a more simple and meritorious motive.

We walked after breakfast from Gresse and attended divine service in Stornoway at 2 o'clock. It was chiefly in Gaelic interspersed with prayers in English, and with two or three musical performances in the way of psalms.

124

By the by, there was a short sermon too in our language, preached like most such performances in Scotland, extemporaneously.

Monday, 20th May ✿ ✿ ✿
Millar, the Excise man and the Illegal[105] Whiskey Stills

IN PURSUANCE OF our intention of seeing something of the island while we were upon it, we arranged yesterday with some fishermen at Gresse to meet us at an early hour this morning, and row us north to Tolsta Head in the first place, and thence to the Butt. However, we were rather later than we intended in setting out and, when we got to Gresse, found the fishermen gone; so we had some more breakfast with the McIvers, and then they procured us another boat, manned by some labourers from the farm, and we set off about 11 from Gresse.

All went well for a while, till we rowed about four miles on our way, when so heavy a tide swell met us from the north as we rounded the first headland, and then after shipping a stiffish sea or two, and endeavouring in vain to prevent the men from talking and induce them to row a little, we found it so impossible to make the strokesman, who had a wide mouth, shut it, that we gave up our intention of sailing to the Butt, and landed about four miles north of Gresse to walk.

The morning had commenced with rain, and then when we set off for Gresse, it came on fine, but changed just as we landed, thickening most suspiciously and settling in gradually to a splendid Scotch mist. Never mind, we had a guide and a compass, certain whisky and a bottle of Cherry Brandy, to say nothing of cold meat etc., so we need not fear a wet coat, and off we set, the day becoming worse with each step. It was a thick mist and through it, impelled by a sharp, cold northeaster, drove a heavy pelting and incessant rain, which commenced with our landing at 1 o'clock and did not finish till after we were housed for the night.

We kept on very confidently by our guide's direction till 4 or 5 o'clock, and then began to feel impatient at not having reached our destination, which was only called twelve miles from Tolsta where we landed. We began to consult our compasses and, after noting our course by them for 10 minutes, found to our extreme provocation, though a little to our amusement, that our friend Donald was rambling about quite at random in the thick fog, now heading north, now south, now east, now west; for he absolutely boxed the compass in his vague roamings.

Things now looked bad. It rained heavily and we could not see twenty yards before us. It was now past six. We met a woman rambling over the heather, wet and draggled like ourselves. *'Ask her the way, Donald,'* said we, *'and give her some whiskey.'* (Putting the bottle containing our remaining stock into his hands).

Jabber, jabber, jabber – away they rattled in the lisping Gaelic of the Lewis, and then they grinned and shook hands and had a pull at the bottle. . . . *'Well, Donald, which is the way?'* Oh, he knew the way very well, but this was what he had said all along and, at length, it was quite evident that he had never asked the woman, but had merely indulged in general conversation for a quarter of an hour. It may be supposed our temper was somewhat tried by all this . . . the mist cleared, we saw houses at two or three miles distance . . . it was the village of Ness . . . we dedicated some few minutes to the conclusion of a bottle of Cherry Brandy and cold fowl . . . We pushed on and reached Mr. Millar, the exciseman's house at Ness at half past 8, having walked rapidly since 1 o'clock. Our error therefore must have been a great one, as the distance is not more than 12 miles.

I think I am correct in stating that there are only two places of public entertainment in Lewis: at least, that there is only one out of Stornoway at Callernish. We were instructed, in the absence of such accommodation, to go unhesitatingly to the best house we could see and demand admittance. We had moreover, an introduction to Millar (the excise man) at Ness, and were received by him in a kind unpretending way, and in a short time were feeding away on the best he could give us.

Millar proved an intelligent obliging fellow, but for this evening was very severe upon the Methodists. He entertained us not a little with narrations of different adventures with smugglers, of whom he had seen a good deal, here and in Inverness-shire. They seldom, as in Ireland, defend their stills, but stand mournfully looking on at their seizure, and generally if treated kindly, and required to do so, assist in removing and destroying them. During the two years Millar has been in Lewis, he has made 193 seizures of malt, and destroyed 42 stills.

One morning amidst the bitter revilings of some of the superior ones (members of the family) he went to the house and found the inmates most closely wrapt in the deepest devotion. Of course he felt uncomfortable enough, but by way of form, proceeded to the bed, which was clustered round with contrite sinners, and making his way between them, lifted the draperies of the bed. His *mauvais haute* vanished. Great was his satisfaction. And no future scruple about intruding on a prayer meeting ever entered his bosom. He drew a glorious prize from beneath the bed!

And after securing the malt, proceeded instantly to other houses where he had hitherto found them much engaged, and made the best morning's work he ever had! This and multitudes of other stories connected with his duties, he detailed to us till bed time, when we retired pretty well knocked up, as our walk, by the rate and time had been one of five or six and thirty miles, and that immediately on leaving shipboard, and on the coarsest day I was ever out in.

☞ **Tuesday, 21th May** 🕸 🕸 🕸
Temples, Agricultural Implements and Utensils,[106] more Whiskey

OUR INTENTION was to have proceeded in our circumambulation of the island today, but our walk had stiffened us a little, and as Millar had promised to shew us a cave where he made a seizure of a still, and which he fancied penetrated to a great distance underground; and as our curiosity had been excited anent[107] the caves of the island, we concluded, as the Americans say, to stay and make a short day's work of it about the rocks at the Butt and other curiosities in the neighbourhood.

. . . We wended our way to the beach of a fine bay on the north west extremity of Lewis, and commenced our search where the level sward, or links, borders on the tide mark . . . The lonely situation of the burial place – exposed to the fierce north-western wind, and the tremendous sea which it hurls on before it – baring and dispersing the bones of the dead upon the bleak shore – and a sort of holy awe, in which these remains are contemplated by the natives, tended not a little to enhance the general interest of this lonely spot.

There is reason to suppose that the real state of the case has but little mystery about it; for I have no doubt that it is merely the place of burial of (perhaps) the generation before the last, who from the scarcity of wood were reduced to deposit their dead between four flat stones, and that they selected the situation, probably, from the convenience of finding stones suitable to the purpose, near to it. The ruin scarcely rising above the sod – which is close to it, we were afterwards informed, is one of the many remains of Roman Catholic chapels which are found in Lewis, and which among the natives receive the name of 'Temples' . . . we proceeded overland to the Butt. On our way we stopped to examine the very perfect remains of another temple – that of St Malachi – which has much celebrity throughout the Western Islands, for the power it possesses of curing insane persons, and those afflicted with a variety of diseases . . . There is nothing at all picturesque in this ruin, or in fact in any we saw in Lewis, except the Danish fort at Doun Carloway.

In our walk to the Butt, I had a good opportunity of observing the husbandry proceedings of this very remote portion of Great Britain, and

Agricultural Proceedings in Lewis, by H. P. Parker

was exceedingly struck with its resemblance to the practice of St Kilda: rows of stones as big as a man's fist form the divisions of the fields; in fact it is what a hunting man would call a regular, '*stone wall country*'. They pull the barley by the roots, instead of cutting it and leaving a stubble; and using it first to thatch their houses with, which like those of St Kilda are made without chimneys, that the roof may be thoroughly saturated with smoke (which improves its qualities as manure for the land). They strip it off after the expiration of a twelvemonth, and mix it intimately with the soil intended for the reception of Barley or Potatoes. This they concur with the St Kildians in pronouncing to be the finest compost they know, and they certainly succeed in raising most excellent Barley.

Their mode of dispatching sheep and pigs partakes, too, of their simple and primitive life, and is as unsophisticated and laconic as need be   they cut their heads smack off, and allow them to run about as long as is convenient to them afterwards.

Their plough, however, is a brilliant piece of mechanism, and throws the simpler contrivance of my worthy island friends, sadly into the shade. It is called in Gaelic, '*Crom na gadd*' and is faithfully represented here. All of it except the small '*share*' and coulter is of wood; it is drawn by four ponies, the leading ones led by a picturesque old man or boy, and the plough itself handled by the superior officer, precisely as shown in the drawing – his right hand being employed in guiding the plough by its single stilt, and his left bearing hard on what may be called the shoulder, to keep it well in. Altogether the 'turnout' is by no means common-place, and decidedly picturesque.

The Harrows are squares or triangles of wood, stuck on the lower side with teeth of wood or iron, and when intended for polishing, assisted by a furze bush stuck through it. This ingenious implement is always drawn by women, who do it in that graceful way, which characterises all their movements, and gives a tone of elegance and refinement to the ruralities of Lewis, which I may conscientiously say I have never seen elsewhere.

'*Cas Chroum*' as they call the spade, is represented lying down in the foreground of the drawing. It is made of two slightly curved pieces of wood spliced together; the extremity of the shorter length being shod with a sort of chisel of iron about 5 inches wide; it is of considerable length and is used over the shoulder, as you see in the right of the picture, there being a wooden peg projecting from one side of the thickest part of the instrument, for the application of the right foot, as in our own spade. It has its advantages of construction over ours, for the land it is used in, inasmuch as its length and mode of application render it an effective and convenient lever in the removal of the large stones which constantly occur.

In like manner, their plough is adapted to the peculiarities of the country, being better calculated for breaking up a friable and stony soil, like most of that near the Butt, than to penetrate and lay over a compact close mass like much that occurs in the cultivation of our own dear land. Its lightness, moreover, renders it easily managed where stones are too bulky for removal, and which must therefore be avoided by it, and the economy of its material puts it more conveniently within the reach of the men of Lewis.

In passing the cottage doors today, I remarked, what I had never seen in use before: earthen[108] and vessels of baked clay, formed entirely with the hand, unaided by any machine to impart a circular motion to the mass of clay under process of manufacture, and thereby ensure a regularity of form; but absolutely pressed and pinched by the hand into the required form. Of course, they were very rough and, being unglazed, incapable of containing liquids. But they were of considerable size, maybe a couple of gallons, and appeared to be in general use for such dry goods as potatoes and oat meal.

The use of such utensils as these may probably convey to my reader a more correct notion of the primitive and unimproved state of being of our countrymen in Lewis, than anything else which I could state.

On we sped till we reached the precipitous rocks which breast the northern seas, and which under the name of the Butt of Lewis, constitute the most north-western part of Great Britain. They are not very great in altitude, but almost make up for any deficiency in that respect by their ruggedness and glorious wildness of character. I have seen the solitary rocks of the furthest Shetland Islands – they are lonely, dreary and poetic; of the Storr and other of the fine rock scenery of the isle of Skye – they are Ossianic[109] and very solemn; of the remote and inaccessible isles of St Kilda – they are incomparably sublime in their stillness and profound solitude, and stupendous beyond any idea I can convey; but the Butt of Lewis is characterised by greater wildness and desolation than anything I have met with. The forms of the individual rocks are often strange and distorted, and as we saw it with a heavy sea plunging and dashing among them, the impression they made on me was one of wild bleak desolation and sterility.

About the N.W. end a small promontory is caverned through, and at the time we saw it, the sea was dashing up to and through it with irresistible grandeur. Nevertheless, with all its peculiar character, and though at the time I made several sketches of the rocks about it, there is nothing, no particular scene – which I think would interest my reader, if introduced here. T'was the whole scene, the succession of one mass of barren rock

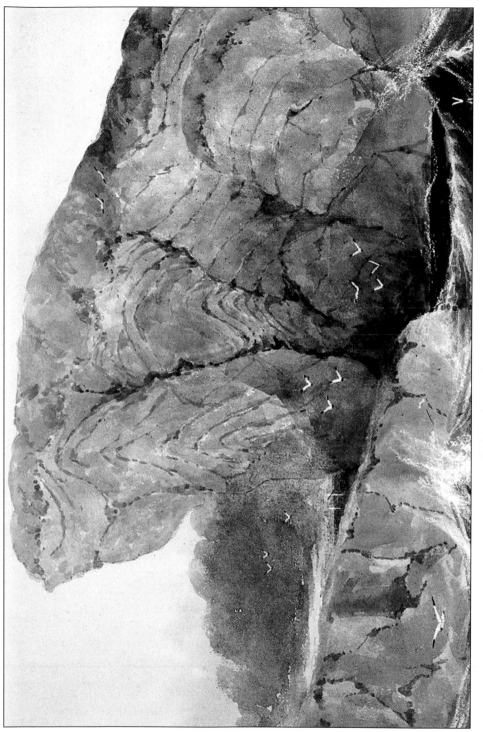

Rocks at the Butt, by G. R. Richardson

and foaming sea – entirely destitute of human form or ought to give individuality to the sketch – to another equally or more striking; and the grey cold day, and heavy, rolling, thundering sea, which constituted the scene, and which was one of the many that I have seen and found alike impossible to describe with either pen or pencil.

Millar was walking along the top of the cliff one summer day, when with a keenness of nose peculiar to excisemen, he caught a sort of smell of peat smoke where no habitation within a distance of some miles could account for its existence. A small run of water trickled past his feet over the ledge of the cliff, so with a rapidity of reasoning highly creditable to his ingenuity, he immediately concluded there must be a still near, but where? The rock appeared quite precipitous, and no indication could be perceived from where he stood, of any cranny or chink which could conceal anything of the kind.

After much examination he fancied, though he could not discern from the top, that a sloping ledge of rock which descended the cliff for a short distance, might lead to some continued mode of access to a small slip of gravelly beach below. So he pursued his examination and, having at considerable risk descended the ledge, found that under a projection of cliff, a narrow and precarious footing presented itself, which led to the beach below.

When he had safely attained this, he soon ascertained that his suspicion had been well founded for, at the high end of the beach, the cliffs overhang at the top receded below into a low dark cavern, in the mouth of which a small still was working away briskly, but unattended by any person.

He smashed the iron pot which formed the lower part of the still and then, fancying the worthy proprietor might have modestly retired to the interior of the cave, he groped away, till he found that a low passage ran off the main body of the cave; and then finding that it penetrated to some distance, and possibly that his intrusion might be inconvenient, he contented himself with securing the head and worm, and made the best of his way to the top of the cliff again with them tied on his shoulders.

Since then our friend had never been at the place, but he often wished for a companion to explore it with . . . finding us bent on seeing anything out of the common way, he eagerly detailed his reasons for wishing to explore the cave, and pressed us to accompany him. Of course nothing could be finer fun for us, and last night when we made up our minds to remain with him over today, our chief motive was the cave speculation.

. . . It was some time though before we could make out where it was situated . . . Here we found the difficulties of the descent had been by no means exaggerated . . . At length, by dint of discarding our shoes St Kilda-fashion, that our feet might embrace more closely the inequalities and projections of the rock, and leaving our guns on the top, we all landed safe, lighted our candles, and entered the arched mouth of the cave.

No appearance of human agency was, however, visible in the rugged scene before us, if we except the rusty fragments of the iron pan, left there by Millar on his visit; and we entered uninterruptedly, and uneventfully on the more intimate investigations of *'Millars mysteries of the cave'*. The main body of the cave is about 45 paces in diameter, low and extremely rugged, both at top and bottom, and full of tracks as it can be. We discovered the entrance of a passage or cavity in the rock on the north-west side of the cave, which penetrated in the same direction. The floor was deep mud, the roof loose rock, and the height about three feet. The ingress was therefore neither cleanly nor convenient; and each individual as he crept along, nearly blocked (or wadded) up the passage, and the tracks of otters (which all the world knows to be a pugnacious, hard biting animal) were most abundant on the mud. The progress of the leader of the party, (one G.C.A.) became gradually more considerate . . . a march of 50 paces brought him scatheless to the end of the passage . . . Another similar passage presented itself on the south side of the cave, penetrating in a south-westerly direction, which we explored and found to be about 120 paces in length and equally uninteresting and Ottery. Towards the end of one of these passages we found some small stalactites, very red from the impregnation of iron, but there were neither remains of antiquity, not natural productions of an uncommon nature to be found.

T'was a bleak boisterous day, and the north-west blew, as if Eolus[110] had had a half holiday. At 4 we returned to dinner after an amusing day, and after a few more anecdotes from our host, who seems more intelligent and observing than any man we have met with, we laid down for the night.

☛ **Wednesday, 22th May** ❀ ❀ ❀
 The Giant's Stone and Family Prayers

A SQUALLY, unpleasant morning, but after breakfast we started from Barvas, nominally 15 miles off, but experimentally more. Millar mounted Cookson on his pony and marched along side of us for 5 or 6 miles, and then we parted.

All this side of Lewis is low, and between Ness – the village we had been staying at, which is about three miles from the Butt – the third mile from Barvas, there is little to interest or amuse the tourist. The country is undulating and, generally near the sea, in a state of partial cultivation, with cottages sparingly interspersed, while inland, it stretches away in bare moor and bog as far as the eye can reach. This state of things is common to all the west of Lewis, from the Butt to Callernish, when it appears to assume a loftier and more mountainous character.

About three miles north of Barvas, on the slope of a hill facing the sea, the eye of the traveller is struck by a gigantic looking object, three or four hundred yards to the east of the exceedingly good road along which he is proceeding, which will prove, if he approaches it, to be a single upright stone of great size. It owes its position, according to the Minister of Barvas, to the Druids, but is called by the Islanders '*Clach an Truiseil*'''' or the 'Giant's Stone', from a legend they have of some gigantic warrior who lies beneath it. The mass of stone must be considerable, as it stands about 16 feet out of the ground, and must be pretty well planted below the surface to support itself. It is flat on the north and south sides, and about 16 feet in circumference.

About 100 paces south-east of it, I think there is a circle of stones, but it is not well defined. If there be one, however, it is 40 paces in diameter, and the stones composing it are low. Of course it is fair to presume it is Druidical.

It had rained heavily and unceasingly all day, and our walk had been rather an uncomfortable one, so we got within a few hundred yards of Barvas, where a road turns off to Stornoway, Cookson left us. Proctor and I went on, and housed ourselves at the Manse at one thirty.

The Minister, Mr. McRae,''' proved a sensible good kind of man, and put into my hands the manuscript of the Stornoway Cooper, of the legends of the Lewis, which proved to be very deficient in dates and data, as well as importance though many of the tales were as wild and extraordinary as can be conceived. Miss McRae played rather well on the piano, and gave me a couple of Gaelic airs which she thought were not in print. The family were out of spirits and depressed at the departure of their friend, the Minister of Ness, who had been driven away by the canting interference of one of the Methodists, though celebrated throughout Lewis for blamelessness of life, and the simple sincerity of his religious professions and practice.

In the evening at some signal that I did not perceive, all the party but the Minister left the room, and he told me they were going to family prayers if I liked to join them. Of course, I did so, and was particularly struck with the simple way in which it was conducted. He prayed in Gaelic, and then a chapter in the Bible was read by all present, each taking a verse in turn, the minister quietly correcting any mistakes, in the reading

Giant's Stone – Clach an Truiseil, by T. M. Richardson

either his own children, or of the servants (for all read in turn), and making a few remarks as the subject seemed to require it.

His eldest daughter, a fine young woman of 19 or 20, who had spent the last five years of her life at school in Edinburgh, required frequent correction in her pronunciation, and at last fairly stuck at the Gaelic for 'blessed', which occurred in the chapter they were reading. It is spelt *'Bianicht'*, but pronounced as if the first letter were half a 'B' and half a 'P', and the last syllable aspirated in a rather difficult way.

After prayers we had some toddy and I seized an early opportunity of retiring.

Thursday, 23th May ✿ ✿ ✿
Ruins at Loch Bragar and Doun Carloway, 'Still' in Action

BREAKFAST AT 9, and then set out for Callernish, four or five and twenty miles off. After walking some miles, we halted to examine a ruin in a small lake to the left of the road called Loch Bragar.[113] It is or has been, precisely similar to the one we saw afterwards at Carloway, but now presents only a circular ruin of ten or twelve feet high, decreasing in diameter with its height, and built with loose flat stones. It differed from the Doun (or castle) Carloway, in having on its east side, a square opening about 3 feet high on a level with the ground, which runs in a straight line towards the centre of the building 7 or 8 feet, and then opens to the left, into an oven-like cavity, large enough to sleep in. What may have been the use of this, I do not pretend to guess, but merely state that which is, for the amusement of such of my friends as may feel interested in the subject.

The next object which we fell in with on this road, is the more perfect ruin of the same description, near the village of Carloway and about a quarter of a mile to the west of the road. Carloway is 6 miles north of Callernish, and under the guidance of our old conductor, Donald, (who wisely kept out of our way while our wrath was up, after his bungling guidance to Millar's, and who still continued in our service), we had struck off the road, to make a short cut to Carloway, and were plodding over the moor, when I spied some picturesque looking smoke rising from a rough patch of rocks we were approaching. Presently an unadorned looking youth without shoes or stockings – clad in fact, in only a flannel shirt, and that portion of a gentleman's garb, which ladies and lexicographers are at a loss to name – bolted from the rocks and sped across the moor like a Buck. *'Oh ho!'* said I, *'There's a still! We'll have a look at it, Proctor!'* And I turned and was walking with Proctor towards it, when the fugitive, turning round, fancied our appearance rather more prepossessing than on his first inspection, I suppose, and first pausing, finally turned to meet Donald, who appeared to be an old friend, and was soon chattering away with him, and as exclusively engaging his attention as the old woman we met with the day we walked to Ness in the rain.

After one or two appeals to Donald, he at length condescended to inform me that the smoke we saw arose from the operation of drying the malt preparatory to distilling; but that our new companion would feel much pleasure in conducting us to the scene of distillation which was at a short distance.

In the meantime, as the Doun lay pretty much in the way to it, we proceeded to inspect it first. It is not (if I remember right) visible from any great distance, but constitutes a very striking object when it becomes so, standing as it does, in a country where no edifice, more lofty than the little cottages of the islanders, occurs to compare with it. It is situated on the gentle slope of a hill with a southern aspect, or rather upon an eminence. The country near to it is more cultivated than much we have seen, and groups of cottages appear here and there on the sides of adjacent hills. A small stream ripples past the foot of the eminence on which it stands, and more in the distance, the blue sea finishes the scene.

This ruin is considered one of the finest and most perfect in existence of its kind, and still retains a height of five or six and thirty feet. The inside is partially filled with loose stones from the building itself, but is still perfect enough, to perceive that passages have encircled it within the thickness of its walls at different heights, which seem to be communicated with the interior by windows or apertures which remain to this day.

The old inhabitants told me through Donald, that they remembered it in a completely perfect state, and that it was then only ten or twelve feet higher than at present, and narrowing more suddenly near the top, till it became nearly round, was covered by a large flat stone. Till lately a doorway to the west was distinctly perceptible, but a great mass of ruin now conceals it: no chamber, like that in the ruin of Loch Bragar, ever existed in it[114]

After sketching the Doun, we placed ourselves in the guidance of our contraband friend, and followed over about a mile of very rough broken ground, with small lakes and pieces of water lying here and there among the hills; for the character of the country had changed from the comparatively moor-land level of the north part of the island, and consisted here of abrupt rocks and hillocks, among which we now made our way. We kept gradually ascending, and at length found ourselves on a steep hill, overhanging a small and very secluded lake. But no appearance

Danish Fort of Doun Carloway, by T. M. Richardson

of a still was visible. At length we wound down a sort of narrow ravine or water course, and turning a little promontory where it discharged itself into the lake, came suddenly on the object of our curiosity, snugly established in a small but deep bay, and entirely shut in by the very steep hill behind it. Several animals of a species similar to the one who conducted us thither, lounged about the scene of action, and a single figure on the top of a lofty hill on the opposite side of the lake shewed that our new friends – for they had been informed of our intended visit, by some of a number of idlers who superintended our examination of the Danish fort, and greeted us most cordially with the good-natured, *'Kimira hajen dhu?'* (how do you do?) – were by no means unwatchful.

Their mechanical arrangements were exceedingly unpretending, but pretty much the same as those in use for distilling throughout the island. A large black iron pot constituted the body of the still, over the top of which a wooden lid was luted[115] or cemented with a hole in the centre. Into this the head was fastened – made of copper and the only material (with the worm) that had been provided for the purpose of distillation alone, all others being convenient articles of household economy. They told us they never kept working in the same place for more than three or four days at a time, for fear of some of the many country people who must know of their proceedings, and who may have no interest in them, giving information. Most of the inhabitants of the village are generally share holders in a smuggling speculation, and the men occasionally relieve each other in the working of the still. The produce was seldom sold, being manufactured for the use of the shareholders, more than for any purpose of emolument, and I was informed, that the practice of smuggling is much on the decline altogether in Lewis.

The poor fellows seemed particularly amused at my sketching their manufactory, and bade me, *'Slan leave'* (goodbye) without the least distrust, laughing and saying I might tell McIver, or the Factor, or any of the respectable people of the island, but not Millar.

From thence we trudged briskly on, and got to the public house at Callernish at 8 o'clock, exceedingly pleased with what we had seen during the day.

☛ **Friday, 24th May** ✿ ✿ ✿
 Druidical Stones at Callernish, return to Stornoway[116]

HAVING breakfasted, we sallied out at 8 o'clock to examine a Druidical circle of upright stones on a hill near the house. It is by far the

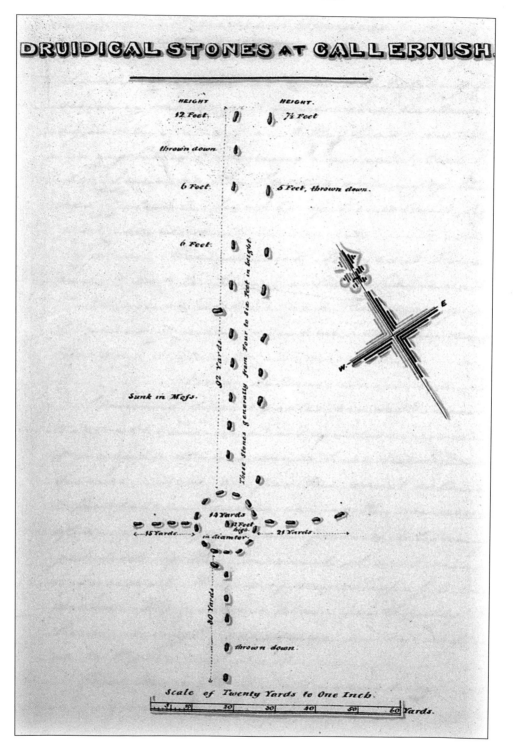

DRUIDICAL STONES AT CALLERNISH.

most extensive and perfect in Lewis, so for the amusement of any antiquarian friends who might get hold of the journal, I took some pains with
the aid of my compass, to lay down the ground plan faithfully.

I was wrong in saying the 'circle' is the most extensive in Lewis, as it is
only 14 paces in diameter, but a large cross is formed by two rows of
upright stones, whose centre is coincident with that of the circle, and the
whole group forms by far the most numerous and complete relic in Lewis;
and situated as it is, on an eminence, is highly curious and picturesque
object. Many of the stones are 12 feet out of the ground, and the landlord
of the public house informed us, that some one had tried how deep they
descended into it, by pushing a sharp pricker of iron diagonally against
their foundation, some years ago, and found them to be planted nearly an
equal depth. The loftiest are generally at the end of the longest limb of
the cross, though one or two are seen in the circle – the centre, if I
remember right, especially. The longest limb of the cross is double, two
lines of stones running parallel to each other 'E.N.E.' direction. However
the subjoined plan will convey so clear an idea of the whole, and it is so
carefully laid down, that I think further verbal explanation will be unnecessary. I don't know that I should have been at the trouble of making a
ground plan of it, but the landlord of the public house told us of two
eminent antiquaries had had a learned dispute about the number of stones
comprising it, so I thought if the subject were sufficiently important for
them to dispute, it might be amusing to some of my readers to have a
correct plan thereof, as well as the two others we saw and mapped down.

I felt anxious to know what the people about said of these remains, not
doubting that some curious legends would be attached to them, but was
much disappointed to find, that before our host (who is a Scotchman)
came here two years since, all tradition and local legends had been con-
demned by the Methodists, as well as the curious old music and heroic
songs of the Hebrides, and that even the mention of such things is now
going into disuse, and their ever having existed will, in a few years, be
entirely forgotten.

About a mile along the road to Stornoway from Callernish another
group of stones may be seen on an eminence to the right of the road. It is
a circle of 9 stones, 18 paces in diameter, and of 3 or 4 feet high each, and
4 more irregularly placed within it; and about a furlong west of it there are
5 more upright stones on a similar eminence ranged in a semicircle, and
no vestige of others which might have been supposed to have completed
the group or circle of 24 paces diameter.

I have been at more pains than I should in this somewhat dry matter,
and subjoin a perhaps unnecessarily exact sketch of the different relics we

DRUIDICAL CIRCLE
NEAR CALLERNISH.

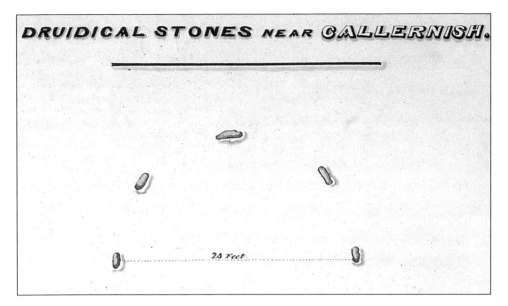

DRUIDICAL STONES NEAR CALLERNISH.

24 Feet

saw, because I think it likely they may be in a more perfect, unmutilated state, than any thing of the kind in a comparatively more civilised country. For as no change (or at any rate a trifling one) has taken place in this remote people for a great length of time, so the vestiges of antiquity have escaped from dilapidation and the baleful effects of change and innovation.

In conclusion – there is another assemblage of stones 2 or 3 miles S.S.E. from Callernish, situated like the others, on a small hill. In the little village of Carloway I likewise observed a single upright stone: and that, I think, concludes the list of Druidical and Danish remains in Lewis.

Cookson had promised, if the *Peggy* should not be ready to sail this week, to be at Callernish by 1 o'clock today and join me in a further ramble in the southern part of Lewis. But he did not '*shew in*' at the appointed time, so having spent the morning in drawing Druidicals and hunting for *carabus clathratus* (a very beautiful and rare beetle which I had found thirty miles south of this two years since in considerable abundance, and which we now pill-boxed half a dozen), Proctor and I started at one for Stornoway. The road, like the one we had hitherto seen, was excellent, but my companions being somewhat over-laden, did not make much way, and I had to walk – about sixteen miles, to myself, and met Cookson marching up the town of Stornoway at six o'clock. He greeted me with the comfortable information, that good sloop *Peggy* can sail tomorrow afternoon, and I dedicated the evening to thin shoes and a lounge.

☞ **Saturday, 25th May** ❁ ❁ ❁
Leaving Lewis on the Sloop Peggy.

HAVING BEEN absent almost entirely from Stornoway during our sojourn in Lewis, this morning was a good deal taken up in preparing for our voyage, though in the course of it I found time to accompany the Factor to Mr. Stewart McKenzie's house, and examine the huge map of Lewis which I have before alluded to, and by which I was now enabled to correct the small rather incorrect published map I had with me.

The house seemed a very comfortable one and possessed a library and other desirable resources, but these are destined, for the next five years, to form the amusement, not of the worthy proprietor, but of an English gentleman, a Sir Frederick Johnson, who has taken the shooting in Lewis for £450 a year: a bargain which I fancy he will soon regret, as from what I saw of the quantity of Grouse on the island, in my walk over the north part the other day, I should consider their numbers scanty. Of the Red Deer we could gain no certain information. It is probable that there may be between 500 and 1,000 in Lewis and Harris. At least a most kind friend who farms that part of Harris called *The Forest*, which is the most abundant in game, told me that was his opinion when we stayed with him during a former Hebridean excursion; but were game of every kind in the greatest profusion, I cannot imagine that it would be a desirable take for any sporting man, as – except once a fortnight – it would be possible to send away what might be killed.

About 40 years since two or three hares were introduced, and they have increased wonderfully on the island, and wild fowl must, I should think, be very abundant in winter.

On the whole there is little in Lewis to induce a tourist to visit it. It is, I think, almost the only spot my ramblings have led me to, that I should not feel desirous of re-visiting to see something more of. I have seen nearly enough of Lewis and formed the general conclusion, that its north part is chiefly level, uninteresting moor, interspersed with numerous, boggy un-picturesque lakes, but very destitute of incident in its interior. Its shores, unlike many of the islands, are more bold and precipitous on the east than on the west side, and rise, I should think, in some places to a 100ft or more, and contain a few fine caves.

The Remains of Antiquity, consisting of the Druidical circles, the *Danish Fort*, as it is called – but I pretend not to judge the propriety of the name – and the ruins of the Roman Catholic Chapels, which tell of a time when that religion was almost exclusively in use in Lewis, exist, I believe, almost entirely along its west side, and would afford to an, antiquarian a most curious subject for enquiry and research.

Off the coasts of this island, and therefore so far pertaining to it, that in the sort of sketch I have given of it, it would look almost like an omission to pass them by, are several small groups of islands. Of these the Shiant Islands to the S.E. have already been mentioned when we landed on them the day we reached Stornoway.

Another group of seven islands, called the Flannan Isles, or Seven Hunters, lies about 20 miles west of the middle of that side of the island. I had been very desirous of paying them a visit, as they abound in Sea fowl and except by McCulloch, have not been seen, I should think, by any Englishman; and because my acquaintance with the Hebrides would then have been rather complete; but we could not find time to do it, and Cookson does not like Boat work. They are farmed for sheep pasturage, and only visited twice a year by the tenant.

In addition to the Shiant and Flannan Isles, are two very remote ones about 30 miles N.E. of the Butt, Barra and North Rona[117]: that is the former N.E.x E, 30 miles off; and Rona (or *Sulisker*, as it is sometimes called), 12 miles E from it. They form part of a Farm on the north end of Lewis, and are visited once or twice a year by the tenant, who employs a family upon the former island to tend his sheep. Their case must be lonely enough in good sooth.

Of course sea fowl breed in great numbers, and on Sulisker (which has its name meaning *Seal Skerry*, from the circumstance that seals are in greater abundance than in almost any part of Great Britain).

A few years since, some men went from the Butt to kill these animals on Sulisker, but were nearly drowned at Rona by the swamping of their boat, and got on shore with much difficulty. Nothing was heard of them in Lewis for some weeks, till at length a small trader, belonging to Stornoway, met a Greenland Whaler at sea, and told the crew that, calling at Barra for water, they found the seal hunters there and, at their urgent request, gave them a sail as far as Sulisker, and then left them. As it was some time since this had happened, and it was well known that no house or any shelter existed on Sulisker, great anxiety was evinced about them, and Captain Oliver[118] who commands a Revenue vessel at Stornoway, offered to go and fetch them back if any of their relatives would accompany him, to show the poor fellows that it was all right. But not a creature would go, and I think the Captain went at last and brought them off.

So much for Lewis. We dined at 4, went on board at 5, and got our anchor in, and our sails up, as soon as possible, though to little purpose as it blew a headwind for clearing the Butt, and we made but little way.

GCA and his party went on to explore in the Faeroe Islands, the Westmann Islands and Iceland. They left Reykjavik on July 4th returning on the Peggy, but not to Stornoway. After reaching Cape Wrath on July 21st, a following wind helped them through the Pentland Firth and on the 24th they turned south down the Aberdeenshire coast and on to Northumberland. They passed Holy Island, Bamburgh and Dunstanburgh, arriving back in Newcastle at breakfast time on Friday 26th July, 'the very day 11 weeks from which we started!' – to complete the 900 miles, they estimated, from Reykjavik.

Editor

Notes on the 1831 Expedition

1   *Ardincaple* A steam packet ship carrying mail, freight and passengers on a
    regular route between Newcastle and Newhaven, Edinburgh. It nearly sank off the
    Berwick coast during a storm in 1833.

2   **Isaac** – Brother of George (GCA) and Richard Atkinson, who accompanied them
    on the expedition as far as Portree, then returned home. He was soon to leave for
    Jamaica.

3   **St Abb's Head**   One of the most striking headlands of the Berwickshire coast.
    The cliffs rise 300ft from the sea with a squat lighthouse at 224ft. Named after
    Aebbe, the daughter of Aethelfrith of Northumbria, who, in the 7th C founded a
    nunnery there visited by St Cuthbert in 661AD.

4   **Bass Rock**   An impressive volcanic plug rearing up 350ft (107m) in the Firth of
    Forth and now home for 30,000 pairs of gannets or Solan Geese which have
    increased considerably in recent years. Possibly named after a man called Bass,
    the rock now has given its name to the gannet, *Sula bassana*. There has been a
    fortress on the rock above the landing place for centuries; in 1651 it surrendered to
    Cromwell's forces and later a prison for Covenanters who resisted Charles II's
    attempted destruction of the Church in Scotland. The remains of a little chapel,
    built around 1491 and dedicated to St Baldred stands on one of the few level bits of
    ground at about 200ft above the sea. In 1902 a lighthouse was erected and manned
    but is now fully automatic. Tree Mallow grows in abundance.

    It was too rough to land on the Bass Rock when Pennant took a boat round it
    in 1771. In his Journal he noted an advert concerning the harvest from the rock,
    '*SOLAN GOOSE – There is to be sold, by John Watson, Junr. at his Stand at the
    Poultry, Edinburgh, all lawfull days in the week, wind and weather serving, good
    and fresh Solan Geese. Any who have occasion for the same may have them at
    reasonable rates. Aug 5, 1768. Edinburgh Advertiser.*' (Pennant, T, 1771)

5   **Wolf's Craig (and Fast Castle)**   Three and a half miles west of St Abb's Head,
    stands the remains of a notorious castle, chosen by Sir Walter Scott as the model
    for *Wolf's Craig* in his novel, *The Bride of Lammermoor*. The castle is perched on
    a rock stack, only reached by a gangway after a steep descent from one of the
    highest cliffs on the east coast. At one time it was used by wreckers and robbers,
    and the tradition of a fabulous and as yet, undiscovered, treasure hidden within is
    legedary. At the end of the 14th C it was the stronghold of the Home family.
    Margaret Tudor, the sister of Henry VIII, stayed here en route to marry
    James IV in 1503.

6   **Dunstanborough**   The most extensive of the Northumbrian castles, it sits
    perched on a 100ft ridge of basalt overlooking the sea. Most of what is seen was
    built between 1313–1322 by Thomas of Lancaster, a grandson of Henry VIII. By 1550
    the castle was in ruins but later proved an inspiration for Turner who painted the
    scene three times.

147

7   **Ewbank, John Wilson, RSA 1799-1847** Darlington-born landscape, coastal and marine oil painter who became apprentice to a house painter, Thomas Coulson of Newcastle, and later moved with him to Edinburgh. Coulson spotted his talent and allowed him to study under one of the leading Scottish landscape painters of the day – Alexander Nasmyth. Ewbank first exhibited in Edinburgh in 1821 and later at the Royal Academy in London, as well as Newcastle and Carlisle. In 1826 he became a founder member of the Scottish Academy, painting pictures for their first exhibition in 1827. His technique and subject matter were strongly influenced by the Dutch 17th C painters, particularly Van de Velde. Sadly in 1834 he left the city in disgrace and returned to Newcastle, where he was obliged to forfeit his position as a Royal Scottish Academician. In 1823 a series of his views of Edinburgh were engraved by Lizars. His work is represented in the British Museum, the National Gallery of Scotland and widely among collections in the NE of England.

8   **Newhaven** The port for Edinburgh with a good harbour and fish-market.

9   **Ambrose's Hotel.** A popular Edinburgh coaching inn.

10   **MacGillivray, William 1796-1852.** An outstanding ornithologist, artist and author, who later became Professor of Natural History, Aberdeen (see Introduction). William's uncle, Roderick MacGillivray, farmed at Northton, Harris and was visited by GCA and his party.

11   **Hutton, William 1797-1860** A friend of GCA through the Natural History Society in Newcastle. Hutton was largely responsible for the formation of the Society and shared duties as the Hon. Secretary with Nathaniel J Winch. He had shown an interest in natural history from early days, especially geology, and developed a comprehensive collection of minerals and Carboniferous plants which was subsequently presented to the Hancock Museum, Newcastle Upon Tyne. Working with Lindley he produced Lindley and Hutton's *'Fossil Flora'* – a foundation work on fossil botany. He was elected a Fellow of the Geological Society of London and of the Royal Society .

12   **McQuarry, Col** of Glenforsa, Mull The MacQuarry's clan territory was the island of Ulva, west of Mull, which they owned for 800 years until forced to sell at the end of the 18th century and move onto Mull. One of Ulva's most famous sons, Major General Lachlan Macquarie (1761-1824), became Governor of New South Wales in 1809, and retired back to the Old Gruline House in Mull eleven years later. It was to his brother, Colonel Charles Macquarie, that GCA had an introduction. When Lachlan went to Australia he asked Charles, who had the adjoining estate of Glen Forsa, to buy all the estates between Gruline and Ulva which nearly bankrupted Lachlan.

13   **French King and Holyrood** From the 12th C criminals could claim sanctuary in Holyrood Abbey, and though murderers and thieves were subsequently excluded, debtors were protected from the arm of the law. The sanctuary was surrounded by a high wall four and a half miles in circumference and the debtors were safe to leave the compound only on Sundays. "The 'French King' referred to in the diary would have been the deposed Charles X. He was the younger brother of the executed Louis XVI and as the Comte d'Artois had escaped revolutionary France. He had fled to England, but his debts and inappropriate behaviour had made it advisable to pack him off to the sanctuary in 1796. Although he returned to ascend the French throne in 1824, by 1831 he had been deposed and was once again in exile

at Holyrood with his immediate family." (Dr R.Fawcett, *pers. comm.*). He received a monthly allowance of £500 from the British Government and remained in the sanctuary for six years on his first visit before his debts could be settled and he was free to return to France. He stayed for two years on his second visit which began in 1830.

14 **Buck's Head, Argyle Street, Glasgow**   A Coach Staging Point

15 **McLean's Hotel, Broomielaw, Glasgow**   A convenient hotel for the steamer. The first Broomielaw Bridge over the Clyde was opened in 1772, in 1833 another designed by Thomas Telford and the widest in the UK was opened in 1836.

16 **McKinnon**   The Columbian Consul, whose mother lived at Corry on Skye with whom they later stayed on their return journey. Visited McKinnon with an introduction from Gilfillan, Isaac's master in Liverpool.

17 **Paddle Steamer – The '*Highlander*'**   A wooden paddle steamer built at Glasgow in 1821, and just nine years after the first sea-going steamship in the world, *Comet I*. With a length of only 78ft, sleeping accommodation was not possible and passengers had to leave the ship at night.   First class passengers often used '*Lumsden's Steam Boat Companion*' to help them in finding suitable accommodation. The *Highlander* made the first recorded steam ship sailing to Skye in 1822. She regularly plied the Glasgow to Oban route (through the Crinan Canal), and on to Tobermory, visiting Staffa. These paddle steamers created a new clanking sound among the Highlands and Islands '*throbbing, thumping and belching smoke*'.   (Campbell, 1977)

18 **The Crinan Canal**   Running the nine miles between Ardrishaig and Crinan is the smallest of the three Scottish sea-to-sea canals, it was built with the help of three great engineers, James Watt, John Rennie and Thomas Telford. It was suggested by John Knox to cut through the Kintyre peninsula to save 85 miles. The prospectus appeared in 1793 stating that the Canal would bring coal from Glasgow, provide a market for fish and prevent emigration to America. Slates from the Easdale quarries were later transported south through the canal. Construction began in 1794 but was hit by many problems and a shortage of money. Eventually the canal was opened in an unfinished state in July 1801 when water was allowed in slowly. In 1816 Telford was made responsible for repairs and the canal had to be closed from March to November 1817. Having a depth of only 10ft it was too shallow, there was also a very short level section of 1,224 yards with four locks on one side and 5 on the other. Problems continued, with paddle steamers perpetually churning up the water, causing damage to the banks of the canal.

19 **Hewitson - William Hewitson 1806-78**   Born in Newcastle, Hewitson was friendly with Albany and John Hancock, Joshua Alder, William Hutton, all founder members of the Natural History Society of Northumberland, Durham and Newcastle upon Tyne, as well as being a neighbour of Richard Wingate the taxidermist. He became Curator of the Insect section of the Hancock Museum, and in 1833 he went on a three month expedition to Norway to collect specimens and to visit sites of breeding birds which winter in Britain, returning with eggs of Capercaille, Fieldfare, Turnstone and of a duck then unknown in England – the Goldeneye. He produced valuable works on Natural History; between 1831-38 he published, '*British Oology*' in two volumes, and 1852-77, '*Illustrations of Exotic Butterflies*'.   He wrote 29 papers describing many new species to science.

20 **Slate Quarries**   These lie to the south of Oban – Easdale and Seil. McCulloch writing in 1819 commented, '*The quarries of Seil, like those of Eysdill, have long been known, and their produce is the subject of a very extended commerce.*'

21 **Dunally = Dunollie Castle** The castle is perched on a rocky promontory on the northern outskirts of Oban guarding the Bay. It was a fortified dun in the C7-8, the stronghold of the Lorn Kings, covering northern Dalriada. The 13th C Towerhouse and bailey, survives. It was the seat of the MacDougall's, Lords of Lorne, until its abandonment in 1746 when the family built Dunollie House.

22 **Dunstaffnage Castle** Situated some three miles north of Oban. Dunstaffnage was the capital of Dalriada, the kingdom established in Argyleshire, when the Scots first crossed over from Ireland. The Stone of Destiny was said to have rested here on the way from Ireland to Scone around 843. The visible remains are of the mediaeval castle, its mid 13th C curtain walled castle with late 15th C gatehouse in the form of a square with towers at each corner. This was another stronghold of the MacDougall's, commanding the narrows at the entrance of Loch Etive as well as the junction of the Sound of Mull and the Firth of Lorne with good anchorage nearby. When the MacDougalls were defeated by Robert Bruce in 1309 it was granted to the Campbells of Argyle. Flora MacDonald, who aided the Young Pretender's escape from Benbecula, was held here as she was being taken from Skye to London.

23 **'Maid of Isla I'** A paddle steamer built in 1815 as the '*Waterloo*' which worked alongside the '*Maid of Isla II*', built in 1826, providing a passage from Glasgow to Port Askaig on Isla and on to Portree on Skye. Passengers were conveyed overland from East to West Loch Tarbert. '*Maid of Isla II*' was much improved – 100ft long, fitted with powerful engines and bunk accommodation.

24 **Sir John McCray (McCrae, McRae) = Sir John Macrae K.C.H.** '*He was the son of Archibald Macrae of Ardintoul and Janet, one of the daughters of Macleod of Raasay who so impressed Boswell and Johnson. John joined the Cameron Highlanders and served with Sir John Moore in the Peninsula and later in the Netherlands, Burma and India where he was A.D.C. to the Marquis of Hastings, who was married to his cousin Countess of Loudoun, daughter of 'Miss Flora' of Raasay. He retired as a Colonel and lived at Ardintoul and Raasay. He died in 1847 and an iron cross in the wall of the ruined chapel at Clachan Duthaich marks his grave.*

Sir John was an accomplished player of the bagpipe, having probably received tuition from Raasay's famous piper, John Mackay, and is said to have played before Queen Victoria. He was also deeply interested in oral tradition. On one occasion he approached an outlying fort in India, at night, carrying dispatches, and could hear the sentry singing a Gaelic song which he had heard in his youth and was anxious to learn. He was able, fortunately, to do so in time as the singer was killed in action on the following day. He taught the song to Peggy Robertson in Hushinish, Harris in his old age and she, in turn, was the one from whom Alexander Carmichael noted the song shortly before her death.

John Macleod, the last Macleod chief resident in Raasay was Sir John's cousin, although considerably younger. Atkinson's Tour notes is the only evidence known that John Macleod served in the Army.

Sir John's brother, Alexander, also served in the Army and was later Tacksman of Hushinish in Harris. He died in 1874 and is also buried at Clachan Duthaich. The ancestor of the Macrae sisters, who contributed so much to Margaret Fay Shaw's, 'Songs and Traditions of South Uist', accompanied him to Harris and remained in his service.' (Dr A. Maclean. *pers. inf.*)

25 **Tobermory** The Capital of the Island of Mull. *Tobar Mhoire – The Well of Mary*. In the18th C it was established as a fishery centre and the island's main shipping hub, now replaced by Craignure. Tobermory's east facing harbour and excellent anchorage, considered the best in the Hebrides, attracts many yachts and gives access to Staffa, the Treshnish and the Outer Isles. The main street is colourful with terraces of houses above and steep wooded surrounds. In Oct 1588 the Spanish Galleon, the *'Florencia'*, sheltered in the Bay and sank with much treasure. 1791 a Customs House and Post Office was set up in the town. In 1831 MacLean of Coll lived in a *'clean house'* half a mile south of Tobermory – he owned the islands of Coll, Rum and one third of Mull. GCA met him on his return journey.

26 **Scuir of Egg (Sgurr of Eigg)** The Sgurr is a corrugated ridge of columnar pitchstone porphyry, which rests on the mass of the south facing hills of the Island of Eigg. It reaches 1,292ft at its highest point, almost completely encircled by cliffs 500ft high, culminating in an overhanging nose. The Sgurr dominates the scene for miles around.

27 **Loons** A family of large, long necked, fish-eating, diving birds, including Red-throated and Black-throated Divers nesting in Scotland, and Great Northern Divers coming as winter visitors. All have a mournful wailing, eerie cry.

28 **Rum Ponies** These were in abundance on the island of Rum when Pennant visited in 1773 and are still present today. They are smaller than the average Highland pony having primitive characteristics of the old Celtic stock with a black *'eel-stripe'* down the back and dark stripes encircling the legs above the fetlocks. They come in many colours with light straw coloured manes and tails. They are strong and used for carrying deer. Midges drive them down from the hills.

29 **Portree** The capital of Skye, with a natural harbour, deep water and well protected from most storms. A fair had been held at Portree since around 1580, primarily for the sale of horses and cattle. From the end of the 17th C the fairs held in the middle of June and the beginning of September had risen to national importance with the tryst ground established on land to the north-west of the township.

Edward Train sketched Mr MacLachlan's house, Portree – He came from Loch Gilphead and is thought to have established a bank in Portree. When Train painted his house by the river at Scorrybreac it had been newly built either in 1831 or the year before.

30 *Reeves, Mr Inspector of Post Offices in the islands with an extensive topographical knowledge of the Hebrides.. In 1836 the situation was summed up by Duncan Shaw of Benbecula,* 'There has for many years been a Packet between the island of Harris and Skye for the conveyance of letters and passengers. There has never, however, been a Post Office in Harris and the consequence is that many letters are mis-sent and frequently entirely lost. The Harris people are most anxious to have a Post Office established at Tarbert, either a sub-office of Portree in Skye or in direct communication with the General Post Office in Edinburgh. The population is not under 5,000 . . . The packet now plies between Tarbert and Loch Uig in Skye. Uig is about fifteen miles distant from Portree. There is, I think, already a Penny Post Office at Uig.' *(Mackay, 1978)*

31 **Rock Pigeons** These two Rock Doves were entered as donations from GCA in the *'Transactions of the Natural History Society of Northumberland, Durham and Newcastle upon Tyne'*.

32 **Mary Ann** GCA's sister who was very interested in his expeditions and who married John Dobson the distinguished Newcastle architect and artist.

33 **Prince Charles' Cave** The cave in which Prince Charles Edward reputedly hid before leaving Skye.

34 **Skye Terriers** *'It sounds as if the gentlemen who bred rare white Skye terriers there and on Rum were the originators of the West Highland Terriers, Westies, breed.'* (R.A.MacLeod. *pers. inf.*)

35 **Breach Sights** GCA's inventiveness is demonstrated in his adaptation to improve the breech sight on his rifle - a simple neat answer to the problem. As far as is known he did not patent his invention, – it is not known by his name. Experts consider that several people would be developing something similar at about the same time. Later he developed a method to measure the height of trees, as well as modifications in blast furnaces and on his wood-turning lathe.

36 **MacCulloch , Dr John (1773-1835)** A native of Jersey, he graduated in Medicine at Edinburgh and later became an Army Surgeon and a friend of Sir Walter Scott. He later turned to geology, and in 1811 was employed by the Government in geographical and other research in Scotland. In 1819 he published *'A Description of the Western Islands of Scotland'* in three volumes, comprising an account of their geological structure with remarks on their agriculture, scenery, and antiquities. In 1824 he published a fourth volume, *'The Highlands and Western Islands of Scotland'.*

37 **Exploring the Storr** Norse, *Staurr* – a stake or point. The Trotternish is a basalt ridge rising north of Portree, culminating in the Storr, 2,363ft. Below the ridge is the mass of jumbled rocks, screes and pinnacles amongst which GCA and Mr Train scrambled.. One of the rock pinnacles, the 'Old Man of Storr', reaches 160ft and stands impressively near the foot of a 600ft precipice – clearly visible from the sea.

38 **Sunderland Tommy** As GCA relates, Tommy on his first voyage from Sunderland as a cabin boy, aged 10, was left behind in Dublin. Attempting to return to Sunderland, a place unknown to all he contacted, he reached Portree where he met GCA. In spite of GCA's attempts to reunite him with his relatives he was still in Portree when GCA returned 1833; he had a job and seemed to be well looked after. The Sunderland Tommy Saga is retold in Tommy's words in GCA's 1833 Expedition. (*see* **Fn. 98.**)

39 **Col McNeil** *'The Colonel McNeil refers to Donald of the Newton family and thus uncle of Dr. MacGillivray. He was a Captain Lieutenant in the Cape Mounted Regiment. He emigrated to Nova Scotia and died in Mira, Cape Breton in 1874.'* (R.A.MacLeod and W.M.Lawson. *pers. inf.*)

40 **Murdoch McDonald** According to GCA Train's sketch of Murdoch was *'just looking as he is represented'.* He was a skilled helmsman and took GCA's party across the Minch, with Sunderland Tommy as a companion. Murdoch was a fisherman living at Portree; a kind-hearted man, who had taken pity on poor Sunderland Tommy, generously providing him with a home for three years since he arrived in Portree from Dublin.

41 **Rowdill (Rodel) Cathedral** –Built between 1520-40 by Alexander MacLeod of Dunvegan and Harris, known as Alasdair Crotach (or humpback), and whose tomb stands on the south side of the choir. It is an impressive sturdy building, cruciform in plan, with a high rectangular tower and contains many interesting

features and sculptures. It is dedicated to St Clement, the third bishop of Rome, who was martyred in AD 99. After the Abbey at Iona, it is the largest Church in the Hebrides. It went out of use after the Reformation although the cemetery continued in use.

42 **Kelp Industry and the Harris Estate** '*GCA and his party arrived in Harris at a time when the new laird was in severe financial difficulty; in fact the estate was almost bankrupt, owing to the collapse of the kelp industry. Three years later in 1834, Harris was sold to the Earl of Dunmore for £60,000 which hardly met his debts. Meanwhile he himself lived in England and left the detail of running the estate to his factor, Donald Stewart, who with his brother had come from Athol via Park in Lewis. He had arranged for his relatives to become tacksmen of the majority of the Harris Estate by this time.*' (R.A.MacLeod. *pers. inf.*)

43 **Philippic** An invective, tirade, used of an outpouring by Demosthenes against Philip of Macedonia.

44 **Mr Bethun** '*referred to was the son of the Rev Alexander Bethune, the minister of Harris from 1806-31. He had three sons Neil, William and Donald. Which one lived at Scarista is uncertain. The minister himself lived at Borve farm in lieu of part of his stipend.*' (R.A.MacLeod. *pers. inf.*).

45 **Parker = Henry Perlee Parker (1795-1873)** An excellent portrait painter living in Newcastle and making a name for himself painting fishermen, pitmen and smuggling subjects. His fame for the latter grew so much that his nick-name was *Smuggler Parker!* See p.128 below for an example of his work.

46 **Northton** The Farm of Roderick MacGillivray who brought up his nephew William and with whom GCA and his party stayed. Situated on the east facing slope of Chaipaval 1,207ft (Northton Hill), the NW ends in Toe Head and to the NE is a beautiful sandy lagoon. The farm has good agricultural land, home of the corn-crake, and overlooks the Sound of Harris to the S and W. The MacGillivrays later amalgamated their farm with the one at Southton, nearby.

47 **Roneval** (Rhoineabhal1) Rising steeply from the sea to 509 ft, it lies just inland from Rodel and to the south of Loch Langavat.

48 **MacGillivray** Dr. Donald MacGillivray was '*the half-brother of Professor William. Born on the day of his father's death, his mother was Effie Macneill of the family who farmed Newton in North Uist, Teaghlach a Chaolais. He was holidaying in Pabbay, also farmed by his uncles, when he appears in the account, in which he is unable to accompany them to St Kilda as he was interested in obtaining an appointment in Uist. He had qualified in the University of Edinburgh. It was in 1832 that he was appointed as doctor in South Uist and he was given tenancy of the farm of Ormaclete as part of his emoluments. The township of Ormaclete was cleared of its population in his favour and subsequently the hill ground also, where many of the displaced had found a foothold. Dr. MacGillivray subsequently served in Barra, although it is not certain whether the farm of Eoligarry was also cleared in his favour. He was however vocally anti-Catholic, which did not make him any more popular. On the day of his death, three men from Boisdale, it is said, were fishing near the western end of the Sound of Barra when a black coach emerged from a rain squall and drove towards them over the waves. It came so near that the men were able to identify the passengers, Dr. MacGillivray, another local oppressor of the poor and the Devil. One account even gave the subject of their con-versation in the coach, Napoleon Boneparte, another 'bad' man!*' (R.A.MacLeod and Dr A. Maclean. *pers. inf.*)

49 **Embarked for St Kilda**   In Mr. MacDonald of Coishlettar's 18ft yawl of about 3 tons burden; it was light enough to haul up the beach for safety at St Kilda. A yawl is a small two or four-oared fishing boat, two masted, fore-and-aft with a mizzen mast stepped far aft..

50 **'Hoy sho wallosho, wallosho'**   = *'here with her altogether'*   GCA's attempt to record the leader's cry to unite the team in heaving the boat up the beach clear of the waves. (See Introduction). For a non-Gaelic ear it is almost impossible to convey. Osgood Mackenzie (the creator of Inverewe Gardens) records his mother's full and accurate description of their visit to St Kilda in 1853, the year after 36 St Kildans had emigrated to Australia. She wrote down their sea shanty - he added the translation:

> 'Iomru illean, iomru illean,
> Robh mhath na gillean, robh mhath na gillean,
> Shid I, shid I, shid i.'

> 'Row, lads, row lads.
> Well done, the lads! Well done, lads!
> There she goes, there she goes.'

51 **Rev Neil MacKenzie**   He had offered to go as a missionary to Labrador, but when this post was filled *'he volunteered to go to any place for which no-one else could be got'* – it was this that led him to being asked to go to St Kilda. He arrived and was introduced to the St Kildans on July 4th 1830. After Acland's visit in 1834 and gift of £20 he was instrumental in helping the natives to divide the land equally to form the new settlement on which the houses were built in an arc above the bay. The sea wall, head dyke, cemetery and saw-pit were all built under his supervision. He was an excellent pastor and recorded many Kildan songs, carried out archaeological work and kept accurate notes on the ornithology. He left St Kilda in 1844 to take up a post in Duror.

52 **Tacksman**   the representative of the owners who normally came to the Islands once a year to collect rent in the form of tweed, feathers, dried fish and fulmar oil. He brought with him seed corn, oatmeal; more recently paraffin and others things ordered the year before.

53 **St Kilda Village**
> 1831 A huddle of about 30 houses, with the new Kirk and Manse
> 1834-38 New planned Village along the Main Street
> 1852 Emigration of 36 St Kildans to Australia on board the *'Priscilla'*, half died on the way or in quarantine on arrival. A loss which the St Kilda community was never able to overcome.
> 1860 October gale removed the roofs off several of the houses. The owner initiated a new building programme resulting in 16 new cottages (rectangular, windows facing the sea, taller, draughty) over the next few years, situated between the old houses which were now used as byres.
> 1914-18 During the War a small naval radio station was manned on St Kilda. The personnel brought news of an easier way of life in Glasgow. Many young St Kildans left as soon as the war was over. Economy no longer viable.

1930 Aug 29th Evacuation of St Kilda brought about by a number of factors – the young men leaving in 1919, an influenza outbreak which killed four senior men, near starvation and long isolation, and the deaths of two young girls eventually broke the St Kildans' spirit and they asked to leave.

54 **Puffins and Bird Numbers**   About one million birds return to St Kilda each year to nest

Including approximate pairs ;-

Fulmars	63,000	Gannets	50,000	Kittiwakes	8,000
Puffins	230,000	Guillemots	12,000	Razorbills	2,000
Black Guillemot	8	Shag	52	Great Skua	120
Herring Gull	60	Greater B-b	56		
Lesser Black-backed Gulls			150		

Huge numbers of Manx Shearwaters, Storm and Leach's Petrels

55 **Yarrell, William**   Yarrell worked in a bank and then ran a newsagent just off Piccadilly. In 1826 he gave up the gun in favour of the study of natural history. He was a great collector of specimens and '*found fish sent to him from Scotland and Ireland travelled equally well in whisky*' (Allen, 1976) as a substitute for alcohol or spirits of wine! In 1833 he became treasurer of the newly formed Entomological Society of London and Secretary of the Zoological Society. He wrote, *History of British Birds*, which appeared in bimonthly periods between 1837-43 with further additions until 1889. It quickly became a standard handbook.

56 **Bullock, William**   A Liverpool goldsmith with a reputation as a ruthless collector, and whose dubious claim to fame is as the person who, in 1812, hunted down and killed the last Great Auk in the Orkney Islands. He built up an extensive collection of specimens which he opened to the public as *The London Museum of Natural History*. He developed new methods of relaxing and preserving skins of animals.

57 **Rockall and Basil Hall**   Rockall G. Sgeir Rocail – '*skerry which roars hoarsely*' Basil Hall was a Lieutenant on HMS '*Endymion*', a 40 gun frigate, and the first to set foot on Rockall, that tiny spike of granite 70ft high, 191 miles west of the nearest land, St Kilda and 230 miles from Manish Point on North Uist. The date of landing was Sunday 8th Sept. 1811 (not on the 8th July 1810 as often reported). Hall commented, '*The stone of which this curious peak is composed is a dark-coloured granite, but the top being covered with a coating as white as snow, from having been for ages the resting-place of myriads of sea-fowl, it is constantly mistaken for a vessel under sail*'. Ownership of Rockall for Britain was claimed in the 1980's by John Ridgeway, the Atlantic rower, who spent a month living on the rock in a tiny shelter bolted to the rock on a narrow ledge, now known as Hall's Ledge. Basil Hall's book, *Fragments of Voyages and Travels*, was published in three volumes in 1831.

58 **St Kilda Islands Described**

59 **Boreray**   (1,259ft) *The Fortified Isle*. Surrounded by spectacular cliffs surmounted by irregular rock pinnacles, turrets and towers, with deep caves at sea level. St Kildans stayed in Tigh Stallir, and later in 3 bothies, at about 800ft built into the steep hillside when they went to attend the sheep or collect gannets or puffins. Never inhabited permanently. Home to 63,000 pairs puffins, 24,000 pairs of gannets, 6,000 pairs fulmars.

Stac Lee   (564ft) *The Blue Stac*. The stac rises vertically 700ft from the sea bed, home to 13,500 pairs of gannets, no puffins. A bothy built at 120m to hold 2-3 men who were landed early for the gannet harvest in case the weather changed and they lost all the gugas, young gannets.

Stac an Armin – (644ft) *The Warriors Stac*. The highest sea-stac in Britain, a massive rock wedge with a vertical face and overhang to the west. Home for the winter of 1727 for three men and eight boys who had been landed in August for the gannet harvest. An outbreak of smallpox prevented a crew being available to man the boat to rescue them. Home to 12,000 pairs of gannets.

Soay – (1,239ft) *Sheep Island*. Almost surrounded by perpendicular cliffs 800 – 1,000ft high. Due to changing weather conditions, difficulty in landing and access it is considered the least visited island in Britain. St Kildans stayed in bothies a week at a time to collect puffins, they also landed to catch the Soay Sheep, a very primitive breed, for winter food. 50,000 pairs puffins, 17 pairs Great Skuas, 13 pairs of St Kilda Wrens.

Dun – (583ft) *Fort* A natural rocky fortress and breakwater one and a half miles long, grassy puffin burrowed slopes to the east, indented rocky cliffs and caves to the west facing the full force of the Atlantic. 50,000 pairs puffins, 12,000 pairs fulmars.

Stac Levenish – (203ft) Possibly *Grey Island*. This pyramid shaped rock guards the approaches to Village Bay with further protection from Na Bodhan, *The Submerged Rocks*.

Conachair – (1,397ft) The highest point on the archipelago with fantastic views on a clear day, not just the 4 miles to Boreray and the Stacs but the 40 miles to the Flannan Islands in the north, 50 miles east to the Outer Hebrides, 100 miles east to the Cuillins on Skye. 6,000 pairs of fulmars nest on the face of Conachair and GCA watched two lads with fowling rods catching guillemots at the foot of the cliff and produced an excellent sketch.

60 **Stacs in Soay Sound**

    Stac Dona (87ft) *The Bad Stac* on account of it being poor for birds.

    Stac Soay (200ft) *Sheep Stac* has a huge hole gouged out of its middle by the sea.

    Stac Biorach (240ft) *The Pointed Stac* – like a steeple. Required the ultimate in climbing skills even by St Kilda standards and was rarely climbed. GCA watched and recorded his description of two lads who climbed it successfully.

61 **'Slan leave ullah'** GCA's farewell to the St Kildans, learnt from the Rev Neil McKenzie – the actual Gaelic would have been *'Slan leibh uile'* – 'Health to you all'.

62 **Leaving St Kilda** A frightful return journey taking two days, involving rowing nearly 50 miles through two nights, via Haskir. Here they were caught in mist and nearly wrecked on the rocks, then on to Berneray to obtain refreshments, and the last leg to Rodel.

63 **Hashkir = Hasker** *Deep-sea Skerry (Norse)* A group of islands 35 miles from St Kilda and 8 from Grimnish Point on North Uist. It is without harbour or shelter and, as it is difficult to land on the greasy slabs to the west, rarely visited except by grey Atlantic seals and nesting sea-birds. No grass grows there, the only plants must be able to survive the constant sea spray, predominantly sea pinks, sea campion, sea plantain and Babbington's Orache. A lighthouse was built in 1997 at the

southern end on the highest point, 123ft, of the main islands, Haisgeir Mhor, *Great Hasker.* The island has Castle Cliff to the north and many interesting rock arches and vertical rock structures. Half a mile to the SW is Haisgeir Eagach, *Notched Hasker,* consisting of a row of five irregular sharp pointed stacks. In 1953 Robert Atkinson excavated a bothy on the main island but found no interesting antiquities.

64   **Mr. Bethun** = Mr Alexander Bethune, Minister of Scarista. *'Son of Neil Bethune, Orbost, and Janet Macleod, Feorlig. He was the missionary minister at Durness, appointed to Harris in 1805. He married Isobel, daughter of Sheriff Macdonald of Castletown who lived at Skirinish Snizort.'* (R.A.MacLeod.pers.inf.)

65   **Hushinish** GCA was trying to track down Mr Train. Hushinish is situated at the end of the road along the northern edge of West Loch Tarbert, and past the old whaling station at Bunavoneadar. The road passes Amhuinnsuidhe castle on the shores of Loch Tarbert, on the edge of the Forrest on Harris before reaching the curving silver sands of Hushinish. The island of Scarp lies opposite to the NW.

66   **Flannan Islands** or The Seven Hunters. A group of islands in three clusters 21 miles west of Lewis. The main group being Eilean Mor, *Big Island*, which includes St Flann's with its 9th C Chapel, and the Lighthouse, famed for the three keepers who disappeared in December 1900.

67   **McCrae of Hushinish** *'Alexander Macrae was the younger brother of Sir John Macrae, their fellow passenger of 20th May. He was also a close associate of Donald Stewart the Harris factor, (despite young Stewart's description of him recorded in the next day's entry), and later held extensive tacks in both Harris and Lewis. He is also mentioned in connection with the lease of Mealista. It is of interest that a letter from Macrae came to the East Coast of England by 'a kelp vessel'.*(R.A.MacLeod. pers inf.).

68   **Gashkir** (Gasker 105ft) *The Journal suggests that Gasker was Lewis property. If so it must have been part of the Mealista tack.* (R.A.MacLeod. pers. inf.). The island lies nearly five miles off Hushinish Point. Home to 2,000 Grey Seals in the autumn coming in October to calve and mate. Only surpassed by North Rona with 7,500.

     Phoco barbate (Fabicius 1776) now *Erignathus barbatus*, the *Bearded Seal* is a truly Arctic species, circumpolar, and a very rare visitor to Britain as an occasional straggler in winter. It can exceed in size the Grey Seal, with bulls 10-12 ft, cows 7ft. The Grey Seal of British Waters was thought to be the Bearded Seal until 1825.

69   **Glen Ulladil (Ulladale)** From the middle of the glen rises a perpindicular cliff, overhanging in places and with immense masses of rock at its base. The rock is the end of a long ridge. To the north of the rock is Glen Ulladil. *'Among the rocks on the southern side is the cave. It is situated about the middle of the glen, and nearer the top than the bottom of the rocks forming the side or boundary. At this place are three ruts or furrows in the rock, of considerable size and nearly parallel. In the side of the one next this great rock is the cave, formed by a hollow left between strata of the rock . . . .I ascended in the rut and entered the cave. In doing which I experienced some difficulty as the stones were slippery with melting snow and ice, and the entrance to the cave is at the best very difficult, being such that one man might easily defend himself against a whole army. On entering the cave I found it snug and warm; so I sat me down and read aloud a considerable portion of the Pleasures of Hope.In one end is a well. On leaving the cave I returned along*

the base of the cliffs, ascended the Robber's Stair for a considerable way. From the top of this I had an excellent view. The lake was just below me; and beyond I could see the whole plain. I was overcanopied by the rock, which projected about fifteen feet beyond its base. I picked up some mineralogical specimens.' (MacGillivray. W in Ralph R., 1996)

70   **McCloud's Cave** = Macleod's Cave. *'The Macleod referred to was the Old Trojan who skulked there after the '45. His history is well documented in the History of the Macleod's of Berneray.'* (R.A.MacLeod. pers. inf.).

71   **Luskintyre – Stewarts**   *' Their artist friend, Mr Train, who had not ventured to St Kilda, had occupied his time in visiting North Harris staying with the Rev Bethune at Scarista and with the Factor, Donald Stewart at Luskintyre. Alex Macleod, proprietor of Harris (3rd of Harris and 8th of Berneray) appointed Stewart, a shepherd from Park, Lewis (originally from Atholl), as Factor. Stewart secured the farm of Luskintye and cleared the population from most of west Harris, including Borve, Govaig and Hushinish which he gave to a relation, Alexander Macrae.. Following the collapse of the kelp industry Macleod was heavily in debt and sold Harris to Lord Dunmore. The Factor's family regaled GCA with the legend of a monster in Loch Laxdale, at the head of the Laxdale river above Luskintyre Bay. Donald Stewart's son was William of Ensay and his descendant, John Stewart had Scorrybreck Farm, Portree until 1923.'* (R.A.MacLeod. pers. inf.).

72   **Sweet!**   Many visitors to St Kilda complained of the malodorous smells which clung to their clothing. Captain A.T.E.Vidal visited the islands on 'H.M.S.Pike' less than a month after GCA had been there. He commented, *'The air is full of feathered animals; the sea is covered with them; the houses are ornamented by them; the ground is speckled with them like a flowery meadow in May. The town is paved with feathers; the very dunghills are made of feathers; the ploughed land seems as if it had been sown with feathers; and the inhabitants look as if they have been all tarred and feathered, for their hair is full of feathers, and their clothes are covered with feathers. The women look like feathered Mercuries, for their shoes are made of a gannet's skin; every thing smells of feathers, and the smell pursued us all over the islands, for the captain had concealed a sack-full in the cabin.'* Fulmars smell even worse!

73   **Jameson's Inn, Portree**   Formerly known as MacNab's Inn built in the earlier half of the 17th C. Defeated at Culloden in his attempt to gain the crown, Charles Edward Stuart came to Skye in June 1746 with a price of £30,000 on his head. The inn is famous as the place where Charles said his good-bye's to Flora MacDonald, who had aided his escape. Today it is known as the Royal Hotel.

74   **Island of Rasa – Raasay.** The island acts as a breakwater between Skye and the mainland and protects the harbour of Portree. It is fifteen miles long by four wide, stretching from the mountains of Storr and the mouth of Loch Sligachan. After the break-up of the Lordship of the Isles it became a home of robbers and pirates It was ruled for 400 years by the MacLeods who originated from the Isle of Lewis. In the 1745 Jacobite Rising which split the Highlands, the MacLeods supported Prince Charles and actually gave him protection for a short period, but suffered greatly for their loyalty. The island was visited by Johnson and Boswell in 1773. On 6thJune 1854, 129 people emigrated to Australia from Raasay.

75   **Eleemosynary** of or pertaining to alms; gratuitous. They were hoping to receive charity from Sir John!

76   **Rasa House**   (Raasay)   At the time of GCA's visit the house actually belonged to John MacLeod, the XIIIth Chief, who was an officer in the 78th Highlanders. It was occupied by Sir John Macrae. The house originally built in the 1730–40's but burnt as a reprisal in 1745 had been rebuilt as a fine mansion by the time of Johnson and Boswell's visit in 1773. The present Regency front was added by James MacLeod who died in 1824. It must have been a glorious house in those days but hard times hit the lairds in the first half of the nineteenth century. James' son, John, struggled on but was the last of the clan to live on the island. He sold the house and the island in 1846 to George Rainy of Edinburgh before leaving for Australia. Rainy ran the island for sheep and as a deer forest. Raasay House was considered to be the island's prize possession, dominating the view from the sea, situated in the lovely curve of the bay with a rocky headland behind rising to the summit of Dun Caan, 1,456ft. (Stack, P. 1979)

77   **Pipers on Raasay**   This small island has produced some remarkable pipers. In 1767 John MacKay was born on Raasay and became the most knowledgeable piper of his day and raised the island's tradition. He claimed his tradition from the MacCrimmons of Borreraig and then the MacKays of Gairloch. He left the island to become piper at Drummond Castle in Perth. His four sons were excellent pipers but Angus (1813-59), his third son, was outstanding, managing to blend the old with the new. He became piper to Campbell of Islay and in 1838 published a collection of 61 ancient piobaireachd or Highland pipe music. He left transcripts of a further 183 at his death in 1859. In 1843 he became piper to Queen Victoria.

78   **Sconser**   The birthplace of John Mackenzie, active as a mountain guide for over half a century, and, who at the age of ten climbed Sgurr nan Gillean on the Cuillin Ridge.

79   **Sligachan**   Cattle Markets were held here, on the route of the old drove road leading to Kyle Rhea where the cattle had to swim across the Sound. The Sligachan Inn was the meeting point for climbers in the Victorian Age.

80   **Whisky Smugglers**   A good many illicit whisky stills were in operation in GCA's time. The sketches throw light on the characters!

81   **Mrs. Mackinnon of Corry** – *'It is not clear who was the chatelaine of Corry at the time of Atkinson's visit. It is probable that she was Anne, the daughter of Farquhar Macrae of Inverinate, who married Sheriff Lachlan Mackinnon.*

It has been said that Anne Macdonald of Kingsburgh, who had helped to entertain Prince Charlie, lived until 1840 reaching an age of 95 years. This cannot be so as she was a grown woman, possibly married to Ranald Macallister, in 1746. As widow she married Lachlan Mackinnon of Corry, the Sheriff's grandfather, as his third wife and, as such, entertained Johnson and Boswell. The lady who lived until 1840 was probably her daughter, Flora Macallister who married Charles, younger of Corry and apparently had no family apart from Sheriff Lachlan Mackinnon.' (Dr A.Maclean. *pers inf.*).

82   **Loch Coruisk** – One of the greatest sights in Britain; no other loch has inspired so many writers, including Walter Scott. The ring of the Black Cuillins encircle the loch and stand up magnificently with their serrated peaks. Coming off them along the east of the loch is an offshoot, the ridge of Druim nan Ramh. Probably the finest view is to the head of the loch where the rocks of Sgurr Dubh descend 3,089ft to the shores of the loch below, which it is only 20ft above sea-level. The area has a wild beauty, remote and desolate in its savage grandeur. Turner painted the scene.

83 **Spar Cave**   A limestone cavern on the Strathaird peninsula, which was discovered around 1770.

84 **MacLean of Coll**   Hugh, the Fifteenth MacLean of Coll, lived at Drumfin House near Tobermory, and owned Coll, Rum and a third of Mull. *'Mr MacIntyre, parish minister of Torosay, who had frequently seen Hugh, fifteenth of Coll, describes him as having been a man of dignity, commanding appearance, kind, affable, and just. His father, Alexander, removed from Coll in 1828 to Mull, and the family never returned to live again in Coll.*

In the immediate neighbourhood of Tobermory is a beautiful loch, called Mary's lake which was owned by Hugh. The spot is a beautiful one, situated between two finely wooded hills, extremely precipitous in their descent. This pleasing spot Hugh improved and on the banks of the lake erected the elegant mansion of Drumfin. Hugh was born in 1782, and at first preferred military service, and rose to the rank of lieutenant-colonel, and for some time served in the Guards . . . .Hugh received the estate burdened, and also added to the indebtedness. It was deemed advisable to sell the whole estate, which was done in April 1856. Hugh was first married in 1814 to Janet, daughter of James Dennistoun, by whom he had four daughters. Hugh married again in 1825 to Jane Robertson. During the later years of his life, Hugh lived in London and died in 1861.' ('History of the Clan MacLean', MacLean J.P. 1889).

R.A.MacLeod makes the comment, *'Hugh would have been circa 49 years old at the time of Atkinson's visit in 1831, but as his father did not die until 1835, his son was not Chief of the Clan until the latter date.'*

85 **McNeil of Canna**   *'Donald MacNeil, was the son of Hector MacNeil of the Taynish branch of the Clan, a merchant in Kintyre who married a daughter of Alexander Macdonald of Boisdale in South Uist. Because of his wife's close ties with Macdonald of Clanranald, Hector became tacksman of a major portion of the island of Canna. Donald, who succeeded his father there in 1810, was able to buy the whole island from Clanranald in 1827. Donald MacNeil was an able proprietor who never married, but had several illegitimate children, despite being 'a clerical looking gentleman'. One of these, also Donald, succeeded him in 1848 and was only then able to conduct clearances on Canna.'* (John Lorne Campbell, 'Canna' and Dr A. Maclean. *pers. inf.*)

86 **Nankeen remainders**   from Nanking, China. A kind of cotton cloth originally made in Nanking from a yellow variety of cotton, later yellow or pale buff and known as the colour of '*nankeen*' – trousers were then made of *nankeen*.

Notes on the 1833 Expedition

87 **Dr Hooker, Professor of Botany**   Later Sir William Jackson Hooker, who was Professor of Botany at Glasgow. His field classes influenced generations of students. In 1830 he published his, *'British Flora'* and later a popular handbook, *'Bentham and Hooker'*. He became the first official Director of the Royal Botanic Gardens at Kew in 1841. His son, Sir Joseph Dalton Hooker followed him as Director of Kew.

88 **yclept**   (Old English) called, named, styled.

89 **Dr Schouler** = Dr John Scouler, (1804-1871) Born in Glasgow, he studied Medicine and was considered by Dr Hooker to be one of his most brilliant pupils. He extended his studies in Paris, and in 1824 became surgeon on the brig *'William and Anne'*, chartered by the Hudson Bay Company to explore the Pacific Northwest coast of America. He took with him as a plant collector, David Douglas, then assistant curator of the Glasgow Botanic Gardens, who introduced many of our garden and cultivated trees. Scouler was the first botanist to explore the State of Oregon and has over twenty plants named in his honour. In 1829 he was appointed Professor of Natural History and Curator of the Museum at Anderson's University, Glasgow. Here he quickly built up the collection. In 1834 he was appointed to a similar post in Dublin which he held for twenty years until his retirement on grounds of health. He published little but had a breadth of interests in natural history – botany, zoology, geology and ethnology. In later years he was known as living alone among his books, his specimens and his tobacco smoke in his lodgings, ambling daily to the Andersonian Institution, until his death in 1871.

90 **Captain Edward Sabine**   later Sir Edward (1788-1883) In 1803 he joined the Royal Artillery, becoming a specialist is astronomy and magnetic surveys. In 1818 he accompanied Sir John Ross on his expedition in search of the North West Passage in the capacity of astronomer, naturalist and collector. He also accompanied William Edward Parry on his expedition in 1819-20. Sabine's Gull, *Xema sabini*, is named after him; it breeds circumpolar in the high Arctic. It was first discovered on the northern shores of Baffin's Bay, on what are now known as the Sabine Islands in Melville Bay, north-west Greenland. GCA was given a skin collected by Sabine of the Brunnich's Guillemot now *Uria lomvia*, primarily an Arctic species with shorter, thicker bill with white on the lower mandible, distinguishing it from the Common Guillemot now *Uria aalge*. The two species overlap in their range a little and this skin was one of a few used to make the original distinction between the species.

91 **'Highland Chieftain'**   Built in 1817 as the *'Duke of Wellington'*. In 1820 she was enlarged and renamed *'Highland Chieftain'*, replacing the *'Comet 1'* on the Fort William route. In 1825 she ran a weekly service to Inverness by way of Oban and the Caledonian Canal in conjunction with the *'Ben Nevis I'*.

92 **Oban** In 1832 Oban was a buzz with activity, '*On two days of the week, and at certain hours, three steamers and a stage coach are seen approaching – The Inverness steamer from the north hoists its black signal on Loch Linnhe, - That of Glasgow from the south advances from the Crinan Canal – the lazy and crazy Highlander (now the new Staffa) emerges westward from the Sound of Mull – while the Diligence stage coach arrives from Inverary in the east.*' Johnson, J. 1834

93 **MacLean of Coll** *See Fn. 84.*

94 **Mrs. Cuthbertson's** At Tobermory. GCA appreciated her ministrations. Her house was known as the Red House, being a substantial three-storey building of red sandstone, it is now painted light green and named 'Rockburn'. It is situated 100 yards inland from the old pier, opposite the present clock tower; in GCA's time it lay just behind the old Inn. It is possible that Felix Mendelssohn stayed there in 1829 when he visited Staffa, for he wrote, '*we have found quarters in a respectable private house perfectly charming it is here!*' James Johnson stayed there in 1832, recording that, '*The arrival of the steamer twice a week is an event. The principal inn soon overflows and in the struggle for beds he who is least successful is most fortunate. Our ejectment into the street threw us into the comfortable house of Mrs. Cuthbertson, seated on an eminence and commanding a romantic prospect. A dozen tourists gathered round the festive board while the mountain dew circulated briskly and hilarity prevailed 'til midnight.*' (Johnson, J. 1834). Mrs. Cuthbertson's husband, Robert, was an inspector in the Fishery Office at Tobermory

95 **McKinnons at Broadford** *See Fn. 81.*

96 **Sir John Macrae on Rasa** *See Fn. 24.*

97 **Portree Inn , Jamieson's** *See Fn. 73*

98 **Sunderland Tommy** – GCA relates the story in Tommy's own words (see also 1831 May 26 and **Fn. 38**). In spite of GCA's attempts to get him home he is still in Portree 1833, now aged 16, comfortable and with a job. However, the following year he does return to Sunderland, and calls on GCA in October 1834. Tommy tells us that his mother lives in the High Street, Sunderland and his aunt not far away. Unfortunately we do not know their Christian names. However, from the 1841 census for Sunderland, we find Thomas is married to Elizabeth aged 22 from Sunderland and that they have a son William aged 4, Tommy, being a Mariner, is probably at sea at the time of the census. They are living in Stamps Lane, just off the High Street.

In the 1851 census, Thomas is home, now aged 33, a Mariner living in Stamps Lane (the houses were not numbered) with his wife Elizabeth 32. William, their son, is now 13, with brothers Francis, 9, Thomas 7 and Charles 2. There were further additions to the family by 1861, when Thomas is home as a Mariner, aged 44, with his wife Elizabeth, 41 , and still resident in the Parish of Holy Trinity Sunderland at 25 Stamps Lane. By now William, aged 23, is unmarried and working as a Painter, with brothers Francis, 19, a Ship Wright, Thomas, 17, a Sail Maker and Charles, 13, a Scholar; Elizabeth, 10, and Joseph, 7, are also Scholars, with the youngest of Tommy's large family comprising John, 3, and Baby Alice at a mere 6 months.

99 **St Nicholas Steeple** GCA compared the height of the Old Man of Storr with the steeple of the parish church in Newcastle upon Tyne, now the Cathedral.

100 *Lt. Col. Murray* Lieutenant Colonel Sir W.R.Murray of Ochtertyre. *His book, 'Honored the express approbation and Patronage of His Most Gracious Majesty'*

according to the title page is called 'Sketches of scenes in Scotland drawn in outline', *illustrated by D. Morison, Junior, FRSA Scotland with 54 lithographic plates,
Quarto volume, Perth 1834. He has two sketches relating to the Storr, a long view
from south of Portree and a close up of the Old Man of Storr. His short chapter
begins with an unnamed reference to Atkinson's description,* 'A Party of Tourists
from England have left the following remarks, written upon a map of Inverness-
shire, in the Inn at Portree: "Of all the scenery in Scotland there is none more
grand or imposing than that of the Storr, in the Isle of Skye. It is so strange and
terrific, so lonely and unnatural, and so perfectly dissimilar from anything else,
that description would be powerless from absence of comparison, and weak from
poorness of expression. If such an idea be not too fanciful, it suggests to the
mind, more than aught else, the burial-place of a race of giants. The view from
the summit is very fine, comprising, to the west, the whole of the long island and
the western part of Skye: to the east and south-east the islands of Rona, Raasay,
Scalpa, and the coasts of Ross and Inverness: and to the south, the magnificent
range of the Cullin hills. The scenery of the Storr itself is utterly unlike any thing
else, and much too grand for description:- nothing but the eye can know it, nor
aught but the mind retain it – language and painting, would be alike thrown away
upon it!!"

The Colonel comments, *'After such a caveat, it requires some courage to
approach the Storr with both pen and pencil; but the sketcher may step in where the
Painter is afraid to tread. He feels that if he, in common with the painter, fail in con-
veying even the faintest impression of the wild magnificence which reigns in this the
most desolate and most stupendous of Nature's temples – he may at least give the
forms of the objects so correctly, as to aid the recollections and descriptions of
those who have been on the spot, and to convey to others some idea of the character of the scenery, which is by no means over-rated in the apparently hyperbolical
eulogium of the English travellers.'*

The concluding paragraph of the Colonel's sketch is significant, *'Until of late
years the Scenery of the Isle of Skye was difficult of approach, and seldom visited.
The establishment of the Steam Packets on the western coast has brought it within
a day's sail of Glasgow. No passenger who can spare a day on his voyage to the
north, should omit to land at Portree. The Inn is good, and the Storr is only 6 miles
distant, accessible by a tolerable bridle road. Whoever may be induced so to turn
aside, or to step on board the packet for the sole purpose of visiting this spot, may
take the quotation with which we commenced, and the remarks which follow it, in
their fullest acceptation; he may form any anticipations however sanguine, **they
will be surpassed.***'

See GCA's Journal for 1831 for Tues 14th June – his Eulogy on Storr

101 **MacDonald's Table**   Lord MacDonald's Table is an impressive slab shaped island,
and lying three miles north west of Hunish Point is one of a group forming the
northernmost point on Skye.

102 **Shiant Islands**   *The Enchanted Islands*, A group of three islands, Garb Eilean,
Rough Island, and to the south, joined by a shingle beach is Eilean an Tigh, *Home
Island,* with the little shepherd's house standing on a grassy patch south of the
beach. Garb Eilean is the largest of the islands with huge columnar basalt cliffs
rising to 500ft, and where the sea eagle used to nest. On the large grassy slopes
thousands of puffins have their burrows, and among the basalt boulders at the
foot of the cliffs by the shore thousands of razorbills have their nests, sitting out

among a few shags. Eilean Mhuire, *Mary's Island*, stands away to the east, and when visited by GCA supported a pair of eagles. There is a small ruin of St Mary's Chapel near the summit.

103 **Lord Seaforth, Admiral Hood, Mrs Stewart Mackenzie** Lord Seaforth (Francis Humberston Mackenzie) was the Colonel of the 78th Regiment and a Member of Parliament. After his elevation to the Peerage in 1797 he and Lady Seaforth lived at Seaforth Lodge, Stornoway. He was involved in the fishing and the kelp industry and in 1791 made the first attempts at road building, completing four miles in six years. He tried to improve the condition of his tenants, and in 1811 made a start in lotting the land in the place of the runrig system. Lady Seaforth taught the women of Lewis spinning, knitting and weaving.

'*Lord Seaforth's four sons died before him, and on his death in January 1815, his title became extinct while his estates passed to his eldest daughter, Mary Frederica Elizabeth, Lady Hood, whose husband, Admiral Sir Samuel Hood, had died eighteen days earlier. Admiral Hood had been Commander-in-Chief in the Indies . . . and so Lady Hood inherited the Seaforth possessions. Lady Hood married James Alexander Stewart of Glasserton in May 1817, after which Mr Stewart assumed the additional surname of Mackenzie. The Hon Mrs Stewart Mackenzie, as Lady Hood became, the last of her race to possess Lewis, was a most outstanding person and possibly the ablest of the Mackenzies.*' (Macdonald, D. 1978). She accompanied her father to Barbados while he was Governor there, and her first husband to the Indies. After the failure of the kelp industry and abortive attempts at sheep farming the estate was put into the hands of Trustees by 1833. Mr Stewart Mackenzie was appointed to the Governorship of Ceylon and later, Lord High Commissioner of the Ionian Isles. He died in 1843 and, in 1844, his widow sold Lewis to Mr James Matheson, a native of Sutherland who had travelled on business to London, India and China, for £190,000.

104 **Sloop 'Peggy'** The vessel chartered to take the party to the Faeroes and Iceland. It was a 54 ton, one masted vessel, rigged fore-and-aft with a mainsail and jib.

105 **Illegal Whiskey.** '*In 1827, a Highland newspaper stated that there was not a drop of illicit whisky to be got from the Butt of Lewis to Barra Head, owing to the vigilance of Captain Oliver on the revenue cutter Prince of Wales. Yet, in 1834, Factor Knox reported to the proprietor that the tenants along the north shore of Broad Bay were better off than those in other districts owing to their distillation of whisky.*' (Macdonald D., 1978)

106 **Agricultural Implements:-**
CasChroum = Cas-chrom – *the crooked spade*, the most important of the implements. It was reckoned that one man could dig over as much ground in a day as four men with an ordinary spade. It was also very useful on boggy land, rocky slopes and later in road making.
Cromnagadd = Cran-nan-gad – *one handled plough*, could be drawn by 1, 2 or 4 horses with one man leading and the other guiding the plough.
Harrow – GCA mentions the pulling of this being done by women, but it was occasionally pulled by men and youngsters.
Cas-dhireach – *the straight spade* was a straight piece of wood tipped with iron with a step or pin on the right hand side for exerting pressure.
The modern type of spade was introduced with road making.

107 **Anent** – concerning, in respect of, in reference to

108 **Earthen Jars - Home-made Pottery** The area supported a celebrated hand-made domestic pottery industry making *Barvas Ware*. *'Clay vessels called craggans, primitive in appearance and shape, were made in all communities, although Barvas and Tolsta were noted as having the best clay for manufacture. When making a craggan, the clay was kneaded until it was smooth and of the right consistency, then fashioned by hand without the use of a potter's wheel. The thick circular bottom was made first, and the rest built on to this, until the desired size and shape was achieved. The craggan was then left standing to dry for a couple of days before being placed in the centre of a fire and filled with the glowing embers until it was sufficiently fired. Milk was then boiled in it to complete the operation.'* (Macdonald D. 1978)

109 *Ossianic* – Ossian was the legendary Gaelic warlike poet of the 3rd C AD, known through the work of the Scottish poet James MacPherson who published several volumes of poems attributed to Ossian in 1818. These inspired the writing of Gaelic poetry in the Ossianic vein at the end of 18th C and the beginning of 19th in Scotland. Scholars were divided about their authenticity believed, *'MacPherson had woven themes from the old traditional ballads connected with Fionn Mac-Cumhail and his band, into a fantastic epic poetry of his own.'* (Campbell, J.L. 1994)

110 **Eolus** = Aeolus - Greek – *'god of the winds'*. Aeolis is part of Asia Minor colonised by Greeks.

111 **Clach an Truiseil – *The Giant's Stone***, which in island tradition is reckoned to have been the petrified remains of a giant, lies on a gentle slope near Balantrushal on the west coast of Lewis. It stands some 18ft 10ins above the ground, 6ft in width and nearly 4ft at its maximum thickness, with a girth of 15ft 7ins at its base.

112 **Mr McRae** The Rev William MacRae, Church of Scotland minister of Barvas, was one of the moderate clergy who *'did much for the community in providing medicines and legal advice'*. In 1836 he reported on the terrible winter of rain and snow leading to *'absolute famine and general mortality among the cattle.'* (Macdonald D., 1978)

113 **Loch Bragar** – known as *Loch an Duna,* where GCA examined a ruin, the remains of a broch which in 1700 was three storeys high with double walls, now reduced to 14ft. There is also a Norse Mill at Bragar which was in use until 1940.

114 **Doun Carloway** Not a Dun (fort) but a broch of the later Iron Age, and one of the four best preserved examples (the others being the Broch of Mousa in Shetland, and the two brochs in Glenelg, SW Ross-shire). It stands to a height of 30ft, commanding a wide view of the approaches of Loch Roag. Roger Miket comments that Atkinson's record is singularly remarkable in not merely recording local memory of a time when the broch was roofed, but that this roof was reputedly a corbelled one. *As far as I am aware this is the only reference to brochs having had the sort of roof familiar in the later shielings.'* (pers. comm.).

115 **Luted** From the Latin – *lutum* = mud. In this case a sticky mud, clay or cement used to make a joint air-tight.

116 **Druidical Stones at Callernish** The famous Standing Stones of Callernish – Considered by Magnus Magnusson to be *'one of the great prehistoric monuments of Europe'* – a religious centre going back 4,000 years and on a par with Stonehenge and Avebury. In the middle of the last century 5ft of peat which had accumulated since the stones were raised was removed to expose their original height;

Atkinson's record and illustration is all the more valuable in recording the stones before this work was carried out. The tallest is nearly 16ft. Within four miles lie seven smaller stone circles, just some of over twenty examples of megalithic monuments, reinforcing the importance of the area in prehistoric times.

117 **North Rona, Sulisker, Barra**   These next three paragraphs are rather confusing to modern travellers. He has followed Dr MacCulloch's (1819) naming of the islands, *'These islands, although at a considerable distance from each other are usually associated by the joint appellation of Barra and Rona, but they are scarcely known except to the mariners who navigate the north sea and to the inhabitants of Lewis, of which estate they form a part. They are the northernmost of the Western islands, the Thule of the other islanders, who consider them as placed 'far from the sun and summer gale,' and beyond the limits of the habitable world. To have visited Barra and Rona gives a claim to distinction scarcely less in their estimation than to have explored the sources of the Nile or the Niger.'*

North Rona has a chapel and a cell and the remains of three low houses occupied until 1844, but which today stand to a height of only 2 ft. The island can boast the largest Grey Seal breeding colony in Britain. Sula Sgeir, which is really *Gannet Rock*, is home to 9,000 pairs. It has a little chapel and bothies still used by the gannet hunters from Lewis today. The name Barra has dropped out of use.

118 **Captain Oliver**   Captain Benjamin Oliver commanded the revenue cutter *'Prince of Wales'* sent to the Hebrides around 1807 to reduce smuggling which was rife. He was greatly feared by those who continued in the trade, with a record of ten ships and their crews captured during in his fourteen years activities.

Links with the Natural History Society Extracts

---

1. GCA's Lecture on St Kilda

To the Natural History Society of Northumberland and Durham and
Newcastle upon Tyne – reported in their Transactions No. VII

A NOTICE OF THE ISLAND OF ST KILDA, ON THE NORTH-WEST COAST OF SCOTLAND. *By Mr G. C. Atkinson. Read January 16, 1832*

During an excursion among some of the less-explored Hebrides, made last spring, I was astonished at the frequent occurrence of the most magnificent rock scenery, in its most imposing forms, and, the more so, that it is almost unknown. The Isle of Skye abounds in it, and Harris, which is the only other I saw much of, has some magnificent precipices; but both are inferior to the solitary isles of St Kilda, which far exceeded any conception I had formed of their grandeur, and seemed so interesting to me, both on that account and from their inhabitants, that, I beg leave to present the following notice of them to the Natural History Society, under the impression that a description of that which was so abundant in interest to me, may not be devoid of it to others, and perhaps induce some more competent person to visit and describe more fully, these magnificent islands.

Remote Situation

From the infrequency, I imagine of the visits of strangers to St Kilda, a most unreasonable degree of difficulty is attributed to the undertaking; so much so, that McCulloch is not exaggerating when he observes, in his amusing *Letters on the Highlands and Western Islands, 'In Scotland universally, we had heard of the voyage to this island as of a mighty problem of navigation,'* for I can add in corroboration, that on our return, the fact of our departure for it had been reported throughout the islands, and the oft-repeated questions about it soon became sufficiently tiresome.

It will be asked, *'What, then, is the usual communication?'* The island belongs to McLeod of Harris, and is visited twice a year by his tacksman, who generally goes from a small island, called Pabbah, situated somewhat nearer to it than Harris, to which it lies nearly opposite. Thus the Pabbah men, who probably have not much intercourse with the larger islands, form a kind of exclusive channel of communication with St Kilda, which accounts in some measure for its being comparatively unknown to the other islanders. Considering, therefore, its remote situation, and the difficulties, real and imaginary, with which its attainment is regarded, it is scarcely to be wondered that this interesting island is so little known.

I will not say that the voyage is entirely without danger, for St Kilda is so exposed to the Atlantic, that only vessels capable of riding at anchor in safety on its heavy swell, or small enough to be hauled up on the beach on arrival, are safe to go in. Of course the latter, to general tourists, will be the most convenient mode, and was the one adopted by my brother and me last summer; hiring a boat for £5 at a small village called Coshlatter, on Harris with three men as its crew. It was 18ft in the keel, yaul built, and contained several wisps (small bundles) of straw for us to sleep on, a sack of oatmeal, a peat fire in an iron pot, and five or six bottles of whiskey. We sailed from Rowdill at 10 o'clock pm on the 30th of May, and entered the small bay on the south east of St Kilda, at 11 next morning, after a pleasant 13 hours' trip in a beautiful night, so light throughout, though there was no moon, that I could easily consult my watch at midnight.

As it was about the time of the tacksman's visit, the natives thought it was his boat, and were anxiously waiting to receive us, and although our nearer approach undeceived them, bestowed on us and our crew every care and attention. Mr. McKenzie, the minister, met us on the rocks at the landing which is close to the village, and took us home to a most acceptable cup of tea: and to his kindness we were indebted for hospitable entertainment during our stay, as well as for much of the information concerning the islands, that I now relate.

The group called St Kilda situated about 60 miles west from the Sound of Harris, consists of three islands, and their adjacent rocks. Of these St Kilda, properly so called, is alone inhabited; it is about four and a half miles long, from north west to south east, and two or two and a half wide. Soa, which lies 200 yards to the west of it, is nearly triangular, and about a mile across; and Borera, five miles to the north east, rather larger. Martin, who published an excellent history of these islands more than a century ago, called St Kilda 1450ft high; but McCulloch, who I should think measured it more accurately, makes it 1380. The highest precipices are on the north side, where they descend unbroken to the sea from the very summit of Conachar, the loftiest hill in the island, presenting to the eye the finest precipice in Great Britain. Soa, is not nearly so lofty, or so precipitous; but Borera is of about the same height and more inaccessible, containing on its north side, which like St Kilda is the steepest, some most stupendous and extraordinary scenes.

Of these islands, the largest alone possesses an abundant supply of water, the others only having a single bad spring each; but on St Kilda it is most abundant and of excellent quality, each spring being celebrated for some particular virtue it is imagined to possess, and named accordingly.

The Inhabitants

We were much struck with the good looks of the inhabitants as they turned out, men, women, and children, to receive us. They are of rather short stature, but present neat compact specimens of the human form, set off by lively intelligent countenances, adorned almost always with beautifully white teeth. Their number is a little more than a hundred and has remained nearly unchanged for centuries; the lack of increase being generally attributed to want of surgical aid for their women in childbed. I did not hear that longevity is common among them, but from the hale countenances we saw and the temperance of their habits, I think it must be so. The dress worn on the island is much the same as that of fishermen at our remote fishing villages, coarse blue jacket and trousers, and sometimes with, though frequently without, shoes and stockings. These latter, however, are worn with a soling of sea fowl feathers compactly sewed to them and must be very safe to traverse the slippery precipices in. Hats or caps they seldom wear. The women wear a gown of the same blue woollen material of which the men's coats are made, drawn in at the waist, but as they are not generally, I think, so good-looking as the men, this negligence is not becoming.

Their habitations lie in a cluster, within a hundred yards of the bay on the south-east side of St Kilda, and are about thirty in number; as the manners of the people are very uncleanly, and all the refuse of the fowl and other filth, is carefully accumulated, within them, to be removed annually, mixed with the straw thatchings thoroughly saturated with smoke, to manure their barley, it may be imagined how unsavoury they become. The inhabitants sleep in apartments like rabbit-holes in construction, excavated from the earth surrounding their houses, and fasten their doors – a rather unnecessary precaution – with simple but ingenious wooden locks of their own manu-facture.

On our departure for St Kilda, we were assured that we would imbibe a smell, from living among them, that would adhere to us for five or six weeks: fortunately the newly built parsonage house, of which our informants had been unaware, presented a comfortable and in-odorous habitation while we staid.

No specific trade or profession is followed by any of the Kildeans; each man farms, weaves, makes shoes, and does joiner work for himself and children alone, nor though naturally kind and obliging in an admirable degree, will they, without a recompense, lend assistance to a neighbour. All their thoughts are bent on the one subject of fowling, and all energies of mind and body centred in it. To say it is of as exclusive importance to them, as the capture of whales is to a Greenland crew, would convey but a slight idea of the value of fowl to the Kildean; for to the one his profession is matter of choice, and his mode of life may be changed at will for any other which appears more agreeable; to the other, it constitutes his only means of livelihood and sustenance, and that not for a season, to be alternated with other fairer scenes and less hazardous occupations, but for the whole period of existence, as they never leave the island, only one or two instances occurring of their being found over the whole of Scotland. From their childhood the rock is the only field of their industry or hardihood, and the produce of it almost the only desirable object to them: constituting at once their food, the staple commodity of the island, and very generally its circulat-ing medium, for the use and value of money is scarcely known, and all bargains among themselves, and between them and the tacksman, are calculated in fowl.

With regard to morality, they are in a curiously primitive state, which may be attrib-uted to the absence of the usual inducements to crime, aided by the utter impossibility of escape in the case of detection. Moreover, they cannot indulge in that beginner of mischiefs, intoxication, as no fermented or spirituous liquor is made on the island, and the supplies of the tacksman are very small. Dishonesty is therefore very rare; murder has not been committed within the memory of man, and adultery is unknown. In dis-position they are cheerful, gentle, and obliging, strongly mindful of their promise, and highly tractable.

With such materials to work on, Mr. McKenzie has the prospect of being of much utility to them; in fact, though he had only been there a year, he had got them to attend the church very attentively and regularly twice a week. Gaelic is the only language spoken, but one man, I believe, understanding any English. Mrs. McKenzie, a Glasgow lady, does not speak it, and therefore was, I am inclined to think, very glad to see us, as it must have been six months since she exchanged a sentiment with anyone but her husband.

The complicated machinery of the law, seems as unknown, as it would be useless among them; but all the interests of the community are managed by a general assembly of men, on a house somewhat larger than the rest in the middle of the village: on the broad wall of this they sit, (*I should observe, that the rafters of the houses rise from the inner side of a broad low wall, which leaves the thickness of the wall as a seat, or shelf to place household utensils on) and portion out the rock to the climbers, examine into the state of ropes which have lain by for the winter, and settle any disputes which may have arisen among their number; anything of more weighty import being left for the decision of the tacksman on his visit.

Skills of the Natives

The whole front of the vast precipices at St Kilda is abundant in narrow shelves and ledges, covered with the richest vegetation; and on these the Fulmar and other fowl deposit their eggs, and the daring skill of the natives is usually called forth. The fowlers generally climb in pairs, each being furnished with a stout rope eight fathoms long, one of which connects the two climbers by the waists, and the other is carried coiled on the neck of the one who has least to do: thus they scramble from shelf to shelf, assisting each other apparently so slightly by the little touches and checks of the rope which are observable between them, that their movements are almost unintelligible to a beholder; though when it is considered, how slender a thread will determine a nicely balanced object, it will readily be imagined that much of their skill consists in these movements. In descending a smooth, perpendicular face of rock, of twenty or thirty feet in height, they have a method of assisting each other which struck me as remarkably ingenious: In it both ropes are employed, each climber having one end of his own rope firmly attached to his waist, while the other remains at liberty. Suppose it is their object to place A on a ledge 20 feet below where they both stand; B chooses as deep a niche of the rock as he can find, and leaning far back into it, fixes himself firmly in his situation; A then lays hold of the rope attached to B's waist, and B simultaneously seizes that tied to A, and A, leaving the ledge with his feet, begins to let himself down by the rope at his companion's waist, relieved at the same time of one half his weight by B, who is supporting him by the other rope. Sometimes, when a deeper descent is made, and ledges do not present themselves, a longer rope is employed, and climbers are let down one by one by their companions, to places where their usual system of climbing in pairs is available.

Yet with all their skill, no season passes over without the destruction of some of these men, and there is scarcely a portion of rock of any extent which has not some mournful tale attached to it.

The only weapon, they use in capturing the birds, is a clumsily made rod of thirteen or fourteen feet in length, with a noose of horse hair, stiffened at its junction to the wood, with slips of quill; this is cautiously thrust forward until it encircles the head of the victim, and then rapidly and unceremoniously withdrawn with its struggling burden. This is the most destructive and common method, and is used against the

Gannet, Fulmar, Guillemot, and Razor Bill, the numbers of which destroyed by it, are almost incredible.

Breeding Birds

The Gannets are entirely confined to Borera, and nestle on the shelves of its tremendous precipices, at all elevations, and in immense numbers; the fowling rod is employed for their capture, and the more hazardous expedient of visiting the rocks at night, and securing the bird who acts as sentinel: if this be accomplished, an abundant capture ensues, as the others, relying upon him, are easily taken from their nests as they sleep.

The Fulmar is infinitely the most esteemed fowl the Kildeans have, affording, in itself, one great component part of their food; in the single, large, brittle, white egg it lays, a delicate and nutritive animal substance, superior to the egg of any other sea bird; and in its young, another branch of their food in very high esteem. When captured this bird ejects from its nostrils a considerable quantity of amber-coloured oil, much valued by the inhabitants for the cure of rheumatism applied externally, and for almost all the '*ills that flesh is heir to,*' taken internally. The young birds afford this in great abundance, and what they eject is received on capture into a wooden bowl, and carefully preserved. The food of the Fulmar seems still unascertained; the stomach of one or two which I opened, contained a small quantity of sorrel and oily animal substance, too much decomposed to ascertain its nature. From the heavy, inactive flight of the bird, I should imagine its prey cannot, generally speaking, be of a very active description; and I am inclined to think, from the pulpy nature of the contents of the stomach of those I opened, that molluscous animals floating near the surface of the sea, may not improbably be the food of this Genus, and that the sorrel, almost always found in their throats and stomachs, may be used by them to assist in the digestion, by correcting some particular quality of this kind of food, which seems to render animals of this description unacceptable to other sea fowl. May we not fairly suppose, that the oily secretions possessed by them is owing, in some measure, to a particular kind of food; and without saying any thing of the rather absurd opinion of its feeding on whale's blubber, is it not probable that whatever its food may be, it is something with which we are not unacquainted. The only places where the Fulmar breeds in Great Britain, are, here in immense numbers, and a few on the South Isles of Barra, in the Outer Hebrides. They make no nest, but place their egg on the rich vegetation of the narrow shelves on the higher parts of the rocks.

In capturing the Guillemot, very little skill is required. The stupidity they evince is almost incredible, scarcely stirring from the ledges they sit on until the climber, in his descent, has displaced them to gain footroom for himself; and when the fatal noose approaches, making no more active exertions to avoid its embrace than by shuffling to the extremest part of the ledge, and endeavouring to catch it in their bills.

On the first coming of the Guillemots in March, they sometimes catch immense quantities by the following contrivance:- a short time before dusk, a fowler clambers into some sheltered nook, which he knows to be a favourite resort of these birds, and having provided himself with a dead bird, or the stuffed skin on one, he displays its white breast before him: on the return of the birds from the sea, they perceive this, and imagining it, I suppose, to be a companion, who has already comfortably settled himself for the evening, come pouring in, in myriads, to keep him company. The fowler has then only to take them, one by one, from beside him, and quietly twist their necks.

Puffins are in exceeding abundance; they seem like a dense flock of midges as they skim noiselessly by, and, on the south side of Borera, where they chiefly dwell, sit in such close masses on the rocks and stones projecting from the grassy slope, that we often knocked two or three at a time from their seats, which rolled away down the hill, with the stones we hurled at them, apparently killed, but generally deceived us, by taking wing, and skimming merrily on again. The inhabitants assured us if the feathers be plucked from a live Puffin, and only just sufficient left in his wing to allow him to fly with, his next plumage will be white; they endeavoured to point out one of these birds, a few of which are about the islands, but without success.

In company with the Puffin, the Manx Petrel associates himself, but is so scarce, that although we devoted a day to it, and were assisted by half the population, we only found two nests. These were in somewhat larger and more intricate holes than the Puffin usually makes, and displayed rather more appearance of a nest, being composed of half a hat-full of dry grass, and contained one white egg each, and a supply of fresh sorrel leaves. The quantity of oil is not so abundant as in the Fulmar, and the bird is of a more slim and elegant make. I was rejoiced to find Mr. Bewick's figure which was taken from a badly-stuffed specimen, exceedingly good.*

The Stormy Petrel breeds in small numbers among the rocks and huge stones about the east of Soa; it comes forth at night and amuses itself all day by singing in its hole, in a harsh note, like a Starling's; it lays an oval white egg, exceedingly brittle, as large as a Blackbird's.**

The remaining animal produce of St Kilda consists of about 20 small ponies, employed to bring the turf which they use as firing, from the hills; some kyloes (a small breed of long-horned Scots cattle), whose milk, with that of the sheep, they manufacture into excellent cheeses; and a quantity of wild-looking sheep; small, like the other quadrupeds, in size, but affording the most delicious mutton. On Borera, they are often striped and mottled in a curious manner, and long in the leg, giving one very much the idea of reverging to a state of nature. Dogs conclude the list. They equal the human population in number, and are a most mongrel set: it has been stated they assist in the capture of Puffins and subterranean fowl, but I have reason to think this a mistake. From the steep nature of their shores they have seldom seals, and never any otters.

Agriculture is not much attended to; a small quantity of excellent barley grows near the village, the different properties being divided by rows of stones, as big as a man's fist. A few potatoes are likewise raised, but nothing more.

Except from the rocks, fishing is not pursued, for they have only one very clumsy boat, and manage it miserably; so in fact, fowling is their only occupation.

---

*In an expedition to the Shetland Islands this summer (1832), I find that the Shearwater is comparatively abundant there, and in high esteem as an article of food; one of our party procured nearly a dozen eggs in the north of Unst.

** In some parts of Zetland this bird breeds in great numbers; on two islands, Oxnay and Papa, in the Bay of Scalloway, particularly. The former of these I visited on the 15th of June, 1832, and, by turning over the large cobble stones (as big as a man's head) till I came to the earth, a yard below, I caught, I dare say, two dozen of these little fellows; they did not seem to have commenced breeding, as, though I saw cavities of last year's nests, I did not get an egg. They are so weak in the leg that they cannot stand, and shuffle along on the whole length of the leg, most awkwardly. From the same cause they cannot rise from a level surface, but must have a tuft of sod, or stone to rise from.

The birds which we observed on St Kilda, are as follows:-

Goshawk	*Falco palumbarius*	Stormy Petrel	*Procellaria pelagica*
Starling	*Sturnus vulgaris*	Fork-tailed Petrel	*Procellaria Leachii*
Common Wren	*Troglodytes europoeus*	Scarf or Cormorant	*Carbo cormoranus*
Oyster Catcher	*Haematopus ostralegus*	Gannet or Solan Goose	*Sula alba*
Kittiwake Gull	*Larus tridactylus*	Guillemot	*Uria Troile*
Herring Gull	*Larus argentatus*	Black Guillemot	*Uria grylle*
Fulmar Petrel	*Procellaria glacialis*	Razor-bill	*Alca torda*
Manx Petrel	*Procellaria anglorum*	Puffin	*Mormon fratercula*
Great Auk	*Alca impennis*		Temm.
Great Black-backed Gull	*Larus marinus*		

In conclusion – with regard to the scenery of this group of islands, it is so decidedly unlike any thing else I have seen, that I scarcely know how to venture on the description, and should have been almost tempted to omit it, but that it constitutes their most decided and wonderful peculiarity. To convey in writing, any idea of size, requires some similar known object to refer and compare with that under description, and the nearer the two resemble each other, the more correct is the impression likely to be which is formed from that description. I have seen much very fine scenery, but never anything so vast and imposing as to serve even to ground a notion of St Kilda on, and, for my own part, I know no rocks which it would not be absolutely ridiculous to select for the purpose of comparison.

I have said the Islands St Kilda and Borera rise from the sea perpendicularly, nearly on every side, and that they each in some places present to the eye an unbroken precipice of nearly 1400 feet in height. If it be remembered that Arthur's Seat, near Edinburgh, standing on an uneven surface, and presenting no precipitous boldness of outline, is far from being an insignificant object, yet is only about 800 feet in elevation; let it be conceived, how imposing a mass must be presented by an island in the open sea, rising almost perpendicularly in gigantic grandeur to a height so much greater, with no speck of earth to rest the eye on, or interfere with the vastness and independence of these tremendous rocks. Nothing can be more interesting, or more instructive and ennobling, to the mind of man, than the contemplation of the works of his Maker, which are daily before us, but when scenes of such immensity and grandeur present themselves, that even imagination has not pictured them, the soul must indeed be unsubdued which does not bow with admiration and awe. It would be difficult to explain the feeling that predominates in the mind in the contemplation of such a scene, but one of conscious insignificance and littleness must arise, when human beings are suspended and crawling among these cliffs, and our faculties are scarcely able to distinguish their diminished forms in the chaos of rocks which surround them.

Whatever I might say on the subject, however, cannot convey an adequate idea of the rocks of St Kilda; but if laying before the Natural History Society so imperfect a description of this most unknown part of the British dominions, I am the means of inducing others to visit these islands, with a portion of satisfaction I experienced in doing so, it will be matter of sincere pleasure to me, and tend to convince me that even this brief notice has not been in vain.

Editorial Comment

1.   **Common Wren/St Kilda Wren** – The marked differences in plumage, song and size, compared with other British examples were not noticed until 1884, when Seebohm described it, from specimens collected by Dixon in that year, as a new species under the name of *Troglodytes hirtensis*. It is now recognised as a sub-species, *Troglodytes troglodytes hirtensis*. There are about 200 pairs on the archipelago.

2.   **Goshawk/Peregrine**. Mentioning Goshawk in the above list GCA was following Mr. McKenzie's identification. GCA collected two young peregrines from the nest on Boreray, the minister called them Goshawks, but GCA was quite convinced they were Peregrine Falcons – cf the sketch and entry for June 1st 1831.

3.   **Great Auk. Gair-fowl.** Icelandic Geyr-fugl, Geyr, *Spear*, possibly from its spear-like beak or its shape when swimming fast in the water. The Greenland name is Isarokitsok, *Little Wings*, which are only 9 inches long.

    Martin Martin visited St Kilda, arriving May 29th 1697, and gives one of the fullest descriptions:

    'The sea-fowl are first, Gair-fowl, being the stateliest as well as the largest sort, and above the size of the Solan Goose, of a black colour, red about the eyes, a large white spot under each, a long broad bill: it stands stately, its whole body erected, its wings short; it flies not at all, lays its egg upon the bare rock, which, if taken away, she lays no more for that year; she is whole footed, and has the hatching spot upon her breast, i.e., a bare spot from which the feathers have fallen off with the heat of hatching; its egg is twice as big as that of the Solan Goose, and is variously spotted, black, green and dark; it comes without regard to any wind, appears the 1st of May, and goes away about the middle of June.'

    There can be little doubt that he saw one at very close quarters. He states in the Preface to his, *Voyage to St Kilda*, 1698:

    'He has been careful to relate nothing in the following Account, but what he asserts for truth, either upon his own particular Knowledge, or from the constant and harmonious Testimony given him by the Inhabitants'.

    From this visit he sent a Great Auk's egg to Sir Hans Sloane in London for His Museum.

    The last Great Auk on St Kilda was killed on Stac an Armin, probably in July 1840; the last two birds of the species were clubbed to death on Eldey Island, Iceland on June 4th, 1844.

2. From the Transactions of the Natural History Society

1830 Lecture recorded in the Transactions - No XVI '*Sketch of the Life and Works of the late Thomas Bewick*' by Mr.George C. Atkinson. Read June 15 1830

1831 Lecture recorded in the Transactions - No. VII '*A Notice of the Island of St Kilda, on the North-west Coast of Scotland*' By Mr G. C. Atkinson. Read January 16, 1832.

1833 Report for the year ending August 1st. '*It is with great pleasure your committee direct the attention of the Society to the extensive and very valuable list of presents received during the past year, and to those more particularly now inpart before the meeting. Again we are favoured by the liberality of Mr G. C. Atkinson, with a large collection illustrative of different branches of Natural History, the produce of his labours during a scientific expedition to the remote Islands of Feroe and Iceland, just terminated.*'

1833 GCA Esq., Sheriff of Newcastle in the Chair . . . It was resolved to build the first museum. In the Report for the year ending August 1st 1834 '*At the November Meeting GCA read his paper, entitled 'Notices of the Habits of some rare Birds, as observed by him in Iceland.' And in January and February he read extracts from his journal of a Voyage to Feroe and Iceland.*'

1839 The Report states, '*Owing greatly to the exertions of Mr George C. Atkinson, the museum has been enriched with various remains of Saurian Animals, now become objects of great interest in every Geological Collection.*'

1845 July 30th Report for the year ending, '*Interest taken by the public in the Museum, as evinced by the number of visitors, is not only unabated but materially increased – more than 30,000 having taken advantage of your liberality within the last twelve months. One cause of this large increase has been the Special Railway Trains, bringing strangers from a distance to visit the town in large numbers.*'

1864 GCA was elected a Vice President and was no longer an honorary curator of the Ornithological Section of the society.
     The Society united with, '*Tyneside Naturalist Field Club in respect to publications of Transactions. The Society resumes its functions as a publishing body after a silence of 26 years.*'
     Edit. After the ambitious and excellent start of the published Transactions there had been a shortage of money preventing the continuation of this practice.

Meteorological Report for 1864 edited by GCA

   . . . dealing with a change in weather patterns . . . *'The only question is, can any local circumstance affect the mean temperature at Greenwich. Is it not possible that a good deal may be due to the increase in smoke and vapour preventing the radiation of heat and the exceedingly increased traffic and movement on railways, on the Thames . . . may cause an appreciable amount of heat: much of it also created, as it is, by steam power?'*

1865   *'Mr. GCA kindly furbished the club (Field Club) with the depth of the Tyne at Wylam Bridge as ascertained by the Tyneometer placed there by him in 1861.'*

---

3. Obituary

In Volume 5 of the Transactions of the NHS and Field Club.

'It is with extreme regret that we have to deplore his decease, which occurred on April 14th 1877 at the age of 69. Mr Atkinson was an original member of the Natural History Society founded in 1830: and of the Tyneside Naturalists Field Club of which he was President in the year 1871, and ever took a lively personal interest in its proceedings and in its prosperity. He was an ardent botanist and an enthusiastic meteorologist. He contributed several important and valuable papers on the science of meteorology. He was of very kindly disposition and considerate feeling, and always evinced great pleasure and interest in imparting his information to others. Nothing afforded him more satisfaction than when he was inticing his friends, more especially his young friends, to pursue and engage in the study of the natural sciences. His memory will be warmly revered and cherished. He contributed the following papers.

To Transaction of the Natural History Society :

Vol. 1 p 132	*Sketches of the Life and Works of the late Thomas Bewick.*
Vol.11 p 215	*Notice of the Island of St Kilda, on the north west coast of Scotland.*
	To the Tyneside Naturalists' Field Club
Vol. V p 29, 209	*Meteorological Notes at Wylam-on-Tyne.*
p 36	*Rainfall in the Vale of the Tyne for 16 years 1845-60.*
Vol. VI p 46	*Rainfall at West Denton and Wylam for 14 years 1849-62.*
p 240	*Meteorological Report for 1863.*
	To Transactions of NHS of Northumberland and Durham and Newcastle upon Tyne
Vol. 1	*Meteorological Report for 1864*
p173	*Meteorological Report for 1865*
Vol. V p 63, 154	*Two Instalments of a Catalogue of the more Remarkable Trees of Northumberland and Durham with plates. pI, II, III.'*

4. CGA's Donations to the Hancock Museum

GCA became an avid collector of specimens for the museum of the newly formed Natural History Society of Northumberland, Durham and Newcastle upon Tyne, of which he was both a founder member in 1829, and later the Curator of the ornithological section. The *Transactions of the Society* . . . frequently refer to specimens he and other members of his family (brothers Richard and Robert, also George in Jamaica, indicated separately) had donated;-

1829   Wild Cat *Felis Catus*, shot in the Highlands of Scotland

1829   Stormy Petrel *Procellaria pellagica*, shot on the Tyne near Benwell Boathouse during very fine weather in Oct 1829; its flight was very similar to that of the swallow, and it occasionally skimmed the water as swallows do.

1829   Nov. - Hedge Sparrow *Accentor modularis*

1830   May - Specimens of Nuts, from a submarine Forest, near Whitburn. Mr. Robert Atkinson.

1830   July - Nine specimens of Vegetable Impressions, from Percy Main Colliary, Mr Robert Atkinson, Percy Main.

1830   Sept.30. - Vitreous Sand Tube from Drig, Cumberland

1830   Oct. - Eggs of 127 species of British Birds

1831   May - Two specimens of Rock Dove *Columba livia*, Temm.

1831   July - Eggs of 14 species of British Birds from St Kilda – Gannet, *Sula alba*; Puffin, *Morman Fratercula*; Shearwater Petrel, *Procellaria Anglorum*; Fulmar Petrel, *Procellaria glacialis*; Stormy Petrel, *Procellaria pelagia*; Black-headed Gull, *Larus atricilla* and *Larus marinus*; Herring Gull, *Larus argentatus*; Razorbill, *Alca Torda*; Foolish Guillemot, *Uria Troile*; Black Guillemot, *Uria Grylle*; Rock Pigeon,*Columba livia*; Shag, *Procellaria graculus*; Common Sandpiper, *Tringa hypoleucos*.

1831   May Two specimens of the egg of Common Sandpiper,*Tringa hypoleucus*,Linn. Mr Richard Atkinson

1831   Aug. - Specimen of Turnstone, *Strepsilis collaris* and Ring Dottrell, *Charadrius Hiaticula*.

1831   Aug. - Eggs of 5 species of British Birds - Purple Heron, *Ardea purpurea*; Thick-Kneed Plover, *OEdicnemus creitans*; Reed Wren, *Sylvia arinaria*; Nightingale, *Sylvia luscinia*; Black Tern, *Sterna nigra* and 2 specimens of the Sanderling, *Calidris arenaria*.

1831-2 18 species of Shells from Shetland Isles given by GCA and Edward James.

1832   May - 2 specimens of Arctic Gull, *Laurus parasiticus*; 2 of BlackGuillemot, *Uria Grylle*; 2 of Stormy Petrel, *Procellaria palagica*; 1 of the Shearwater Petrel, *Procellaria Anglorum*.

1833   A collection of Minerals from Feroe and Iceland
        A specimen of Surturbrand or Bogwood of Iceland

1833   1 pair of Feroe Slippers, Carved Staff with Iron Pike for the descent of Mountains; and a Necklace of small shells from Van Dieman's Land

1833   The eggs of 4 species of British Birds from the Hebrides.
        18 species of birds and their eggs from Iceland

9 species of Insects from Feroe and Iceland

7 specimens of Bearded Sea Starfish, *Asterias sphoerulata* from Shetland Isles

1834-35 Specimens of Coral from Shetland and Shells from Port Arthur, New South Wales.

Specimens of *Pinna ingens, Venus Islandica,* and 15 other species of Corals from the Shetland Islands.

Specimens of Coprolites

2 cases of Insects from Van Dieman's Land

1834-35 Several birds, 15 skins of birds from Jamaica.

5 species of humming birds

7 skins of birds from Van Dieman's Land.

1836 61 Bird skins from Jamaica, given by George Atkinson, Esq. Jamaica

1837 Several specimens of Brown Haematitic Iron from Devonshire and Bituminous

Ironstone from near Glasgow.

1836 3 Bird Skins (no details)

1836-38 Fish – Specimen of the Porcupine Fish by G. Atkinson, Esq. Jamaica.

1841 Specimen of Brown Spar, from the Magnesium Limestone of Durham. By Robert T. Atkinson

ACCESSION NUMBERS FOR GCA's DONATIONS TO THE HANCOCK MUSEUM

Record number NEWHM : AX5167
Admin. Category subject : ZOOL
Brief Description : Two Eggs of Wigeon, Two of Red-Breasted Merganser
Field Collection
Place – Loch Awe
Acquisition
Person from : Atkinson, G.C.
Date 1872-1874
Method donated
Documentation group : Trans Nhs

Record Number :NEWHM ; AX5205
Admin. Category subject : ZOOL
Brief Description : Two Eggs of Red Throated Diver
Field Collection
Place – Sutherlandshire
Person from : Atkinson, G. C.
Date 1872-1874
Method donated
Documentation group : Trans Nhs

Record Number :NEWHM : AX8076
Admin. Category subject : ZOOL
Brief Description : The Eggs of one hundred and twenty-seven Species of British Birds
Acquisition
Person from : Atkinson, G.C.
Date Oct 1830
Method donated
Documentation group : Early Trans Nhs

Record Number : NEWHM : AX8097
Admin. Category subject : ZOOL
Brief Description : Two Specimens of the Rock Dove, *Columba livia*, Temm.
Acquisition
Person from : Atkinson, G.C.
Date May 1831
Documentation Group : Early Trans Nhs

Record Number : NEWHM. AX8103
Admin. Category subject : ZOOL
Brief Description : The Eggs of Fourteen Species of British Birds Viz., Gannet, *Sula Alba*.
Puffin, *Mormon Fratercula*. Shearwater Petrel, *Procellaria Anglorum*. Fulmar Petrel,
    Procellaria Glacialis. Stormy Petrel, *Procellaria Pelagica*. Black-Headed Gull, *Larus
    Atricilla*. Black-Headed Gull, *Larus Marinus*. Herring Gull, *Larus Argentatus*.
    Razorbill, *Alca Torda*. Foolish Guillemot, *Uria Troile*. Rock Pigeon, *Columba Livia*.
    Shag, *Carbo Graculus*. Common Sandpiper, *Tringa Hypoleucos*. Black Guillemot,
    Uria Grylle.
Field Collection
Place : St Kilda
Person : Atkinson G.C.
Date July 1831
Method Donated
Documentation group : Early Trans Nhs

Record number NEWHM : AX8144
Admin Category subject : GEOL
Brief Description : Vitreous Sand Tube.
Field Collection
Place Drigg, Cumberland
Acquisition
Person from : Atkinson, G.C.
Date Sept 1830
Method Donated
Documentation group : Early Trans Nhs

Record number : NEWHM ; AX8192
Admin Category subject : ZOOL
Brief Description : 18 Species of Shells
Field Collection
Place Shetland
Acquisition
Person from : Atkinson, G.C. & James E
Date Dec 1831
Method Donated
Documentation group : Early Trans Nhs

Record number : NEWHM : AX8194
Admin. Category subject : ZOOL
Brief Description : Specimens of *Pinna Ingens, Venus Islandica,* and 15 other Species
Field Collection
Place Shetland Islands
Acquisition
Person from : Atkinson, G.C.
Date 1833
Method Donated
Documentation group : Early Trans Nhs

Record number : NEWHM : AX8197
Admin Category subject : ZOOL
Brief Description : 7 Specimens of the Beaded Sea Starfish, *Asterias Sphoerulata*
Field Collection
Place : Shetland Islands
Acquisition
Person from : Atkinson G.C.
Date 1833
Method Donated
Documentation group : Early Trans Nhs

Record number NEWHM : AX8204
Admin. Category subject : ZOOL
Brief Description : Specimen of Coral
Field Collection
Place Shetland
Acquisition
Person from : Atkinson G.C.
Date 1834-1835
Method Donated
Documentation group : Early Trans Nhs

Record number : NEWHM : AX8205
Admin Category subject : ZOOL
Brief Description Shells
Field Collection
Place Port Arthur, New South Wales
Person from : Atkinson, G.C.
Date 1834-1835
Method donated
Documentation group : Early Trans Nhs

Record number : NEWHM : AX8236
Admin. Category subject : ZOOL
Brief Description - Three Bird Skins
Acquisition
Place – not recorded
Person from : Atkinson, G.C.
Date 1836
Method Donated
Documentation group : Early Trans Nhs

Record number : NEWHM : AX8280
Admin. Category subject : ZOOL
Brief Description Nine Species of Insects
Field Collection
Place Feroe and Iceland
Acquisition
Person from : Atkinson, G.C.
Date 1833
Method Donated
Documentation group : Early Trans Nhs

Record number NEWHM : AX8287
Admin. Category group : ZOOL
Brief Description Two Cases of Insects from Van Dieman's Land
Acquisition
Person from : Atkinson, G.C.
Date 1834-1835

Method Donated
Documentation group : Early Trans Nhs

Record number : NEWHM : AX8295
Admin. Category subject : ZOOL
Brief Description The Eggs of 4 Species of British Birds
Field Collection
Place Hebrides
Acquisition
Person from : Atkinson, G.C.
Date 1833
Method Donated
Documentation group : Early Trans Nhs

Record Number : NEWHM. AX8296
Admin. Category subject :ZOOL
Brief Description 18 Species of Birds and their Eggs
Field Collection
Place Iceland
Person from : Atkinson, G.C.
Date 1833
Method Donated
Documentation group : Early Trans Nhs

Record number NEWHM : AX8302
Admin Category subject :ZOOL
Brief Description 15 Skins of Birds
Field Collection
Place Jamaica
Acquisition
Person from : Atkinson, G.C.
Date 1834-1835
Method Donated
Documentation group : Early Trans Nhs

Record number NEWHM : AX8303
Admin. Category subject : ZOOL
Brief Description Five Species of Humming Birds, and Seven Skins of Birds
Field Collection
Place Van Dieman's Land
Acquisition
Person from : Atkinson, G.C.
Date 1834-35
Method Donated
Documentation group : Early Trans Nhs

Record number NEWHM : AX8416
Admin. Category subject : GEOL
Brief Description A Collection of Minerals
Field Collection
Place Feroe and Iceland
Acquisition
Person from : Atkinson, G.C.
Date 1833
Method Donated
Documentation group : Early Trans Nhs

Record number NEWHM : AX8435
Admin. Category subject :GEOL
Brief Description Several Specimens of Brown Haematitic Iron
Field Collection
Place Devonshire
Acquisition
Person from : Atkinson G.C.
Date 1836
Method Donated
Documentation group : Early Trans Nhs

Record number NEWHM : AX8436
Admin Category subject :GEOL
Brief Description Bituminous Iron-Stone
Field Collection
Place Near Glasgow
Acquisition
Person from : Atkinson, G.C.
Date 1836
Method Donated
Documentation group : Early Trans Nhs

Record number NEWHM : AX8459
Admin Category subject :GEOL
Brief Description A Specimen of Surturbrand or Bogwood
Field Collection
Place Iceland
Acquisition
Person from : Atkinson, G.C.
Date 1833
Method Donated
Documentation group : Early Trans Nhs

Record number NEWHM : AX8540
Admin Category subject :GEOL
Brief Description Specimens of Coprolites
Acquisition
Person from : Atkinson, G.C.
Date 1834-1835
Method Donated
Documentation group : Early Trans Nhs

Record number NEWHM : AX8579
Admin Category subject : ETHNO
Brief Description A Pair of Feroe Island Slippers
Acquisition
Person from : Atkinson, G.C.
Date 1833
Method Donated
Documentation group : Early Trans Nhs

Record number NEWHM : AX8592
Admin Category subject : ETHNO
Brief Description Pair of Slippers. A Carved Staff, with Iron Pike, for Descending
Mountains. And a Necklace of small shells.
Field Collection
Place Van Dieman's Land
Acquisition
Person from : Atkinson, G.C.

Date 1834-1835
Method Donated
Documentation group : Early Trans Nhs

Record number NEWHM : AX8789
Admin Category subject : GEOL
Brief Description A Collection of Fossils
Field Collection
Place Oolitic Rocks of Yorkshire
Acquisition
Person from : Atkinson, G.C.
Date 1841
Method Donated
Documentation group : Early Accessions Book

Record number NEWHM : AX8862
Admin Category subject :GEOL
Brief Description An Undescribed Fossil
Field Collection
Place Slates of Skiddaw
Acquisition
Person from : Atkinson, G.C.
Date 1841
Method Donated
Documentation group : Early Accessions Book

Record number NEWHM : AX9064
Admin Category subject :GEOL
Brief Description Fossils
Field Collection
Place The Gault, Specton, Yorkshire
Acquisition
Person from : Atkinson, G.C.
Date 1843
Method Donated
Documentation group : Early Accessions Book

Record number NEWHM : AX9389
Admin Category subject :GEOL
Brief Description A Collection of Fossils and Two Specimens of the Ichthiosaurus
Field Collection
Place The Lias
Acquisition
Person from : Atkinson, G.C.
Date 1853
Method Donated
Documentation group : Early Accessions Book

Record number NEWHM : AX9451
Admin Category subject : ZOOL
Brief Description Case of Bird Skins
Acquisition
Person from : Atkinson, G.C.
Date 15 Sept. 1856
Method Donated
Documentation group : Early Accessions Book

BIBLIOGRAPHY

ACLAND, A, 1981 *A Devon Family – the Story of the Aclands*, Phillimore

ALLEN, D. E., 1978 *The Naturalist in Britain* Penguin Books

ATKINSON, G.C., 1832 *Sketch of the Life and Works of the Late Thomas Bewick*
    Transactions of the Nat. Hist. Soc. of Northumberland, Durham and
    Newcastle upon Tyne, Vol. 1.

    1838 *A Notice of the Island of St Kilda, on the North-west coast of Scotland,* read on
    Jan 16, 1832, Transaction of the Nat. Hist. Soc. of Northumberland, Durham
    and Newcastle upon Tyne, Vol 2

    1989 *Journal of an Expedition to the Feroe and Westman Islands and Iceland in
    1833,* Edited by Seaton A.V. Bewick – Beaufort Press

AYRIS, I., 1997 *A City of Palaces* – Richard Grainger and the Making of Newcastle upon
    Tyne, Newcastle Libraries and Information Service

BOSWELL, J., 1785 *Journal of a Tour to the Hebrides*

BROUGHAM, H., 1871 *Life and Times of Henry Lord Brougham,* 3 Vols (Vol 1) Blackwood,
    Edinb.

CAMPBELL, J. L, 1994 *Canna – The Story of a Hebridean Island.* Canongate, Edinb.

CAMPBELL, M., 1977 *Argyll – The Enchanting Heartland* Turnstone Books

CLARKE, W.E, 1912 *Studies in Bird Migration* 2 volumes, Gurney and Jackson

COOPER., D., 1979 *'Road to the Isles – Travellers in the Hebrides* Routledge and Kegan
    Paul

FISHER, J., 1956, *Rockall* Geoffrey Bles

GODDARD, R .T., 1929 *History of the Natural History Society of Northumberland Durham
    and Newcastle upon Tyne.* Newcastle

HARMAN, M., 1997 *'An Isle Called Hirte – A History and Culture of St Kilda to 1930* Maclean
    Press

HALL, M., 1982 *The Artists of Northumberland.* Newcastle

HADFIELD, C., 1950 *British Canals* David and Charles

HASWELL-SMITH, H., 1996 *Scottish Islands – a comprehensive guide to every Scottish
    Island.* Canongate, Edinburgh

HEWER, H. R., 1974 *British Seals* New Naturalist Series, Collins

HODGE, G., 1872 Obituary of G.C.Atkinson in Transactions of the Natural History Society
    of Northumberland and Durham, 4, 524-6.

JOHNSON, J., 1834 *Recess in the Highlands and Lowlands* London

JOHNSON, S., 1775 *A Journey to the Western Isles of Scotland* Cassell and Co.(1892)

LINDSAY, J., 1968 *The Canals of Scotland,* David and Charles

LUNN, A. G., 1983 'Physical Geographers, Quaternary Geologists and Conservationists' in
    A History of Naturalists in North-East England. Ed. A.G.Lunn, 81-97.

MACAULAY, REV. K., 1764 *The History of St Kilda* Repr Mercat Press, Edinb. 1974

MACCULLOCH, J., 1819 *A Description of the Western Islands of Scotland, 3 Vols,*
    Constable, Edinb.

    1824 *The Highlands and Western Islands of Scotland,* London

MACDONALD, D., 1978 *Lewis – A History of the Island* Gordon Wright, Edinb.

MACDONALD, REV DR. J., 1823 *Journal and Report of a Visit to the Island of St Kilda* Edinb
    SSPCK

MACGREGOR,.A., 1994 *Sir Hans Sloane – Founding Father of the British Museum,* British
    Museum.

MacKay, J., 1978 *Island Postal History No.1 Harris and St Kilda* Published by the Author

MacKenzie, Rev N., 1911 *Episode in the Life of the Rev Neil MacKenzie at St Kilda from 1829–43.* Privately Printed

MacKenzie, O.H., 1924 *A Hundred Years in the Highlands* Edward Arnold, London

MacLean, L., 1838 *Sketches of St Kilda with the Journal of an Excursion to St. Kilda.* Glasgow: McPhun

Martin, M., 1698 *A Late Voyage to St Kilda, Repr. Mackay 1934*

1703 *A Description of the Western Islands of Scotland* , Republished by James Thin, 1976

Murray, W.R., 1834 *Sketches of Scenes in Scotland drawn in Outline,* Perth

Pennant, T., 1771 *A Tour in Scotland. 1769.* John Monk, Chester

1774 *A Tour in Scotland and Voyage to the Hebrides: 1774.* Monk of Chester

Quine, D., 1982 *St Kilda Revisited,* Dowland Press, Frome

1989 *St Kilda Portraits,* Dowland Press, Frome

1995 *St Kilda,* Colin Baxter Island Guides Series, Colin Baxter Photography Ltd.

Ralph, 1993 *William MacGillivray,* Nat. Hist. Museum, HMSO

1996 *William MacGillivray – A Hebridean Naturalist's Journal, 1817-18* Acair Press

Stack, P., 1979 *Island Quest – The Inner Hebrides,* Collins and Harwell

Welford, R., 1893 *Men of Mark twixt Tyne and Weir.* 3 Vols, Newcastle

OTHER DOCUMENTS

Journal of the Andersonian Naturalists of Glasgow, 1958-71,
     John Scouler M.D.,Lld., FLS.(1894-1871), by Blodwen Lloyd, Msc., Ph.D
History of the Geological Society of Glasgow 1858-1908,
     Edited by Peter Macnair and Frederick Mort. Publ. Geological Soc. 1908

Index

(Page numbers in *italics* indicate illustrations)